TAROT & MAGIC

THE TREASURE HOUSE OF IMAGES

SECOND EDITION

Gareth Knight

© Gareth Knight, 1986, 2012

This expanded edition first published in Great Britain in 2012 by Skylight Press, 210 Brooklyn Road, Cheltenham, Glos GL51 8EA

Chapters 1-6 originally published as *The Treasure House of Images* in 1986 by The Aquarian Press, Wellingborough. Facsimile edition published in the USA as *Tarot and Magic* in 1991 by Destiny Books, Vermont.

Designed and typeset by Rebsie Fairholm
Publisher: Daniel Staniforth

www.skylightpress.co.uk

Printed and bound in Great Britain by Lightning Source, Milton Keynes
Typeset in Adobe Caslon Pro. Titles set in TierraNueva Norte.

British Library Cataloguing in Publication Data.
A catalogue record for this book is available from the British Library.

ISBN 978-1-908011-35-0

To my mother and father
wherever they may be
on the journey to
the Land of the Heart's Desire

Contents

	Acknowledgements	7
1	The Evolution of the Tarot	9
2	Tarot Trump Imagery	23
3	The Language of the Tarot Images in Pattern and Sequence	75
4	Tarot Pathworking	96
5	Tarot Ritual and Divination	111
6	Journey to the Centre: Working with the Archetypes	123
7	The Mystical Tree of the Tarot	174
8	Images and Number in the Lesser Arcana	182
9	The Fourfold Structure of the Greater Arcana	195
10	A Narrative Approach to the Lesser Arcana	207
11	Preparation for Divination	219
12	Divinatory Methods	226
	Index of Trump Images	232
	Index of Books Cited	234
	Index of Packs Cited	236

Acknowledgements

All students of the Tarot today must be indebted to two books which have revealed much knowledge that was hitherto obscure or unknown. These are *The Game of Tarot* by Michael Dummett and *The Encyclopaedia of Tarot* by Stuart Kaplan.

Michael Dummett has little sympathy for occult interpreters of the Tarot, and not without reason. He is all the more to be respected for his patience in analysing much that must have been hardly congenial to an Oxford Professor of Logic, and I for one am grateful for the benefit of such devoted application of academic discipline in establishing the historical facts of a subject close to my heart.

Stuart Kaplan, as one of the great Tarot card collectors of the world, and a publisher of some of them, is also to be thanked for sharing his accumulated treasures with the rest of us.

I am also grateful to the curators of the Bibliothèque Nationale who assembled a once-in-a-life time exhibition of Tarot when I happened to be in Paris.

This book concentrates on the magical applications of the Tarot and to this end I am grateful to those like-minded spirits who attended my workshop on the subject at Hawkwood College in December 1984 where much of the practical work described herein had its origin.

Also my thanks go to Daniel Bloxsom for appearing out of the blue at the appropriate time and engaging me in an illuminating and wide ranging correspondence on the subject.

And finally my thanks to the spirit of the Tarot itself. Despite all the abuse it may have had from less than spotless hands and intentions in the past, it revealed itself to me as a very wise and gentle source of wisdom and encouragement, deserving much respect.

Gareth Knight

The Evolution of the Tarot

THE TAROT IS A structured system of magical images. The date and place of its origin is not precisely known but the historical evidence points to some little time before AD 1450. Some have claimed a greater antiquity for it, with roots in ancient Egypt; but although, as archetypal images, many of the figures may well have correspondences in remote antiquity, the particular characteristics of the Tarot system indicate that it is an artefact of the Renaissance period, grafted on to the newly popular games of playing cards.

Although the Tarot has come down to us as part of a card game it does not pre-date the ordinary playing card pack. Playing cards were introduced to Europe soon after 1375. The first references appear in 1377 and they are widespread all over Europe by 1400. In 1392 Charles VI of France commissioned the design of a pack of cards but there is no evidence that they were Tarot cards – although they were for some time confused with the mid-fifteenth century Gringonneur Tarot cards in the Bibliothèque Nationale.

The Tarot is characterized by the twenty-two cards that we nowadays call Trump cards, although they were originally called *trionfi* or Triumphs. Trionfi are first mentioned in 1422 and the term *tarrochi* from which the word Tarot derives does not appear until 1516.

Another, less well known characteristic of the Tarot is the introduction of the Queen to the court cards of each suit. Originally the court cards were King, Knight and Page. The fourteen card Tarot suits introduced the Queen who, in the course of time, ousted the Knight from the thirteen card suits of modern playing cards.

The suit emblems of all cards were originally Swords *(spade)*, Wands *(bastoni)*, Cups *(coppe)*, and Coins *(denari)*. When card games spread to France, Switzerland and Germany however, modified suit emblems were introduced and became nationally accepted. We inherit in the familiar Spades, Clubs, Hearts and Diamonds of today, the French system, which first appears in 1480.

The German Leaves, Acorns, Hearts and Shells and the Swiss Shields, Acorns, Roses and Shells appeared between 1430 and 1460. The suit emblems that we associate with the Tarot are the original Italian devices, and seem to originate from Turkish dominated Egypt, with possible roots in Persia or even India. A few playing cards in the Istanbul Museum show suits of curved Swords, or Scimitars, Cups, Coins, and curved Wands that may derive from polo sticks. There is a strong tradition in Italian suit design for curved swords and wands with spatulate ends, and this may have been their origin – Mamluk Egyptian cards imported possibly through Venice. There are three Court Cards but with abstract designs because of the Muslim prohibition on depicting human figures.

A common theory that it was the gypsies who brought either playing cards or the Tarot to Europe does not seem likely, for gypsies did not arrive in Europe until 1417, by which time playing cards had been known for forty years. And the first mention of Trionfi, although soon after, seems associated with aristocratic circles. In all the records referring to gypsies before the nineteenth century there is no mention of telling fortunes by cards – their particular speciality was palmistry. Indeed telling fortunes by cards does not seem to have occurred to anyone prior to the mid-eighteenth century, and subsequent gypsy use would appear to have been the result of *gorgio* influence upon them rather than the reverse.

The earliest examples of Tarot Trumps or Trionfi that we have date from about 1450.

This was a time of great interest in meditation upon magical images, following the translations of Greek hermetic works by Marsilio Ficino under the patronage of Cosimo de Medici. A number of the works of the artist Botticelli are thought perhaps to have been commissioned for magical purposes. *The Primavera*, or the *Birth of Venus*, or *Venus Overcoming Mars* could be cited as possible magical images, and his *Fortitia*, or Strength, could certainly have come straight from the Tarot Trumps.

The Visconti-Sforza cards are typical of a number of sumptuously produced hand-painted and gilded sets that would hardly seem suited for actual playing at cards, even by the most opulent of princes. If they were *objets d'art* for display, and it seems that they may have been popular as wedding gifts, then they could equally have been subjects for meditation as magical images by those who were in the know. Even the Popes were interested in magic in those days – sometimes quite enthusiastically.

One of Marsilio Ficino's recommended methods of natural magic was the placement in certain designs and configurations of lamps or other symbols to counteract unfortunate astrological forces or psychophysical distempers. The Tarot Trumps would have made excellent figures for this use.

However, between 1450 and 1480 there is clear evidence that whatever the possible magical uses, the Trionfi were definitely in use as a game. A document known as the Steele Manuscript, that dates from this time, records a sermon by a Dominican father against the evils of gambling games. In the course of this he lists, in numbered sequence, the Tarot Trumps.

It is worth our reproducing this list, for it confirms that the same images were in use that have come down to us today. And we also find that they are in a different sequence. Of this, more later:

1. El bagatella	12. Lo impichato
2. Imperatrix	13. La morte
3. Imperator	14. El diavolo
4. La papessa	15. La sagitta
5. El papa	16. La stella
6. La temperentia	17. La luna
7. L'amore	18. El sole
8. Lo caro triomphale	19. Lo angelo
9. La forteza	20. La iusticia
10. La rotta	21. El mondo
11. El gobbo	22. El matto sine nulla

This numbered sequence is of interest because it is the only evidence we have of the names and numbers of the Trumps at this time. Names and numbers do not appear on the early hand-painted cards, nor on the earliest printed examples we have of c. 1475.

Of the mainstream of Tarot card design and tradition the earliest non-Italian printed set we have is the Catelin de Geofroy pack of 1557. This is something of an idiosyncrasy as it is copied from a luxury set designed by a distinguished engraver, Virgil Solis, in 1544. There are only three suits, lions, falcons and peacocks, and only seven Trumps survive. However, this fragmentary pack is historically important in that its Trumps are numbered in conformity with the sequence that came to be the standard that has come down to us today.

Between 1500 and 1750 the story of the Tarot is principally that of a popular card game. Although the game originated in Italy, France became the major manufacturing country, with Rouen and Lyons being centres for exporting cards to Spain, Flanders, England, Portugal and Switzerland in the late sixteenth century. We have taxation records that give clear indications of the importance of the industry. In 1595 cards were being manufactured in Paris and in 1599 at Nancy. In 1608 the manufacturers of Lyons tried to get the rival growing industry in Marseilles suppressed. However, in 1631 Marseilles received a royal edict for its activities and became the dominant centre for card manufacture, exporting them even to Italy. It is thus that the Marseilles Tarot has become largely the modern accepted standard.

In 1622 a Jesuit comments that the Tarot is played in France more than chess, and at this time the industry was so attractive to framers of tax laws that some entrepreneurs abandoned France to set up factories in Switzerland, Savoy and even England.

The game was played in Switzerland by 1600, possibly as early as 1515, and was certainly well established in Germany by 1650. In 1664 it had reached Sicily, via Rome, from the North. Evidence for its rise and decline in popularity as a card game can be gleaned from successive editions of the French book of games called *La Maison acadèmique des jeux*. In the second edition, of 1659, detailed description of the game and play of Tarot is given. This continues through successive editions until 1718, when it is dropped.

Coincidentally, 1718 is also the date of manufacture of our earliest surviving Marseilles Tarot pack.

The Tarot rules appear only sporadically in subsequent editions of *La Maison acadèmique des jeux*, and in 1726 it is described as obsolete.

This reflects only Parisian society and Northern France however, for the game continued to be popular in Southern France, Italy, Germany and Switzerland. It was this fact that caused Court de Gebelin to say in his book of 1781 that the Tarot was unknown in Paris.

This book of 1781 is of key importance to the development of the esoteric traditions of the Tarot. It was the eighth volume of Court de Gebelin's *Le Monde Primitif* in which he announced the Tarot to be the remains of an ancient Egyptian book of secret wisdom.

Court de Gebelin (1719-1784), a Protestant pastor, born in Geneva, had wide ranging occult interests. Since the 1770s he had been a freemason and a member of the Order of the Philalèthes, which was an off-shoot of the Order of Elect Cohens founded by Martines de Pasqually (d. 1774). Thus Court de Gebelin's remarks on the Tarot may well not originate entirely from him, but be the revelation of an esoteric tradition propagated in eighteenth-century secret fraternities. As I commented in *A History of White Magic*, the Order of Elect Cohens 'consisted of seven grades leading to that of Rose Croix and was based on belief in Biblical truth together with a general spiritual evolutionary scheme that commenced with man's existence long before the creation story in Genesis. Some of these teachings seem to derive from Jacob Boehme and Dr John Dee.'

Court de Gebelin's aim in writing the nine volumes of *Le Monde Primitif* was to advance his theory of an original golden age – a concept by no means unknown to the traditions of the ancient world. He proposed to substantiate this by the allegorical interpretation of myths and the etymological study of language.

As part of this great design he cited the game of Tarot as a surviving example of ancient wisdom. He claimed:

+ that the symbolism stemmed from ancient Egypt;
+ that Egyptian priests had rendered these symbols into playing cards to preserve them through the ages;
+ that from the Egyptians it passed to Imperial Rome, and thence with the later popes to Avignon, from whence it spread throughout Provence;
+ that the word 'Taro' derived from ancient Egyptian words *tar* for 'way' and *ro, ros, rog* for 'royal';
+ that the twenty-two Trumps corresponded to the twenty-two letters of the Hebrew alphabet.

As an addendum to this part of *Le Monde Primitif* Court de Gebelin added an essay by an anonymous M. le Comte de M***.

This supported the theory of ancient Egyptian origin for the Tarot, and indeed:

+ referred to it as 'the Book of Thoth';
+ derived the word Tarot from Egyptian language as meaning the doctrine or science of Thoth;
+ said that the Tarot came to Europe through Spain with the Muslims, and was thence carried to Germany by the troops of Charlemagne;

✦ associated the Tarot with fortune telling, described as an ancient Egyptian practice;
✦ drew correspondences with the Hebrew letters as part of the cartomantic method.

In his introduction to this essay, Court de Gebelin also made the assertion that bands of Egyptians known as Bohemians carried the cards throughout Europe. This is the origin of the gypsy theory.

He also provided illustrations of the Tarot Trumps and the Aces but these are crude copies of the Marseilles Tarot rendered by an amateur artist friend.

To be quite frank, Court de Gebelin is a likable but garrulous eighteenth-century gossip of appalling scholarship, but the publication of his assertions aroused tremendous interest in the Tarot, particularly as a fortune telling device.

This was exploited to the full by a professional cartomancer, astrologer, interpreter of dreams and maker of talismans known as Etteilla, the inversion of his real name of Alliette.

Etteilla was perhaps one of the earliest card readers, and fortune telling was rife in pre-revolutionary Paris, a fashion which continued well into Napoleonic times. He had previously used a piquet pack of conventional cards and published a book on his method in 1770, which ran through several editions.

After the interest aroused in the Tarot by Court de Gebelin, Etteilla was not slow to introduce a fortune telling method using the Tarot pack, which, following the mysterious M. le Comte de M***, he called the Book of Thoth. He followed this up with a series of booklets developing the subject and indeed claimed that he had long been aware of the esoteric significance of the Tarot. He said that from 1757 to 1765 he had studied it at the instigation of an old man from Piedmont who had given him his notes on the subject. These notes referred to the Tarot as an Egyptian book compiled by a group of magi presided over by Hermes Trismagistus soon after the Flood. The originals had been inscribed on leaves of gold and deposited in a temple at Memphis.

Etteilla then proceeded to make 'rectifications' to the existing Tarot designs, bringing them in line with his ideas of their true esoteric significance. This was the start of a tradition among occult writers that has continued with increasing proliferation.

For instance, he considered that the oval wreath around the central figure on the World Trump should be an ouroboros – the symbol of eternity – a serpent swallowing its own tail. He follows Court de Gebelin in inverting the Hanged Man and calling the card Prudence. This idea seems to have arisen from Court de Gebelin having seen a Belgian pack wherein this error of inversion is made by a careless manufacturer. He seized the opportunity to introduce the fourth Cardinal Virtue to the Trumps (Justice, Temperance and Fortitude already being present), describing the figure as 'an upright man who has one foot poised before the other ready to take a step and examining the place where he is going to step. The title of this card was therefore the man with suspended foot, pede suspenso.' (See Figure 1.)

Figure 1

From 1783 Etteilla advertised his 'corrected' pack for sale, though none of these survives. They are, however, well described in his books, and modified sets were subsequently issued by his followers after his death in 1791. Grand Etteilla Pack I appeared in about 1800, and II and III in the 1840s. They are still available, but Etteilla's fertile imagination soon lost connection with the original Tarot and his work is really an idiosyncratic fortune telling system.

In this he was followed by a whole generation of society clairvoyants practising cartomancy. The most celebrated was Mlle. Marie-Anne

Adelaide Lenormand (d. 1843) who claimed the patronage of the Empress Josephine. From 1825 many fortune telling packs were published and although some claimed a Tarot origin, the connection was generally very tenuous. An extensive ephemeral literature accompanied these packs, lasting through to about 1875.

A more serious continuation of the esoteric Tarot tradition is to be found in the works of Alphonse Louis Constant (1810-75) who wrote under the pen-name of Eliphas Lévi. *Dogme et Rituel de la Haute Magie* appeared in 1855/6, *Histoire de la Magie* in 1860, *Le Clef des Mystères* in 1861 and *Le Science des Esprits* in 1865.

Like Court de Gebelin he considered the Tarot to be a book of ancient wisdom. He called it the Book of Hermes and considered it to have come from a time long before Moses, ultimately from the patriarch Enoch. He had little time for Etteilla or the plethora of contemporary fortune telling packs and insisted on the need to go back to the Marseilles Tarot.

He related the twenty-two Trumps to the twenty-two letters of the Hebrew alphabet and the ten numeral cards of each suit to the ten Sephiroth of the Tree of Life. He saw the Court Cards as representing stages of human life and linked the four suits to the four letters of the Holy Name of God. He accepted the Trump sequence of the Marseilles Tarot but placed the Fool between Trumps XX and XXI. He also expressed the desire to issue an esoterically rectified Marseilles Tarot but never achieved this ambition.

In 1852 he was approached by a writer and former librarian named Jean-Baptiste Pitois (1811-77), who took lessons from him and wrote subsequently under the pen-name of Paul Christian. *L'homme rouge des Tuileries*, of 1863, took the form of a supposed manuscript written by an old monk, copied from a breviary based upon seventy-eight gold leaves that had been arranged in a great circle in an Egyptian temple at Memphis. There is no mention of correspondences with the Hebrew alphabet, although the figure is alleged to have been known to the rabbis as the Samaritan Oracle. It is, of course, the Tarot, though with a full blooded Mystery nomenclature deriving largely from Egyptian assumptions.

I	The Magus
II	The Gate of the Sanctuary
III	Isis Urania
IV	The Cubic Stone

V   Master of the Mysteries of the Arcana
VI   The Two Roads
VII   The Chariot of Osiris
VIII   Themis, or The Scales and the Blade
IX   The Veiled Lamp
X   The Sphinx
XI   The Muzzled or Tamed Lion
XII   The Sacrifice
XIII   The Skeleton Reaper or Scythe
XIV   The Two Urns or Genius of the Sun
XV   Typhon
XVI   The Beheaded or Lightning Struck Tower
XVII   The Tower of the Magi
XVIII   The Twilight
XIX   The Blazing Light
XX   The Awakening of the Dead or Genius of the Dead
O   The Crocodile
XXI   The Crown of the Magi

It will be observed that the sequence follows that of Eliphas Lévi.

In 1870 Paul Christian published *A History of Magic*, in which he describes an initiation ceremony under the pyramids of ancient Egypt. The candidate is led up seventy-eight steps and passes through a hall of images of the Tarot Trumps. However fanciful this may be in historical terms it nonetheless has the hall-marks of a powerful creative visualization exercise or initiatory 'path working'. Thus for those concerned with practical occultism his ideas should not be lightly dismissed. It may give the clue to nineteenth-century occult praxis in some of the secret fraternities and their antecedents.

There is a lull in published work on the Tarot until 1888 when Eugène Jacob, the husband of a professional cartomancer, devoted fifty pages to the subject in an astrological work, written under the pen-name of Ely Star. He follows Paul Christian quite closely but places the Crocodile (The Fool) at the end of all the Trumps and numbers it XXII.

1888 was an important year in two other respects in that it saw the foundation of two influential occult societies, the Cabalistic Order of the Rosy Cross in France, and the Hermetic Order of the Golden Dawn in England.

The French order was founded by Marquis Stanislaus de Guaita (1861-97), who was a great admirer of Eliphas Lévi. In 1887 he met an amateur artist named Oswald Wirth (1860-1943) and together they set about realizing Eliphas Lévi's expressed intention of 'restoring the twenty-two Arcana of the Tarot to their hieroglyphic purity.' In 1889 an edition of 350 copies of the Trumps was published. They were numbered 0 to 21 and given an appropriate Hebrew letter correspondence in accordance with the system of Eliphas Lévi. The designs followed the Marseilles pattern but with esoteric modifications.

Dr Gerard Encausse, a co-founder of Stanislaus de Guaita's society, used the Oswald Wirth illustrations together with those of the Marseilles pack in the first published book devoted exclusively to the Tarot. This was *Le Tarot des Bohèmiens* published in 1889 under the pen-name of Papus. The method of interpretation is a numerological one based on the four-fold symbolism of the Tetragrammaton, the Holy Name of God. It is influenced by both Eliphas Lévi and Paul Christian.

Another work published in France before the turn of the century was by R. Falconnier, an actor in the Comèdie Française, and enthusiast of the Egyptianized Tarot. Indeed, the extended title of his book, published in 1896, says it all: *Les XXII lames hermetiques du tarot divinatoire, exactement reconstituées d'après les textes sacrés et selon la tradition des mages de l'ancienne Egypte.* Designs for the cards were taken from original frescos and bas-reliefs in the Louvre and the British Museum but they nonetheless retain a very French flavour.

In similar vein a *Tarot Hieroglyphique Egyptien* was issued in 1897 by Madame Dulora de la Haye. Twenty-two cards only, with explanatory text incorporated on the pictures, that is in effect a mélange of Etteilla and the Marseilles Tarot.

The English interest in the Tarot may have been stimulated directly by Eliphas Lévi. He visited England in 1854 and 1861 and is known to have had contacts with individuals who later became prominent members of the Societas Rosicruciana in Anglia, founded in 1866, namely Lord Lytton (1802-73) and Kenneth Mackenzie (1833-86).

Mackenzie was particularly interested in the Tarot, discussed it with Lévi, and wrote a book on the subject that was, however, never published. He was an important influence on Dr William Wynn Westcott (1848-1925) who was one of the founders of the Hermetic Order of the Golden Dawn.

The Tarot played a significant part in the Golden Dawn curriculum, although the Knowledge Papers on the subject were probably the work of another founder member, Samuel Liddell MacGregor Mathers (1854-1917). He had published a booklet on the subject in 1888 in which he referred to the French occult authorities on the subject and used the sequence and numeration of the Trumps promulgated by Eliphas Lévi. For the most part it was an elementary instruction book on divination. It is interesting that he used a different sequence in the Golden Dawn papers.

Eliphas Lévi's works were now being translated into English by A. E. Waite, who had already translated Papus' *Tarot of the Bohemians* in 1892. Lévi's *Dogme et Rituel* was translated in 1896 as *Transcendental Magic*, and also a hitherto unpublished work by Lévi on the Tarot, the *Sanctum Regnum*. This translation carried a preface by Dr Westcott which stated that the Lévi/Christian/Papus sequence, and Hebrew letter attributions, was incorrect. He alleged that this was a blind to preserve the secret tradition from profanation by the uninitiated, and that he had seen a manuscript, some 150 years old, in cipher, giving the correct version.

This kind of portentous secrecy and mystery mongering was typical of the Golden Dawn leaders. Whether there was such a document is open to conjecture. It may have been yet another 'blind'. There is circumstantial evidence at least to suspect that the Hermetic Order of the Golden Dawn and the Societas Rosicruciana in Anglia may have been influenced by, if not derived from, a German Rosicrucian tradition. This might well account for the differences from the French tradition. Although all published work on the esoteric Tarot throughout the nineteenth century was French, the British occultists were adamant in refuting, at first in private and then publicly, the French system of correspondences.

A major event in Tarot exegesis occurred in 1910 with the publication of A. E. Waite's *Key to the Tarot* issued with a full pack of esoterically designed cards. These included the innovation of picture designs for the numbered suit cards as well as the Trumps. This pack incorporated the Golden Dawn system of attributions and sequence and it is important in having influenced much subsequent esoteric pack design. Waite had been a member of the Golden Dawn briefly in 1891/2 and again from 1896, until in 1903 he took over control of a society that was beginning to splinter into factions. He dissolved his part of the Order in 1914, and founded a new group, the Fellowship of the True Rosy Cross, in 1916.

Another Golden Dawn member who played an important role in the development of esoteric ideas on the Tarot was Aleister Crowley (1875-1945). He joined in 1898 but by 1907 had formed his own group and in 1912 published a study of the Tarot in his journal *The Equinox*.

His most prominent contribution however was in 1944 with the publication of a full length study of the cards, called *The Book of Thoth*, together with a set of highly original and competently executed cards painted by Lady Frieda Harris. This again is generally based upon the Golden Dawn system but with some idiosyncratic developments of considerable complexity and subtlety.

More in the main stream of the Golden Dawn tradition was the work of Paul Case (1884-1954) in the United States, who had originally headed up the Chicago temple of that body. He later founded his own group, the Builders of the Adytum (B.O.T.A.) which still functions in Los Angeles. He published *The Tarot* in 1927 and issued a pack in 1931, with a modernized version of the Waite Trump designs in black line outline so that the student could personalize them by painting in the colours. He reverted to the old tradition of geometric patterns for the suit cards.

Hitherto, the principal impact of the Tarot in the United States had been A. E. Waite's translation of Papus, which crossed the Atlantic in 1910, and copies of Waite's cards by the de Laurence Publishing Company in 1918.

Manley P. Hall also wrote knowledgeably about the Tarot in his monumental *An Encyclopaedic Outline of Masonic, Hermetic, Qabbalistic and Rosicrucian Symbolical Philosophy* of 1928, which is now more familiarly known as *The Secret Teachings of All Ages*. From this project was developed a new set of designs by his artist J. Augustus Knapp which generally follow the rectified Marseilles tradition first effected by Oswald Wirth. In France, a new and revised version of Wirth's pack was published in 1926.

Another American promulgator of the Tarot was Elbert Benjamine whose *Sacred Tarot* of 1936 closely followed the French/Egyptian tradition of Falconnier, with closely reasoned but idiosyncratic Qabalistic correspondences.

In 1937 to 1940 the Golden Dawn system was revealed to the American public and the world in four volumes of the Order's papers published by Israel Regardie (1907-85). It had been the practice in the Golden Dawn for members to copy a set of their own from a single master set. Regardie had made his own set in this manner in 1923, by which time certain modifications had been introduced. However, in 1977, with Robert Wang doing the artwork, Regardie published a copy of such a pack, modified to be as close as possible to the original Golden Dawn master set.

For a period of twenty years after the Second World War there was a dearth of Tarot exegesis apart from a little book by Frank Lind and a set of traditional type cards issued with a six lesson course by the Insight Institute.

At the time I wrote *A Practical Guide to Qabalistic Symbolism* in the early 1960s it was very difficult to find a pack of Tarot cards. Even the Marseilles pack was not to be found unless one travelled to the appropriate part of Europe where the game was still played. And A. E. Waite's *Key to the Tarot* as well as the works of Regardie and Crowley and the others were rarities on the second-hand book market.

Since 1970 the scene has been utterly transformed. There has been an explosion of books upon the subject and also of esoteric packs, with reprints of most of the older versions too. A whole host of specialist packs cater for every conceivable taste. There are packs designed to appeal to students of witchcraft, Tibetan Buddhism, astrology, Mayan legend, even Pop/Rock. No doubt many of these will prove to be ephemeral but this burst of publishing activity indicates that in the Tarot there is a response to a modern need.

How this need may be met in more practical terms we hope to show in this book, but first, by analyzing the evolution of the design of each card, we must identify the basic idea or archetype that each one expresses.

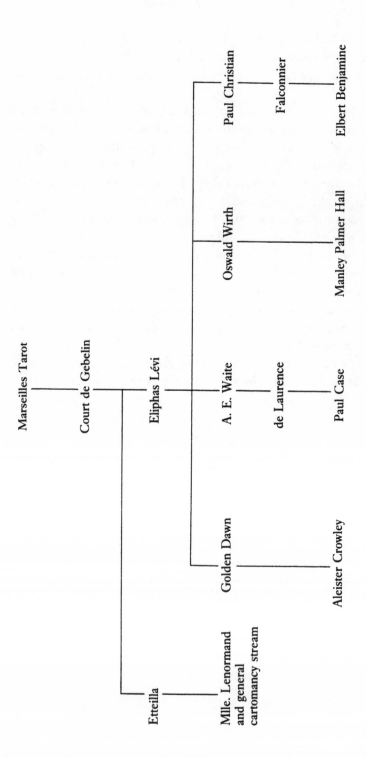

Marseilles Tarot

Court de Gebelin

Etteilla

Eliphas Lévi

Mlle. Lenormand
and general
cartomancy stream

Golden Dawn

A. E. Waite

Oswald Wirth

Paul Christian

Aleister Crowley

de Laurence

Paul Case

Manley Palmer Hall

Falconnier

Elbert Benjamine

Table 1

22

Tarot Trump Imagery

I N THE SURVEY of Tarot Trump design that follows we have made a number of assumptions in the interest of clarity.

1. We have used the Marseilles Tarot sequence, because this has become the generally accepted standard. There are other orders possible which we discuss in the next chapter.
2. We have chosen as headings the Trump titles which are most widely accepted or at least understood by students of the esoteric Tarot.
3. We have used a line-drawn Marseilles design for reference, as this is the source from which most esoteric packs derive.
4. We have sought only to cover the main stream of esoteric design. That is, we have omitted the cartomantic packs of Etteilla and his imitators and the Egyptianized designs of the Paul Christian/ Falconnier stream.
5. We have not discussed esoteric designs beyond 1910. That is, we have confined ourselves to the three principal packs of the turn of the century, those of Oswald Wirth, the Golden Dawn and A. E. Waite. Most later esoteric packs derive from one or other of these lines of tradition. (See Table 1.)
6. We have structured our remarks into the following broad headings:
   a) Hand-Painted Images (i.e. circa 1450-1500)
   b) Early Printed Card Tradition (i.e. circa 1500-1700)
      Designs after 1700 proliferate wildly according to whims and fashions of card makers and their customers.
   c) Esoteric Versions (i.e. occult society based packs of 1889-1910).
   d) Commentary – our own notes and observations from study of these designs.
7. Short titles have been accorded to the packs cited, details of which are as follows:

Hand-painted

Visconti Sforza: Pierpoint Morgan Library, New York and Accademia Carrara, Bergamo. (15 and 5 Trumps)

Gringonneur: Bibliothèque Nationale, Paris. (16 Trumps)

D'Este: Cary Collection, University of Yale. (8 Trumps)

Fournier Visconti-Sforza: Museo Fournier, Vittoria, Spain. (2 Trumps)

Cary-Yale Visconti-Sforza: Cary Collection, University of Yale. (11 Trumps)

Brera: Brera Gallery, Milan. (2 Trumps)

Rothschild: Rothschild Collection, The Louvre, Paris. (1 Trump)

Von Bartsch Visconti-Sforza: Museum of Fine Arts, Montreal. (1 Trump)

Collection Piero Tozzi, New York. (4 Trumps)

Victoria & Albert Visconti-Sforza: Victoria & Albert Museum, London. (2 Trumps)

Guildhall: Guildhall, London. (1 Trump)

Rosenthal Visconti-Sforza: Rosenthal Collection, London. (5 Trumps)

Castello Ursino: Museo Civico, Castello Ursino, Catania, Italy. (4 Trumps)

Printed Cards and Sheets

Rosenwald: Rosenwald Collection, National Gallery of Art, Washington, D.C. (5 Trumps, c. 1500)

Parisian: Bibliothèque Nationale, Paris. (22 Trumps, c. 1650)

Catelin Geofroy: Museum für Kunsthandwerk, Frankfurt. (8 Trumps, 1557)

Colonna: British Museum, London. (4 Trumps, c. 1610)

Rothschild: Rothschild Collection, The Louvre, Paris. (6 Trumps, c. 1500)

Beaux Arts: Bibliothèque de l'École Nationale Supérieur des Beaux Arts, Paris. (6 Trumps, c. 1500)

Italian: Metropolitan Museum of Art, New York. (5 Trumps, c. 1500)

Swiss: J. P. Mayer cards. Cincinnati Art Museum. (6 cards. c. 1680)

Marseilles: Common. Before 1740 to present.

Esoteric

Oswald Wirth: Stanislaus de Guaita & Oswald Wirth Paris 1889.

A. E. Waite: A. E. Waite and Pamela Coleman-Smith published by Rider, London 1910.

Golden Dawn: S. L. MacGregor Mathers and associates, c. 1888, reconstructed by Israel Regardie and Robert Wang 1977, published by U.S. Games Systems Inc., New York.

The Fool

Hand-Painted Images

The Visconti-Sforza Fool has the appearance of an ill-cared for idiot. He stands in rags, his bare feet show through holes in his stockings, and seven feathers are stuck in his hair. His ill-shaven face has a blank look, and over his shoulder he carries a long club.

In the Gringonneur cards the Fool has more the aspect of a clown, with a widely grinning vacuous face. He has a pointed cap with asses' ears and is arrayed in a form of motley, though bare legged. He plays with a string of balls or bells and about his feet four boys gather stones to throw at him.

The D'Este Fool is similar but less dressed, being virtually naked save for his head dress. This is more the conventional jester's tricorn, a belled centre point with long ear-like side points. He carries a stick with some kind of baubles attached.

Early Printed Card Tradition

On a seventeenth-century Parisian set he is more fully dressed in jester's clothing, and carries a stick with a puppet fool's head at which he gazes.

In the Marseilles Tarot he is similarly dressed but carries a bag on a stick over his shoulder. He has a staff as a walking stick and is pawed from behind by a dog. (See Figure 2.)

Esoteric Versions

Oswald Wirth saw Le Fou much as the Marseilles card, although the harassing animal is feline rather than canine. A fallen obelisk and a crocodile also appear in the background.

Whereas the Wirth figure's face looks coarse and imbecilic, A. E. Waite stresses the innocence of youth. He shows the Fool about to walk off a high precipice in the mountains. The bag over his shoulder has an eye on it and in his other hand he holds a white rose. A white dog beside him jumps for joy.

The Golden Dawn stresses innocence even more by depicting the Fool as a naked child, stretching his hand to pluck a golden rose from a tree, accompanied by a leashed black wolf or wolf-like dog.

Figure 2

Commentary

In the game of Tarot the Fool has a special role, for with his Zero designation, he has no scoring capacity in the ranking of the Trumps. Rather, his function is that of being able to overturn all the rules. He is never played in the usual sense. Rather, the player who holds him shows him at the appropriate moment and this excuses the player from having to follow suit with a higher card that he may wish to reserve until later. For this reason the Fool is often called the *scusi* – the excuse.

It is natural to assume that the Fool is the last surviving Trump in the conventional pack. of cards, where he now appears, with a similar kind of playing function, as the Joker.

It appears however that there was no direct line of descent in this development. The ordinary pack never had a Joker or similar special card. It was a nineteenth-century introduction in America.

However, those who have some experience of the magical power of the Tarot archetypes, and the reality of the Platonic Ideas of the magical universe behind the physical world, may be willing to concede that the Fool has willed his own re-invention or rediscovery. He in particular, of all the Trumps, is too important to be ignored.

The realization of this especial role and significance carries over into the modern esoteric tradition. For Manly P. Hall makes the suggestion that the Fool contains all the other Trumps. In the full page illustration to the Tarot section of his *Secret Teachings of All Ages* he shows this quite strikingly, with a picture of the Fool and a pyramid of the other Trumps superimposed over his body.

A. E. Waite also spoke guardedly, in his characteristic style, of the Fool being 'the most speaking' of symbols, which we may take to refer to its representation of the Word. The Word made Flesh in an esoteric Christian conception of the Tarot would certainly have all the characteristics of the Fool; the apparent insignificance and foolishness that is in reality a power and wisdom that transcends that of the mundane human world.

In his novel *The Greater Trumps* Charles Williams emphasizes this role in his description of the secret room where the original models of the images are kept. This is of course a very real inner condition, although for the conventions of the genre it is described as a physical place in the story. Here, on a table, about which are ranged symbols of the Lesser Arcanum, the Trump figures move about in self-propelled endless dance, in a golden haze and with a slight humming noise. This is a very evocative image, and it is even worth placing the cards out on a table physically in this manner and meditating upon it. The cards speak most strongly to those who physically 'play' with them.

In this set-up the Fool is described as standing in the centre of all the moving Trumps, as stable focus and indeed Lord of the Dance. However, when someone such as Aunt Sybil looks at the table she sees the Fool in fact also to be dancing in amongst the other cards. Sybil is that remarkable person, a fully redeemed human individual, one whose realization of the true and the good is firm and sure, and who expresses this in her daily life. To her the Fool is a living active Fool, just as to the perceptive Christian, the Christ is a Risen and Active Lord in the presence of, and in relation to, all his created archetypes, rather than a formal theological or philosophical concept.

The traditional cards add a brutal side to the concept of the Fool that is akin to the Biblical account of the passers by who mocked the dying God at the crucifixion. This is demonstrated in the cards that show children gathering missiles to throw at the demented beggar man.

This reflects a common human characteristic, the persecution of the strange or the afflicted, a trait which extends even into the animal world. There are, of course, deep paradoxical truths in the wisdom of the innocent, as has been explored in Shakespeare's *King Lear* and Dostoevsky's *The Idiot*.

A. E. Waite's esoteric cards take up the theme of innocence as a quality of the virgin human spirit coming into the world. The Golden Dawn card also more overtly carries the quality of the miraculous child, one who can tame and control the fierce elemental forces or even the wolves of evil intent, and pluck the golden blossom of the Tree of Paradise.

In esoteric allocation of the Hebrew letters to the Trumps, Eliphas Lévi favoured Shin for the Fool, signifying the three-fold fire of the Spirit. The Golden Dawn tradition allocates Aleph which, as Divine Breath, could also be held to be relevant.

The Magician

Hand-Painted Images

The Visconti-Sforza Magician is well dressed, in scarlet trimmed with ermine, including an ornate hat. He thus has the air of a merchant rather than a trickster or thimble rigger. He sits on what appears to be a chest and has various artefacts before him on a table, and a rod in his left hand. The objects are a knife, a cylindrical cup, two small round objects, and what appears to be a white soft hat as might be used by a conjuror for concealing things.

The D'Este Magician stands in a more active pose before a young audience. He is also richly dressed and with a plume in his hat. He holds a cup aloft, another larger cup is upon the table, together with three small round objects.

Early Printed Card Tradition

On the sixteenth-century Rosenwald printed sheets, the Magician wears a two-horned jester's cap and bells and faces straight out of the card, standing behind his table, a stick in each hand, with a number of small objects before him.

In the Catelin Geofroy card he is definitely entertaining three people to a performance of legerdemain, sitting with magic wand. The tricks of his trade are small objects and two down-turned cups under which they might appear.

The Parisian seventeenth-century card also shows him with a two pronged jester's hat. He is performing before an audience and has a monkey and a dog beneath his table.

On the Marseilles card and its derivatives he stands without an audience before a table laden with a number of objects that include

Figure 3

small balls or bells, cups, knives and a bag. He reverts to a wide brimmed hat in place of the jester's cap, though his dress does not appear to be motley. (See Figure 3.)

Esoteric Versions

Oswald Wirth's Bateleur has a tidier table than the Marseilles card and placed upon it are emblems of the suits; a coin, a sword and a cup, which is filled with red wine. The magician holds the wand in his hand, which has a red sphere at one end and a blue sphere at the other.

Waite also puts suit emblems, including a stave, on the table, which now takes on the appearance of an altar. The magician holds another wand high in his right and with his left hand points downward, as if directing force from one level to another. A lemniscate halo is placed over his bare head, and red roses and white lilies bloom before his altar, with more red roses above his head.

The Golden Dawn Magician has a figure of Mercury in the air over his head as well as the traditional broad brimmed hat. The caduceus of Mercury is also emblazoned on the breast of his tunic, and on the square stone altar before him are the four suit emblems.

Commentary

In the original tradition this figure is one who carries a power and glamour about him, whether conceived as a rich merchant from far away places, or as a master of tricks and legerdemain. To an extent, all actors, performers, fairground showmen, even market traders, and by extension, advertising men and 'image' merchants share in this archetypal role.

In the theological context he is therefore an extension of the Fool – in fact almost the polar complement. One who demonstrates a wisdom superior to those whom he tricks or entertains, and so who also has a power over them. As wanderer, whose home is always elsewhere, he carries with him the ambience of another world, another dimension of existence. This is the attraction of the 'other' that leads all the adventurous young to leave home, or to seek the glamour of fame or fortune.

In this aspect he is like the Pied Piper of Hamelin. The esoteric cards conceptualize the magical and philosophical elements of this rather more formally by making the table into an altar of magical operation, and the thimbles and bells and other illusionist's tricks into the four suits of the Tarot with their implied elemental attributions. All of this sense is implied, perhaps more strongly if less obviously, in the traditional card design.

The Magician seems, with the advent of the printed cards however, to have come down somewhat in the world. From well heeled merchant traveller to fair ground or market mountebank. All these occupations are, of course, under the patronage of Hermes.

Eliphas Lévi sought to see the Hebrew letter Aleph in the attitude of the figure on the Marseilles card, but this connection is of doubtful provenance.

In his broad potential the Magician is very much a Hermes figure – the psychopomp of all magic and knowledge and exchange. The chameleon like Mercurius of the alchemical process. The Golden Dawn card lays emphasis on this fact. The power of ever flowing creation and bringing through of power from one level to another is also well expressed in the Waite and Golden Dawn designs.

The High Priestess

Hand-Painted Images
The Visconti-Sforza figure is a seated nun in a brown habit holding a closed book in her left hand and a thin sceptre topped by a cross in her right. Over her tall white pointed wimple she wears a triple golden tiara.

These basic features are repeated in the Fournier Visconti-Sforza card although her threefold tiara appears more queenly than ecclesiastical in design. Almost as if she were a noble lady in charge of a convent – a practice that was not uncommon in medieval and Renaissance times.

Early Printed Card Tradition

The theme is repeated on the Rosenwald printed sheet but she holds a key in her left hand and a closed book on her knee with her right.

Book and sceptre appear in the Parisian printed cards and also the suggestion of pillars and veil behind, which becomes a prominent feature of later esoteric cards.

This feature is similarly apparent in crude and embryonic form in the Marseilles card, where, however, she has lost her sceptre but holds her book open in her lap. (See Figure 4.)

Figure 4

Esoteric Versions

Wirth's Papesse has her book closed, although she retains one finger at a particular page. The book has received an oriental touch by having a Chinese 'tai-ge-tu' sign emblazoned on its front cover. In her left hand she holds crossed gold and silver keys, and a crescent moon tops her three-fold tiara. Behind her the suggestion of pillars in the Marseilles card is made explicit, in red and blue, with a white veil between them, and the floor is of black and white paving, like a masonic lodge.

Waite gives the priestess a scroll in place of a book, on which the word TORA(H) can be seen. At her breast is an equal-armed cross, and her silver head-dress is horned and indicative of the three phases of the moon. Her blue and white draperies flow to the floor with a suggestion of water, to a silver crescent moon by her feet. The pillars behind her are massive black and white ones, of Egyptian style, with lotus capitals, and bearing the letters B and J – no doubt for Boaz and Jachim, the Hebrew titles of the pillars of the Temple of Solomon the King, familiar to masonic tradition. The veil between them is decorated with a pomegranate motif.

The Golden Dawn High Priestess, in light blue draperies on a predominantly light blue card, stands bare foot, holding a chalice, a silver crescent moon at her brow.

Commentary

The original conception of this card seems to have been simply a noble lady of religious vocation. The allocation of the startling title of Popess, indicating an apparent readiness to concede at least equal spiritual temporal status to female as to male, is a notion that traditional religious authorities have found it difficult to come to terms with. The patriarchal bias of Judaeo-Christian religious thought has tended to regard women as spiritually subservient if not inferior. A natural reaction to this unnatural attitude has been the supernatural elevation of the mother of Jesus, through the Cult of the Blessed Virgin, to Mother of God.

The esoteric development of this card has followed the Marian trend so that the symbolic associations now associated with it bring to mind titles that have been accorded to the Virgin – Star of the Sea, Fount of Wisdom and so on.

The root of much of this symbolism is found in the great pagan appreciation of the divine feminine in such goddesses as Isis and Ishtar. This reassertion of ancient channels of devotion has scandalized the Protestant wing of the church.

The High Priestess is ultimately representative of the Holy Wisdom, the *sancta sophia*, the Holy Spirit seen as a feminine principle. This is indicated by the book or scroll that she carries.

The Pillars of the Temple of Solomon are by no means irrelevant to this conception for she might also be regarded as the Shekinah, the Divine Presence that ever accompanied the Ark of the Covenant, from the times of its travels in the tent of the Tabernacle in the Wilderness to its installation in the Holy of Holies guarded by Cherubim in the Temple of Solomon. The Veil before which she sits not only has relevance to the Veil of Isis, the barrier of perception between the planes (that were seven-fold in the legends of Ishtar), but also the Veil of the Temple that was woven by the young virgin, in scarlet and purple silk, in the apocryphal stories of Mary, and which was rent at the Crucifixion, opening to the world the potential of that which had been hitherto concealed and unrevealed since the expulsion from Eden.

The Empress

Hand-Painted Images
The Visconti-Sforza Empress sits crowned with sceptre in her right hand and shield in her left, upon which is the device of the black imperial eagle.

Early Printed Card Tradition
In the Rosenwald sheet the sceptre is in her left hand and she holds an orb in her right. The Parisian tarot returns the sceptre to her right hand and her left hand is empty. This is the same basic pattern as the Catelin Geofroy Card.

In the Marseilles card the sceptre is held in the left hand and has a large orb with cross at its top, and the eagle shield reappears at her right hand. There is also the suggestion of two pillars behind her – or else a high backed throne. (See Figure 5.)

Esoteric Versions
Wirth's Imperatrice is winged, and holds a grand golden sceptre surmounted with a cross , and also a red shield upon which is a white eagle. A halo about her crowned head contains nine five-pointed golden stars. Her blue mantle falls down towards a crescent moon which has a representation of an eye above it.

Waite's Empress is out of doors on a green mound, with wheat growing before her, and trees, a stream and a waterfall in the background. She holds a short green and gold sceptre aloft, and wears a head-dress consisting of a green wreath with twelve golden five-pointed stars. Her robe is decorated with flowers and her throne is supported by a heart shaped shield emblazoned with the sign of Venus.

Figure 5

The Golden Dawn Empress sits before a green curtain on a brown throne on a dais. She wears a flat head-dress with a type of crown decoration upon it, and holds an ankh in one hand and a sceptre topped by a golden sphere in the other. A halo encircles her head, the sphere, and arms of the throne; and a golden bird that is emblematically portrayed beside her head.

Commentary

In the original hand-painted images this represents the simple power of supreme rulership in its feminine aspect.

This is a more outward, or mundane expression, so to speak, of the principle of the High Priestess – just as the Magician might be said to be a more outward expression of the Fool.

It can be found in the archetype that overshadowed great queens such as Elizabeth and Victoria – or that mythical queen who was thought to reside in the heart of Africa.

The principle of sovereignty was a feminine figure going back to the oldest of times, as in the figure of Ériu, the sovereignty of Ireland, which is at root behind and beyond the Holy Grail legends.

In Christian terms the figure is represented by the great Mother Church – an outward, mundane expression of the inner church that is represented by icons of the Virgin. Again there is deep symbolic relevance to the church as Body of Christ; for the feminine principle in outward expression is that of the body, the vessel, ultimately the Grail.

A. E. Waite emphasizes another expression of this great ruling feminine principle by showing on his card the Earth Mother, and the Venus symbol that is upon her heart-shaped shield is a reminder of the inner tradition that Venus holds the pattern for the perfected Earth. This, however, is more immediately a product of the Golden Dawn's allocation of the Trumps and planets to the Paths of the Tree of Life. This is indicated on the Golden Dawn by the presence of a hovering dove, a bird sacred to Venus.

The Empress as a whole might indeed be regarded as, not only the goddess Venus, but all goddesses that rule expression in form, including the principle of motherhood.

The Emperor

Hand-Painted Images
We have a number of extant hand-painted cards of the Emperor.

The Visconti-Sforza Emperor sits with a sceptre in his right hand and an orb in his left. On his head is an ornate hat bearing the imperial eagle.

The Cary-Yale Emperor sits facing us on a raised throne. He is similarly accoutred, and attended by four pages, one of whom, at lower right, kneels bearing a crown.

The Brera-Brambilla card is similar but without the page.

The same basic features are found on the otherwise stylistically very different Rosenthal card; and again on the Fournier card.

The Gringonneur card has much the same features, though stylistically is different yet again, and attended by two pages with hands piously crossed upon their breasts. The eagle hat has given way, however, to a crown, and the sceptre is a form of fleur-de-lys, as are the decorations of the crown.

The Rothschild Emperor has two attendants also, but these are small bearded figures before him that barely reach to his knees. His sceptre is again a fleur-de-lys and the orb may have turned into a great seal.

Early Printed Card Tradition
The simple lines of the Rosenwald sheet show orb or seal in right

hand, fleur-de-lys sceptre in left, and a crown on the head. There is no suggestion of eagles or attendants.

The Emperor of the Parisian card is a crowned standing figure in open country, wearing an enveloping cloak.

This suggestion of being out of doors is maintained on the Marseilles card, but the emperor is again throned, the eagle re-appears at the side of his throne, and in his right hand is a crossed orbed sceptre. His left hand is empty and he wears a chain and lamen of office. (See Figure 6.)

Figure 6

Esoteric Versions

Wirth's L'Empereur is given a trident or fleur-de-lys sceptre, with a crescent moon near its base, and a large orb. Emblems of the sun and moon are placed on his breast plate. He sits on a cubic stone instead of a throne, and the imperial eagle is on the side of it.

Waite depicts the Emperor full face, sitting on an imposing grey stone throne decorated with rams' skulls. Behind him is a chasm with a river at the bottom, and on the far side of it, high red mountains. He holds an orb and a sceptre rather like an elongated ankh. He wears full armour under a purple cloak.

The Golden Dawn Emperor is similar but sits before a green curtain or background. He is barefoot and clad in red court robes. His feet rest upon a white ram, and a white ram's head also tops his sceptre. In the other hand is the orb.

Commentary

The original hand-painted card shows simply a great king or emperor. It is the principle of rulership, of kingship, of empire – so all power of government, of whatever political colour, may be said to be represented here. In fact it is the peak of the pyramid of any organisational structure. This applies not only to mercantile or social systems but to systems generally, all of which, as organisations or organisms of diverse units, have a coherent ruling principle, without which the whole thing falls into decay, disease, chaos or death. In the mundane demonstration of authority Charles Williams summed up the principle in the up-raised arm of a policeman directing traffic. Multiply the function of this raised arm of authority many times and one has the structure of government, law and order in action. This is a force that can be used with wisdom and justice or abused.

It should be said in the context of both the Emperor and Empress cards that the concept of empire is not, in its true sense, the exploitation of one nation by another, even if that is how it is generally expressed in a far from perfect world. Empire should be a step toward the ultimate expression of a peaceful universal order. Ultimately, in religious symbolic terms, it is the descent from heaven of the New Jerusalem, or the founding of a universal Utopia It is the full expression of what the United Nations organisation sets out to express.

Charles Williams in his Arthurian Cycle of poems expresses the conception in the symbol of Byzantium. It is also implied in the great vision of Dante in its cosmic aspect, of universal city.

The ram symbolism on the Waite and Golden Dawn cards derives from their chosen system of Tree of Life correspondences. In so far that 0° of Aries is the conventional position for commencing the marking out of the zodiac, like the convention of the 0° meridian line of Greenwich for terrestrial timing and navigational charting, this symbolism has its relevance.

The Hierophant

Hand-Painted Images

The Visconti-Sforza Pope faces out from the card making a sign of blessing with his right hand and holding a long sceptre, topped with a cross, in his left. The same theme appears on the Von Bartsch card.

The Gringonneur Pope, however, holds a key, and is seen in profile, flanked by two seated cardinals.

The D'Este Pope is likewise seen in profile but as well as holding the key he makes the sign of blessing, and has no attendant figures.

Early Printed Card Tradition

In the Rosenwald sheet the Pope, facing us, has no attendants or accoutrements nor does he make any sign of benediction. He simply sits enthroned with possibly an open scroll on his knees.

The Parisian Pope, however, holds a huge key and also a long staff which may be topped by a banner.

In the Marseilles cards this long staff appears with a threefold cross at its top whilst the Pope makes the sign of blessing with his right hand to two (possibly four) tonsured figures before him. Behind him are two distinct pillars. (See Figure 7.)

Esoteric Versions

Wirth's Pope is essentially similar to the Marseilles card apart from stylistic differences. Waite also, with more massive pillars and crossed

Figure 7

keys at the feet of the figure. The Golden Dawn figure has no pillars but sits alone before a white curtain, holding an open scroll and a shepherd's crook; the throne decorated with bull's heads.

Commentary

The hand-painted cards depicted the principle of spiritual authority on Earth. The esoteric cards extend this conception with minor symbolic additions. The bulls in the Golden Dawn card relate the card to Taurus on their Tree of Life schema – and presumably no pun was intended over papal bulls!

The function relates to that of the Emperor. In fact this card might be said to be a more inner expression of the Emperor, just as the High Priestess is of the Empress.

In outer life the principle of the Pope is seen not only in the papacy but in the seat of authority in all religious confessions, including the least authoritarian, where the authority may be invested in a congregation or committee. The principle can also be applied to all organisations with an idealistic vision, even if that vision be expressed in non-religious or even anti-religious terms. The card indeed sums up the principle of faith and belief, from which any code of conduct or moral standard ultimately derives.

The Lovers

Hand-Painted Images

The Visconti-Sforza Lovers stand hand in hand, facing each other, beneath a winged blindfolded and naked Cupid who holds a long arrow aloft in his right hand, and a long rod in his left, which could possibly be another dart or a bow. He stands on a high pedestal behind the lovers.

In the Cary-Yale Lovers, the pedestal has become a parasol-like canopy and Cupid flies above it, holding two darts.

The Gringonneur card shows a procession of three pairs of lovers and a cloud above them from which two winged naked figures, not blindfolded, shoot with bows and arrows at the assembled company.

Early Printed Card Tradition

On the Rosenwald sheet the male lover kneels on one knee before his beloved, his hands on his heart, in conventional pose, whilst the winged and blindfolded Cupid flies above them with bow and arrow, supported by a cloud.

The seventeenth-century Colonna sheet, of superior workmanship, similarly shows a blindfolded Cupid shooting from a cloud, but the lovers stand holding a flower between them.

The Parisian printed Lovers card shows three figures, dancing or embracing under a tree, with Cupid overhead with bow and arrow, in what appears to be a sunburst.

The Marseilles card similarly shows three figures, but the third has emerged from the background to appear as a wreathed female, her hand on the shoulder of the male lover, who stands facing her with his beloved. Cupid, in a sunburst above them, without blindfold, aims a shaft at the couple. (See Figure 8.)

Figure 8

Esoteric Versions

Wirth's L'Amoureux has the young man plainly standing at a forking of the ways, his hands crossed on his breast, while one way is indicated by a flower decked bare-foot maiden in yellow and green, and the other by a crowned maiden in red and blue. As on the Marseilles card, Cupid flies overhead but his dart is pointed directly at the young man and not between the lovers.

Waite transforms Cupid into a great winged angel standing in the sun, and the lovers appear as Adam and Eve. She has a fruiting tree behind her with a coiled serpent; he has a burning bush. Between them in the distance is a high mountain peak.

The Golden Dawn breaks new ground with a picture of a naked Andromeda chained to a rock, menaced by a monster from the sea, whilst Perseus with sword, shield and winged helmet, dives from the sky to her rescue.

Commentary

The original principle of this card was Love, the key figure being Cupid hovering over the lovers. In the course of time, on the Marseilles card, we find the centre of interest subtly changed. This has caused some difference of interpretation among the esoteric commentators. Some interpret the card as a young man standing at the crossroads of vice and virtue, or facing some other dilemma. This is implied on the Wirth card where the young man stands with one foot on each of the branching ways.

Waite and the Golden Dawn use the ambiguity to launch into lines of thought of their own. Waite makes Cupid an overseeing angel and evokes the imagery of the ancient Biblical mythology of the Garden of Eden and the Fall. The Golden Dawn also reverts to very ancient imagery, for the Perseus and Andromeda story was old even before the ancient Greeks adopted it, probably from Babylonia. It is the age old perennial story of the hero rescuing the damsel in distress.

Whatever the mode of symbolism, the common root is that we have sexual differentiation expressed on the card.

The figure on the Marseilles card who stands before the lovers is perhaps best regarded as Venus, the mother of Cupid. Each of the lovers is at a point of decision in their commitment to each other that love demands.

The Chariot

Hand-Painted Images

On the Visconti-Sforza card a fair lady is depicted, on a platform of a triumphal chariot drawn by two white winged horses.

On the Von Bartsch card she casually holds the reins in her right hand, holds an orb in her left, and, wearing a crown, is seated on an ornate throne.

The card in the Museo Civico, Catania, shows the now more familiar face-on scenario. The chariot is now a box-like affair in which there stands a female figure holding an orb or disk. The horses are not winged and are led by two men.

On the Gringonneur card we have the platformed type of float but face-on. The figure now appears to be male, clean-shaven and youthful in appearance, wearing a sword and holding a halberd. The horses are not led, nor are they winged.

Early Printed Card Tradition

A fragment of a printed Italian card of the fifteenth or sixteenth century shows a scallop shaped chariot in which several people appear to travel, with a winged figure above them who is possibly holding the reins and driving the chariot.

On the uncut Rothschild sheet, plumed horses pull a high edifice on a triumphal car upon which a figure with winged helmet is perched, holding orb in right hand and drawn sword in left. There appear to be two suns in the sky but this could be festive bunting.

The Rosenwald sheet is more prosaic, showing the box-like car drawn by two horses in which a crowned male figure stands, orb in right hand, sword in left.

The Colonna card of the early seventeenth century shows a similar figure, on a throned chariot, the orb and sword in opposite hands.

The Parisian seventeenth-century version is much more actively portrayed, in side view. A triumphal figure sits somewhat precariously, holding a baton or similar device, whilst a young driver before him whips up the horses.

The Marseilles card is a very static face-on representation in a box-like chariot which has appeared before but now with four pillars supporting a canopy. The crowned figure holds a sceptre in his right hand and is equipped with strange epaulettes in the form of faces appearing as crescents. The horses are not winged. Between them on the chariot front is a shield-shaped device with the letters S.M. The conventionalised drawing of the horses, face on, gives the appearance that they are a two-headed single creature. (See Figure 9.)

Esoteric Versions

Wirth places stars on the canopy of the chariot and on the charioteer's crown, and transforms the horses into sphinxes, one black and one white. This follows the suggestion of Eliphas Lévi. The front of the chariot is

Figure 9

embellished with Egyptian derived signs including a winged sun-disk.

These signs also appear on the front of the Waite chariot, as also the sphinxes and the stars, derivative either from Wirth or Lévi.

The Golden Dawn card shows a horned-helmet warrior riding a chariot through the sky, pulled by a black and a white horse. The shaft of the chariot is embellished with a hawk or eagle head.

Commentary

The original hand-painted conception was a simple one, familiar since classical times, of a usually winged figure of Victory in a triumphal chariot. Thus the horses are winged on the Visconti-Sforza card.

Somewhere along the line the sex of the charioteer changed and the chariot was depicted head on, and the strange epaulettes appear. No commentator seems to have adequately accounted for these beyond speculation that they may be oracular devices deriving from ancient Hebrew tradition.

With the starry canopy we have a certain resemblance to the Vision of Ezekiel and the whole range of Merkebah or Chariot mysticism. This is a mystical Jewish conception of God but there are also pagan allusions that could be drawn, such as the sun chariot of Helios.

It is odd that the change of sex of the figure has diverted attention from the original title of Victory, which has an interesting correlation with the fact that this is Trump VII and the seventh Sephirah of the Tree of Life has the tide of Victory.

Justice

Hand-Painted Images
The Visconti-Sforza Justice shows a seated female with scales in her left hand and a drawn sword in her right. Overhead a bareheaded but otherwise armoured knight on a richly caparisoned white horse gallops with drawn sword. The same features appear on the Rosenthal Visconti-Sforza card.

The Gringonneur figure, however, appears without the knight in the background, but has a kind of angular nimbus about her head.

Early Printed Card Tradition
The nimbus also appears in the Rosenwald sheet, which is similar, apart from the scales and sword being in different hands. On the seventeenth-century Parisian printed version the figure of Justice stands, has no nimbus and is blindfolded.

Figure 10

The Marseilles card reverts to a straightforward seated figure, with crown-like head-dress, and sword and scales. (See Figure 10.)

Esoteric Versions

Wirth's Justice follows the conventional lines of the Marseilles card. So does Waite's, though he places her before a veil between pillars. The Golden Dawn figure, however, is Egyptianized, seated between black and white lotus pillars, and with lotus decorations on her throne. Her bare feet rest on a grey wolf and the floor is the chequered paving associated with masonry. A black and white striped Egyptian nemyss is upon her head.

Commentary

The traditional design for this card is the conventional figure of Justice, although the inclusion of a knight is an interesting feature which has dropped from the esoteric designs. This is perhaps a pity as it has resonances with the law-keeping tradition of the knight errant, and also the ancient tradition of one test of justice being battle by champions. Whatever our view of this method of jurisprudence, it was part and parcel of a different world view, which considered that God would and could act on the side of right. We may have lost something of value in our more demotic and reasoned view of the processes of law.

However, there remains at a sterner level the incontrovertible fact that might is right insofar that life is subject to natural law. Thus the balance of nature is to be seen at work here, and in more millennial terms the ultimate fate of the world and those who live on it.

The Egyptian symbolism of the Golden Dawn card is hardly essential, but the Egyptian conception of a judgement after death is strikingly presented on surviving papyri and has obviously impressed modern students of occultism. Balance is, of course, an important concept in magical philosophy and practice; the principle is a universal one and the rule of law and balance works at all levels of existence and in all ages and climes.

The Hermit

Hand-Painted Images

The Visconti-Sforza hermit is an old man with an ornate hat, bearing a long staff and holding an hour glass.

The Gringonneur hermit has a more modest head-dress and a cloak over his girdled robe. He has no staff but holds up an hour glass at which he gazes. In the background is a high mountain.

Early Printed Card Tradition

The sheet in the Bibliothèque de l'École Nationale Supérieure des Beaux Arts shows the hermit on crutches, though winged. He seems to stand in a gateway, and behind him is an obelisk, while a sun shines from the top left-hand corner of the card. All these details suggest attributions of Time.

The Rosenwald sheet likewise shows an old man on crutches but without background symbolism, nor with wings.

On the Catelin Geofroy card the old man has a cross hanging by a beaded chain from his waist. He holds a lantern in place of the hour glass and seems as if he may be knocking at a door. Although somewhat decrepit, he has no need of crutches.

In the Parisian printed set he appears to be either tending a light or even serving an altar.

The Marseilles card depicts the hermit robed, with staff in left hand and lantern upheld in right. (See Figure 11).

Figure 11

Esoteric Versions

Wirth's L'Ermite is similar to the Marseilles card, with the addition of a dragon-like worm crawling before the hermit.

Waite's Hermit has a gold six-pointed star in his lantern and is standing on a snowy height.

The Golden Dawn Hermit, however, stands on a desert plain under a starry sky and has a Hebrew letter Yod in a triangle upon his hood. This is to accord with the Tree of Life Path attribution of this card in accordance with the Golden Dawn system.

Commentary

This figure has undergone a sea change. Originally he was Father Time carrying an hour glass, and sometimes seen with wings or crutches, for time can crawl or fly according to circumstances.

As soon as the hour glass became a lantern it laid the basis for an additional range of meaning, that in fact seems to have ousted the original conception. Nowadays he is seen as a way-shower; a guide, philosopher and friend; a keeper of secret wisdom.

The card can, in fact, carry all the attributes conventionally associated with age, from God the Father and Ancient of Days downwards – though age and ancient wisdom are not necessarily to be associated with decrepitude.

Time might well be reconsidered as a title for this card by esoteric students, for it is by involvement in the world of time that the lessons of life are learned. This is the experience of incarnation and all time is measured in terms of the movement of the Earth and the other celestial bodies in space. The hermit is therefore a universal figure of cosmic proportions.

In the role of guardian of esoteric secrets he also has profound dynamics. The guardian of any mystery system is also its psychopomp. Thus we have the tradition in myth and legend that the seeker at the gate, if he succeeds in gaining entry to the mystery, has to take his turn as guardian. This is clearly demonstrated in *The Chymical Marriage of Christian Rosencreutz*.

Another line of tradition could see the hermit as Joseph, either as head of the Holy Family, or, in the Grail Tradition as Joseph of Arimathea. In both roles he is the custodian of profound mysteries.

The snowy heights that are introduced into Waite's card emphasize the heights of spiritual wisdom. Thus the Hermit is also a light-house, so to speak, and, in olden time, light-houses were also altars. His lantern holds 'the light that lighteth every man that cometh into the world.' His cloak, in this respect, is the Night of Time.

The Wheel of Fortune

Hand-Painted Images

The Visconti-Sforza Wheel of Fortune has a blindfold winged female figure at its centre, no doubt representing Fortuna. At the top of her wheel is an enthroned king; a young man rises upon the wheel at the left; another man falls head first at the right. The falling man has a tail, and the two others, asses' ears. Underneath the wheel, an old man crawls on all fours. The figures are labelled as follows:

> top figure – *Regno* – I rule
> rising figure – *Regnabo* – I shall rule
> falling figure – *Regnavi* – I ruled
> bottom figure – *Sum sine regno* – I am without rulership

The Brera-Brambilla card is similar but without the inscribed words, and the descending figure has no tail. Likewise the Von Bartsch card, with minor changes of detail and inscriptions difficult to decipher. The descending figure has a tail, but the figures do not have asses' ears, though the topmost figure's crown has a configuration that suggests them.

Early Printed Card Tradition

The fifteenth/sixteenth century Italian sheets in the Metropolitan Museum of Art, New York, are crude in execution. No figure of Fortuna appears at the centre and the wheel direction is reversed. At the top is a four-legged beast; descending on the left is a man; and rising on the right is an animal headed man; whilst underneath a possibly female figure seems to lie in repose. The inscriptions are not well produced but plainly are the same as those cited above.

On the Beaux Arts card there is no figure of Fortuna and at the top what appears to be a bear-headed figure in kingly regalia, holding orb and truncheon-like sceptre. Three figures at the bottom and sides cling to the anticlockwise-revolving wheel.

The Parisian card wheel revolves clockwise with three human figures at bottom and sides. The topmost place is held precariously by a man with cloak and trident. Again there is no figure of Fortuna.

The Marseilles card is remarkable for having no human figures, no goddess Fortuna, and only three figures. The rising and falling ones on the anticlockwise-rotating wheel are like monkeys, the one at the top with crown and sword rather like a monkey-faced sphinx. (See Figure 12.)

Figure 12

Esoteric Versions

Wirth's Wheel has fantastic creatures about its rim after the style of the Marseilles card. He makes the topmost figure unmistakably a sphinx, whilst the descending figure is a horned devil with a trident, and the ascending one a figure of the Egyptian god Anubis, the Opener of the Ways, carrying a caduceus. The whole wheel floats upon a moon-shaped boat with twined serpents rising from it.

Waite places his Wheel in the sky with winged kerubic emblems at the corners – man, eagle, lion, bull. The wheel is in the form of a disk or pentacle with the letters TARO and the Divine Name JHVH in Hebrew letters, with a formal sigil in the centre. He also places a sphinx at the top, and has a rising Anubis, but a falling serpent.

The Golden Dawn Wheel is a twelve-spoked one floating in space, its spokes coloured in different shades in accordance with the Golden Dawn's attribution of colours to the twelve signs of the zodiac. Above the wheel is a sphinx; below it a monkey.

Commentary

It is surprising that the figure of Fortune should have dropped from this card – she who turns the wheel whereby men and women suffer the vagaries of 'those two imposters' – 'triumph' and 'disaster'. The assinine characteristics of the ambitious creatures about the wheel came in the course of time to dominate the card, leading esoteric commentators to transform them into figures from Egyptian iconography.

This has led to a more overtly philosophical implication in that Wirth indicates the Opener of the Ways rising, and an evil figure falling, under the presidency of a sphinx. This idea is followed by Waite who adds the further cosmic framework of the Kerubic Emblems and the Tetragrammaton, or Most Holy Name of God. The colour symbolism of the Golden Dawn also implies a system of interlinking zodiacal influences.

The cyclic aspect of this card should also lead us to consider the universal principle of cycles, in time and space and circumstance, that is a condition of existence outside of eternity. Therefore, like the Hermit, this is a card closely linked to the principles of time and space.

Those of an oriental turn of mind will also see within it the cycles of karma; others, such as the followers of Gurdjieff, the principle of recurrence. Given the principle that time may not be the simple linear figure that is commonly assumed, various possibilities of sequence of experience become tenable. A free spirit can presumably enter and leave the turning wheels of time and space at any point in their revolution.

Strength

Hand-Painted Images

On the Visconti-Sforza card a rough looking man, with flying scarf, holds a club on high in a threatening fashion. At his feet is a lion. They both appear to be threatening the same person or object on the card. (At first sight it looks as if the man is belabouring the lion but on closer examination this seems not to be the case.)

On the Gringonneur card we have a maiden (with an angular nimbus similar to Temperance and Justice and the World in this set), standing beside a column which is breaking in two.

Early Printed Card Tradition

On the Rosenwald sheet the maiden (also with angular nimbus in common with Justice and Temperance on the same sheet), is seated beside an unbroken column, which she clasps.

The Parisian card has the stump of a broken column but the maiden who stands over it is demonstrating her power by subduing a lion.

On the Marseilles card the stump of pillar has gone and we simply have the maiden, in wide-brimmed hat, holding a lion by the jaws. (See Figure 13.)

Figure 13

Esoteric Versions

Wirth's La Force follows the Marseilles card closely.

Waite introduces a chain of roses between the maiden and the lion and in place of the wide brimmed hat places a lemniscate figure above her head. In the background is a high mountain.

On the Golden Dawn card the maiden simply stands beside the lion, her hand on its mane, and she holds four red roses, while a yellow veil blows in the wind about her.

Commentary

The Visconti-Sforza card is something of an anomaly in relation to the mainstream of tradition of the card, although there is a lion featured upon it. Generally speaking the traditions are two-fold, either a maiden beside a pillar (which may be broken) or a maiden controlling a lion.

The maiden and the pillar is perhaps the more conventional image, and, as Fortitude, was depicted by many artists, including Botticelli, as one of the Cardinal Virtues. Although the pillar may be broken, or show the maiden apparently breaking it, the image more consistent with the spirit of the card is really an unbroken pillar, for the sense of the image is strength and support. Indeed the maiden could well be depicted as a caryatid, though this idea does not appear to have occurred to any designer.

The strong man with a club on the Visconti-Sforza card can be thought of as Hercules, the archetypal strong man and hero, who has associations with a lion. The more appealing image is however the maiden with the lion with its associations of beauty and the beast, of spiritual will gently but indominatably controlling physical power. Or again, an idea depicted in another fashion by Botticelli in a famous picture, the victory of Venus over Mars.

The Hanged Man

Hand-Painted Images
The Visconti-Sforza Hanged Man is suspended by the left leg from a beam, supported by two posts, rather like a door frame. His hands appear to be tied behind his back and his right leg is crossed behind the bound one.

The Gringonneur hanged man is altogether more active, suspended by his right ankle and flailing around somewhat, holding on to two heavy bags, presumably containing money. The frame of the gallows is more rustic.

Early Printed Card Tradition
The Beaux Arts sheet is similar to the Gringonneur conception but the figure is in much more repose, the left leg crossed behind the right. The same applies to the Rosenwald sheet, though it is the left leg that is tied.

The Catelin Geofroy card shows a conventional gibbet from which the hanged man is suspended by both feet his hands tied behind his back.

The Paris card is without money bags, though the hands are not tied or held behind.

The Marseilles card shows the hands behind the back, the legs crossed, and a ragged framework, seemingly erected over a ditch or abyss.

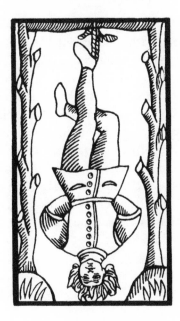

Figure 14

The moon-like pockets and buttons down the front of the man's coat appear on this card, which have given much grist to the imagination of later esoteric commentators. (See Figure 14.)

Esoteric Versions
Wirth's Le Pendu follows the Marseilles card but has coins falling from the man's pockets, gold one side, silver the other.

Waite changes the shape of the gibbet to a Tau cross and gives the man a halo.

The Golden Dawn man is suspended from the roof of a sea cave and the cross and triangle motif suggested in most Hanged Man cards by the disposition of the man's limbs is here accentuated in thin lines of light.

Commentary
This card was often referred to as The Traitor, and no doubt this was the unequivocal meaning to Italians, from the Renaissance period to the present day. It is the mark of extreme social disgrace, and effigies of traitors were publicly displayed upside-down and no less an artist than Botticelli was commissioned to produce works for such a purpose. In modern times the body of the dictator Mussolini was hung up in this way by a vengeful mob.

This may relate to the money bags that the man has on some cards, which could refer to Judas Iscariot, the archetypal traitor, on the common assumption that he betrayed his leader and his God for money.

A traitor represents one with an inversion of all values and there is a higher sense to this inversion that is brought out in the esoteric cards by the serene expression on the man's face and his halo. He is in this respect the willing sacrifice, or the martyr, or one whose actions and beliefs are based on non-material values – or values that differ from the assumptions of the society in which he lives. In this respect the card can represent the Crucifixion, which in Roman times was a mode of execution associated with utter social disgrace, and one particularly applied to traitors or rebels against the state.

Death

Hand-Painted Images

The Visconti-Sforza figure of Death is a standing skeleton, a white cloth or band about its head, holding a bow in one hand, an arrow in the other.

The Cary-Yale skeleton wields a scythe and gallops on horse back over a huddled group of human figures.

The Victoria & Albert Museum card has the figure standing on a floor of black and white paving, holding a scythe over his shoulder. He wears a cardinal's hat and the words SAN FINE come from his mouth. Two sets of beads depending from the hat brim are in the form of a Pythagorean tetractys.

The Gringonneur skeleton is more fully clothed and rides, wielding his scythe, over supine personages of power such as kings and bishops.

Early Printed Card Tradition

The Italian card of the fifteenth/sixteenth century also rides a horse, carrying a scythe, but there are no victims depicted. The Rothschild sheet is similar.

The Rosenwald sheet also features scythe and horseman, with two victims beneath the horse's hooves. The Catelin Geofroy card has the skeleton on foot and wielding a scythe, with a shovel over his shoulder.

The Parisian card is also of the standing skeleton scythesman, which is found on the Marseilles card too, in a field of lopped heads, hands and feet. (See Figure 15.)

Figure 15

Esoteric Versions

Wirth's skeleton mower closely follows the Marseilles card.

Waite follows the tradition of a skeleton on horseback, which he depicts in black armour and carrying a black banner on which is a white rose. Two children kneel before him, a bishop stands, apparently in supplication, and a king lies dead. In the background is a river, and on the horizon the sun rises, or sets, between two towers.

The Golden Dawn follows the Marseilles tradition but introduces a strange multicoloured sun, as if in eclipse, in the sky; and a blue eagle head from which depends a fiery serpent.

Commentary

Printed card manufacturers, in deference to popular superstition, seldom gave a name to this card; and they also contrived to give it the number of 'unlucky' 13 no matter what local variation of Trump sequence there might be. Even today tarocchi players who draw this card consider themselves to be unlucky.

Temperance

Hand-Painted Images

On the Visconti-Sforza card Temperance, in a starry robe, stands in open countryside, pouring liquid from one vase into another. This theme is repeated on the Von Bartsch and on the Gringonneur cards. On the latter the figure has the characteristic pointed nimbus found also on Strength, Justice and the World in this set, and the figure is seated, as also on the D'Este card.

Early Printed Card Tradition

The Rosenwald sheet is similar to the D'Este.

The Catelin Geofroy figure is also seated but pours liquid from a jar into a dish.

The Marseilles figure is remarkable for being winged, and also reverts to the convention of a standing figure in countryside. (See Figure 16.)

Figure 16

Esoteric Versions

Wirth follows the Marseilles scheme. Waite has an angelic figure standing partly on land, partly on water; and a pathway leads to mountains over which is the sun, upon which is superimposed a crown.

The angel also has a solar disc on the forehead, and iris flowers growing at the water's edge are symbolically reinforced by a rainbow over the figure's head.

The Golden Dawn card also has Temperance standing on land and sea. She has a yellow square on her breast and a golden sphere or sun is above her head. In the background a volcano erupts.

Commentary

Temperance is another standard iconographic figure of one of the cardinal virtues. It also has strong alchemical connotations of purification and the tempering of metals. Another sense, that is not so readily obvious, is that in days before piped running water, lords and ladies at table washed their hands (which they used for eating until forks were later introduced) by the assistance of a servant pouring water from one bowl to another. Thus the figure also represents a cleansing process.

The standing between land and water is a comparatively modern esoteric conception, it would seem. The rainbow attributions of the Waite card refer to the position where the card was placed on the Tree of Life in the Golden Dawn system, on the path between Yesod and Tiphereth.

Of interest on the Gringonneur cards is the nimbus given to Temperance, Strength, Justice and the World, which implies a relationship between these four cards that accords with a particular way of laying out the cards (see page 88).

The Devil

Hand-Painted Images

No Devil on a hand-painted card has survived.

Early Printed Card Tradition

The earliest version we have is a fragmented Italian printed sheet where he stands in open country, a tree in the background. He is winged and carries a trident over his shoulder. He has another face on his lower abdomen, with animal ears, which could be part of a garment. He has horns and long ears on his head which could, again, be part of a head-dress.

The uncut Rothschild sheet shows a more grotesque figure, with taloned feet, a tail, a horned and animal-eared head that is definitely part of the figure, another more human head for a torso, and spiky wings and shaggy body-hair which by the shape suggests flames. He is in the process of eating a man and a woman.

The Rosenwald sheet Devil is much less menacing, with a quaint depiction of a human figure with horns, animal ears, and taloned feet, holding a trident and dressed in a tunic, either of shaggy fur or feathers, or possibly flames.

The Parisian pack Devil is similar in principle; a menacing figure, horned, winged and taloned, with a rod or trident.

The Marseilles card differs from all previous designs in having the Devil, who holds a hiltless sword or baton, standing on an anvil-like pedestal to which are attached two human figures with horned head-dresses, and who have tails that they may be holding on behind them. The horns, as those of the Devil, appear to be stag rather than goat horns. The Devil himself has bat-like wings and taloned feet. (See Figure 17.)

Figure 17

Esoteric Versions

Wirth's Diable has devils, not humans, secured to the pedestal. The Devil himself bears a long candle and a lamp, with one arm labelled SOLVE and the other COAGULA. At his loins is the sigil for Mercury. A pentagram is upon the forehead of his goat head, and his feet are cloven rather than clawed. Most of these ideas derive from Eliphas Lévi's illustration of the card.

On Waite, the forehead pentagram is inverted, and the alchemical signs and labels do not appear. The figures below are naked humans, though with horns and tails. Their neck manacles are large enough in diameter to be lifted off over their heads. The woman's tail ends in a bunch of grapes, the man's in a flame. The Devil makes a sign of duality with one hand and holds an inverted torch in the other. His feet are the traditional claws.

The Golden Dawn Devil has a horned head that closely resembles an inverted pentagram. He holds an inverted torch and a horn in the other hand. His feet are clawed. The figures below are human but equipped with horns and skirts, and they are manacled to the pedestal by their wrists.

Commentary

The absence of any hand-painted form of the Devil suggests that in the Renaissance period the evil qualities of the Devil were taken seriously and it was preferred that this card be hidden and not on display. As C. S. Lewis has pointed out in *The Screwtape Letters*, a major victory for the Devil has been the spread of the assumption that he does not exist. Or, that if he does, he cuts a ludicrous and easily identified figure after the fashion of the demon king at a pantomime.

The recognition of the real presence of evil in the world, however, is not the same as elevating its importance to a level with God. Everything of evil is uncreative, parasitic, a corruption or distortion of the health and proper function of a living system. It may be that evil is a menacing presence within the world but in the end it will come to nothing, in the Nothing that is the Limitless Light which dispels all darkness.

In the meantime the weeds may flourish with the good and growing crop. The basis of the parable of the tares and the wheat is that the wheat grows to a greater height than the tares. To try to eliminate the tares during growth would be a difficult task injurious to the growing wheat. At harvest time, however, the wheat ears, having grown higher, can be easily harvested, leaving the tares to be put to the destroying and earth-cleansing fire.

The figures on the card plainly indicate bondage, and most evil could be described as a form of bondage – of compulsive behaviour. Compulsion is the hallmark of neurosis and disease, of addiction and vice. In true service is perfect freedom.

Evil is present not only within the world but within each one of us. One does not have to fear raising the Devil by 'dabbling in the occult' or by any other means. His presence is as close as God's – closer than breathing, nearer than hands and feet. But often we give ear and credence to the promptings of evil rather than good. However, the choice remains ours. It is not really sufficient for all that fall to cling to the excuse that they were pushed!

The sign of duality that appears on the cards signifies the principle of evil. The demonic reflection of the Tree of Life, for example, has as its highest (or lowest) sphere the Dual Contending Heads rather than the One Great Countenance of Kether. The Devil may indeed aspire to establish the principle of dualism – an equal footing with God or good – but in this he has the same ambitions as a cancerous cell.

The inverted pentagram similarly, with its two points upward, is a denial of the power of the spirit over the elements.

Waite demonstrates the ultimate lack of power of evil by making it possible for the chained figures to remove the manacles from about their necks. The prisoners, like the inhabitants of Dante's *Inferno*, are there by their own free choice. When we really abhor evil we will cease to be ruled by it. Hence the Delphic adage 'Man – Know Thyself'.

One of the great lessons of more advanced occultism, and one that is more difficult to learn than almost any other, is that the world about us reflects back to us, in the circumstances of our lives, our own state of soul. Yet we often recoil from the hideous face in the mirror of our environment, seeking to blame anybody but ourselves. This is the confrontation with the Dweller on the Threshold who is, like the Devil and his victims, an image of ourselves.

The Tower

Hand-Painted Images
The Gringonneur card is the sole surviving depiction of a hand-painted Tower. Here it is a massive four-square castle-like edifice that is crumbling and falling at the back, with flames disintegrating its upper tower.

Early Printed Card Tradition
The crudely effected Italian printed sheet has a single square tower standing between two trees at the top of a flight of steps. The top of the tower is ablaze with an arrow of lightning coming down from the Sun.

On the Rothschild sheet we have a scheme similar to the Gringonneur version: a massive building, burning in its upper storeys, and the introduction of a male and a female human figure falling before it. There also appears to be two suns in the sky but this feature is found also on other cards in this series (Star, Moon, Chariot and Wheel of Fortune).

The Rosenwald card follows the Gringonneur style also, but with no human figures. A massive tower disintegrates, with flames at the top. The sun is shown above; there is no lightning flash, but flames appear in the sky between the sun and the tower.

The Catelin Geofroy Tower is full of drama. The tower burns in the background whilst in the foreground is a grotesque devil-like figure, and two human figures, one of whom is playing a violin.

The Parisian card is similar in conception and shows several figures in confusion, including one naked with an animal head.

A Swiss pack of 1680 shows the free-standing tower, with two figures falling from it. A blast from the sun lifts the turreted top of the tower, and stones fall from it.

This is the style developed in the Marseilles Tarot, although here the tower is quite intact below the tilting turret, and the falling masonry becomes a pattern of circles in the sky. (See Figure 18.)

Figure 18

Esoteric Versions

The Wirth card follows the Marseilles card closely, though the top courses of brickwork of the tower are damaged, and falling bricks accompany the coloured spheres. One of the falling figures wears a crown, and the bolt from the sky clearly emanates from a sun face.

Waite's Tower is on a high eminence, and appears to be depicted at night. Its top is like a crown and is thrown off intact, as on the Marseilles card. A lightning bolt strikes fire into the tower itself. Two figures fall, the female one crowned: Clouds are in the sky and the coloured spheres of the Marseilles card are rendered as flames in the form of Hebrew letter Yods.

In the Golden Dawn card a bolt from the sun strikes the tower which is a raging inferno inside, and damaged – although the golden-crown top of the tower lifts up intact. Two part-naked figures fall, and the spheres of the Marseilles card are arranged as two Trees of Life; a conventional white one to the right and a black one with an extra sphere (two Yesods) to the left.

Commentary

Like the Devil this card has not survived well from the hand-painted era. This is probably because of its close association with the Devil in its interpretation as Gate of Hell.

An immediate association of the picture on the card is with the Tower of Babel raised by man's overweening pride. This has an ominous relevance to the contemporary world with man's towering achievements in science and technology and his inability to handle the power that this gives him.

The tale of the Great Tower has resonances throughout history and legend. Thomas Mann in the Prelude to his *Joseph and his Brothers* cites other examples such as the pyramids of Cheops in Egypt and Cholula in Central America:

> The people of Cholula have always denied that they were the authors of this mighty structure. They declared it to be the work of giants, strangers from the east, they said, a superior race who, filled with drunken longing for the sun, had reared it up in their ardour, out of clay and asphalt, in order to draw near to the worshipped planet. There is much support for the theory that these progressive foreigners were colonists from Atlantis, and it appears that these sun worshippers and astrologers incarnate always made it their first care, wherever they were, to set up mighty watch-towers, before the faces of the

astonished natives, modelled upon the high towers of their native land, and in particular upon the lofty mountain of the gods of which Plato speaks. In Atlantis, then, we may seek the prototype of the Great Tower.

There is a more positive side to the card however. This is indicated in the convention that shows the top of the tower gently lifting off to receive the lightning bolt. Similar imagery is described in great detail in the seventeenth-century *Chymical Marriage of Christian Rosencreutz* where it is part of the resurrection process in a sequence of spiritual alchemy.

In all the variations of meaning there is an underlying theme of the power of God, the lightning strike of the Spirit, the Promethean force that re-establishes rulership to its supernatural source.

One could perhaps read in the esoteric tendency to replace falling masonry with symbolic patterns, a desire to rebuild harmonic order from chaos – to restore the true pattern that has been lost by the tumbling figures.

The Star

Hand-Painted Images
The Visconti-Sforza Star shows a maiden with a star-patterned cloak over her robe, holding up an eight-pointed star.

On the Rosenthal Visconti-Sforza card she is crowned, as also on the Victoria & Albert Museum card.

The D'Este card shows two bearded men looking up toward a central eight-pointed star, pointing to it. One of them holds a chart or text.

Early Printed Card Tradition
The Rothschild uncut sheet shows three figures under the star, holding up a crown between them. One of the men seems to be a king, another a jester or fool, whilst the third figure is a woman.

The Rosenwald uncut sheet is a plain central star, between two formal devices above and below that are suggestive of wheels with pointed rays.

The Parisian printed card shows a single seated figure looking up towards a star.

The Swiss 1680 pack has a naked figure pouring two urns out onto the ground, with seven stars in the sky, one very prominent, and a tree in the background. This is the scheme adopted by the Marseilles card

Figure 19

with, however, an extra star, and two trees, with a bird in one of them. (See Figure 19.)

Esoteric Versions
Wirth's L'Etoile follows the Marseilles card but he replaces the bird on a tree by a butterfly on a red flower. One jar is gold, the other silver.

Waite also follows the Marseilles card iconography.

The Golden Dawn differs only by having both jars poured into the water instead of one onto the land. In the background is an additional eight-pointed star that appears immediately over the figure's head, who has one vase red and the other blue. Two trees are in the background, one carrying spheres in the form of a Tree of Life, the other with a white bird flying over it.

Commentary
The earlier versions of this card concentrate upon the star rather than the figure below. However, this figure is important, and indeed on the Visconti-Sforza card the starry cloak of the maiden brings echoes of Astraea, the Virgin of the Stars, and the starry messenger, a form of Isis-Urania, who comes to Christian Rosencreutz at the commencement of the *Chymical Marriage*.

The maiden who pours her vases upon the land and the waters may well be regarded as the Spirit of the Stars, and the dew that is found in the morning used to be termed the sweat of the stars, and was considered to have profound healing and magical powers. Indeed one interpretation of the Mysteries of the Rose Cross is that the rose derives from the Latin word *ros*, meaning dew.

The lore of the stars is a greatly neglected field of esoteric knowledge despite the apparent popularity of astrology. Astrology as commonly practised has become closely involved with the art of mundane prediction and character analysis through the interpretation of theoretical charts. The deeper wisdom is to be gained from going out and standing under the stars and observing them as the ancient navigators, herdsmen, travellers, farmers, and indeed astrologers did. One is more likely to meet the Star Maiden under the stars than in the library.

The Moon

Hand-Painted Images
The Visconti-Sforza Moon is a maiden holding the crescent moon in her hand. Her girdle is prominently featured, and her dress has a pattern of a spiral round her body, like an orbiting celestial body.

The Gringonneur Moon shows two astrologers with chart and dividers under a crescent moon.

The D'Este card shows just one seated astrologer, working at a chart with a pair of dividers, an armillary sphere on a stand behind him, and a crescent moon in the sky.

Early Printed Card Tradition
The Rothschild sheet shows two figures, either female or classically draped, one with dividers and holding an armillary sphere, the other with what is probably a form of sextant. Their heads are wreathed and they point to the moon, which is a crescent, filled in to a full moon with a face. At each top corner appear to be suns with rays – a convention found on other cards on this sheet (the Chariot, the Star, and the Wheel of Fortune, though the latter without rays).

The Rosenwald sheet, as with the Star, shows just the moon itself with a double crescent enclosing a full moon face, and also like the Star between two formal devices like rayed wheels.

The Parisian moon is full face, with features, shining over a scene with what appear to be battlements and various small figures below.

The 1680 Swiss pack shows the pattern also adopted by the Marseilles Tarot; a full moon over two towers on either side of the card, and a dog baying at the moon on each side of a path that runs from a stream or pool in the foreground in which there is a craw-fish. (See Figure 20.)

Figure 20

Esoteric Versions
Wirth's La Lune follows the Marseilles card, but with a clearly defined path leading between the two towers. The two canine creatures are shown as a white dog and a black wolf.

On Waite's card the path starts actually from the water and leads to distant mountains. Otherwise the Marseilles symbolism is followed, with Wirth's dog and wolf.

The Golden Dawn card is similar but with two dark wolves, one on either side of the path.

Commentary
The Visconti-Sforza card follows the same simple principle with this card as it did with the Star, showing a maiden holding the crescent

moon. Similarly she could be regarded, not as the star maiden, but as the goddess of the moon.

Later versions of the card emphasize by implication the hidden laws of life that are studied by astronomers or astrologers – there was no distinction between the disciplines in earlier times.

The Marseilles card follows another line of interpretation with an evocative design that, in true moon fashion, hints at mysteries just beyond the range of intellectual consciousness. It has not inappropriately been named the Twilight. The falling drops may also be regarded as the dew of lunar influence, similar to the star dew mentioned in relation to the Star.

In Renaissance and earlier natural philosophy there was a profound difference between the perceived influence of the moon and of the stars. On the system of crystalline spheres that were held to surround the central Earth, the moon was the nearest and that of the fixed stars the penultimate furthest, with only the sphere of the angels, and God, beyond. This is represented schematically on the Tree of Life with the Moon on the 9th Sephirah, Yesod, and the Fixed Stars on the 2nd Sephirah, Chokmah. Between them are the spheres of the Sun and the visible planets. The powers of the sub-lunary world, which lie within the Earth's shadow, differ considerably from the starry powers of deep space.

Latter-day esoteric comment tends to see the force of evolution represented by the Marseilles card. One is at liberty to read into a card whatever one is inspired to see, but the card was designed in pre-Darwinian times, which leads to the interesting question of whether the original designers were aware of the theory of evolution centuries before it was formulated, or whether we moderns tend to read into old symbols our own assumptions as to what was intended.

The Sun

Hand-Painted Images

The Visconti-Sforza card shows a naked winged boy, a scarf loosely draped across his shoulders and loins, standing on a cloud above a hilly landscape and holding a ruddy-rayed sun-head aloft.

The Rosenthal Visconti-Sforza card shows a full-face sun, adorned with features, over a castle under which is the inscription FORTEZZA. A fleur-de-lys and a five-pointed flamed wheel are in the sky over the side towers of the castle.

The Gringonneur Sun shows a sun blazing in the sky above a maiden with long fair hair who stands in a meadow spinning.

The D'Este card has two figures, beneath a blazing sun complete with face. One, a bearded man, sits in what appears to be the end of a large drainpipe, and converses with a younger man standing before him.

Early Printed Card Tradition
The Beaux Arts sheet shows the full sun-face over a maiden, with hat and long hair, who sits spinning before what seems to be a low ornate wall.

The Rosenwald sheet is a plain rayed sun, with face, shining in the sky with a few flat clouds above and below.

The Parisian card shows, under a shining solar face, a long haired maiden gazing into a looking glass held up to her by a monkey.

The 1680 Swiss Sun is full in the sky, with face, and drops emanate from it in all directions. Below are two children, naked except for loin cloths, embracing. They are standing on a low hillock, or possibly an island, and behind them is a low wall. This schema is adopted also in the Marseilles Tarot. (See Figure 21.)

Esoteric Versions
Wirth shows the Marseilles card children in a fairy ring replete with flowers.

Figure 21

Waite introduces a naked boy riding a white horse and carrying a large red banner. Sunflowers grow behind the rear wall.

On the Golden Dawn card a naked boy stands on land, a naked girl in water, and they hold hands before a curved wall. Daisies grow in the grass.

Commentary

There is a very great deal more behind this card than the superficies of bright enjoyment in the sunshine after the manner of a holiday poster. The Visconti-Sforza boy holding up a radiant head is an image that has resonances with the Mysteries of Orpheus and the Holy Grail, ancient Celtic Mysteries, and the esoteric Christianity associated with Salome and John the Baptist. The maiden in a meadow spinning is another deep and evocative symbol. Also the Sun's face being given features is no mere convention but an affirmation that it is the physical body of a conscious being.

The Last Judgement

Hand-Painted Tradition

In the Visconti-Sforza card a bearded figure looks down with a drawn sword, flanked by two angels blowing trumpets. Below them three figures emerge from a tomb.

The Cary-Yale Visconti-Sforza card has just the two angels, one with a bannered trumpet, the other with banner only, but four figures rise from a tomb below.

The Von Bartsch card includes the bearded figure with drawn sword above the two trumpeting angels, and he is also crowned. Two figures rise from the grave.

On the Gringonneur card there are just the two winged trumpeting angels and seven figures rising from the tomb.

Early Printed Card Tradition

The Beaux Arts sheet card is dominated by a single trumpeting angel who stands, a vast figure, on the landscape, with three figures rising below him. The Paris card is similar.

Two figures rise under a single angel, in a more formal interior context on the Rosenwald sheet. And there is also but a single angel on the Catelin Geofroy card, seated in the clouds, while three human figures rise below.

The Marseilles version shows three figures rising and an angel above appearing with rays from the clouds, with a trumpet from which depends a banner with a cross emblazoned upon it. (See Figure 22.)

Figure 22

Esoteric Versions

Wirth follows the Marseilles card quite closely, but introduces the falling drops that are associated with the Sun, Moon and Tower cards. Waite also, with sea and high mountain peaks in the background; a feature that is suggested in the Marseilles card.

The Golden Dawn card also features sea and a number of additional symbolic elements. The angel above is in the centre of a circular rainbow pathway in the sky and is attended by serpents. He is also surrounded by a white equilateral triangle. Seven Hebrew letter Yods appear in the air, and a letter Shin at the base of the card.

Commentary

This is obviously a card of Resurrection and is an unequivocal reminder that the Renaissance magi were Christian and quite happy to work within a Christian and Biblical iconography.

It is a great handicap to understanding to ignore this fact. If the angel were to be seen as an inter-galactic spaceman arriving on his starship to rescue the beleagured individuals of a dying planet then something of the mighty and wide ranging implications of this conception might become more apparent to those who cannot come easily to terms with conventional religious tradition.

The World

Hand-Painted Images
The World in the Visconti-Sforza Tarot shows two winged naked boys, each draped with a scarf about the shoulders, in an outdoor landscape, indicating a formal sphere above them in which there is a fair many-turreted castle, upon an island in the middle of the sea, with golden stars above the castle in the sphere.

The Cary-Yale Visconti-Sforza card shows a woman in the top half of the card bearing a trumpet in her right hand and a crown in her left. Below a scallop-shaped motif there is a large golden crown beneath which, under an arch, is a scene of various castles and buildings, with sea and a river. Ships embark on the sea, and there is a boat being rowed in the river, between a fisherman on one bank and an approaching knight on horseback on the other.

The Visconti-Sforza card in the London Guildhall follows the former scheme. But a card in the Museo Civica, Catania is a variant of the latter. Here a maiden with a sword and orb, or seal, stands upon a sphere that contains land and seascapes – whilst below are six mountain islands. The Gringonneur card is similar but instead of a sword the maiden carries a sceptre with a cross at the top.

On the D'Este card a winged naked child sits above the sphere, and below is an eagle with spread wings, apparently supporting the sphere. The child holds a sceptre and an orb or seal.

Early Printed Card Tradition
The Beaux Arts sheet has a quite formal design. The sphere is like a circular wreath divided in a way similar to the arms of a Maltese cross, and surrounding a quartered centre in which are emblems of the four elements – clouds, a moon, a fiery altar and a tree. The figure standing above is fully armed with a winged helmet and holds an orb and sceptre. The orb is topped with a cross, the sceptre with a winged orb.

The Rosenwald sheet also shows a circular wreath in which is a land- and sea-scape. An angel stands above it, with wings and halo holding sword and orb.

The Parisian card shows the world itself as a great orb, with cross rising from it, tilted at an angle. Above, a naked figure is partly draped with a curtain or banner.

The Marseilles card shows a naked figure, draped with scarf, and carrying two batons, inside an oval wreath, with angel, eagle, lion and bull at the corners, the first three with halos. (See Figure 23.)

Figure 23

Esoteric Versions

Wirth's Le Monde has a circular wreath in which the female figure appears, and the two batons are carried in one hand.

Waite closely follows Marseilles symbolism. The Golden Dawn also, in general structure, although the wreath is like a necklace of pearls before twelve spheres in zodiacal colours. The female figure also has a moon above her head and a star beneath her feet.

Commentary

It is interesting to compare the Visconti-Sforza and the Marseilles card, for a certain counterchange seems to have taken place. The single draped figure on the Visconti-Sforza Sun appears on the Marseilles World; and the two naked children of the Visconti-Sforza World appear on the Marseilles Sun.

Esoterically there is a close symbolic link between Sun and Earth, which is highlighted in the Qabalistic Tree of Life, where the Lesser Countenance of the Sun sphere, Tiphareth, has his Bride in the Earth sphere, Malkuth.

A strong impression that comes from the Visconti-Sforza design is that the world here shown is an ideal world. It is the New Jerusalem yet to come. This card therefore seems the summation of achievement, as befits, in the game, the highest scoring Trump.

Indeed if the previous card of the Last Judgement represents an awakening of the dead, then this is the new world to which they are awakened. This is amply represented in the wreathed figure on the Marseilles card, surrounded by the four cosmic principles. It is a card of achievement.

THE FOOL

Figure 24

The Language of the Tarot Images
in Pattern and Sequence

A CONCEPTUAL STRUCTURE that will serve as a starting point for us to appreciate the magical dynamics of the Tarot can be found in the design of the Marseilles Trump of the World. That is, a dancing figure within a wreath, with one of the four kerubic emblems at each corner of the card.

These kerubic emblems represent the Elemental powers that are unfolded in the suit cards. The attributions run as follows:

Man (or Angel)	Air	Swords	East
Lion	Fire	Wands	South
Eagle	Water	Cups	West
Ox (or Bull)	Earth	Coins	North

The Trumps are represented by the central figure.

Thus we can take a first step in practical magic by sorting the pack into five stacks, face up, running in sequence from the Aces at the top to the Kings at the bottom of each pile. The Trumps similarly are arranged face up in the centre, with the Fool on the top, running down in numbered sequence to the World. (See Figure 24.)

This in itself is an evocative meditation symbol, for from it the rest of the powers represented by the Tarot can unfold.

One method of unfolding these powers visually is to lay the cards out after the fashion of the mysterious table of Tarot images that is described in Charles Williams' novel *The Greater Trumps*.

This circular table, kept in a curtained room behind locked doors, had upon it twenty-two sculpted figures of the Tarot Trumps that danced of their own volition. In the centre was the Fool, about which the other Trump figures moved, generating a humming sound and a golden light. The lesser cards were represented by the structure of the underpart of the table itself, a single central support opening into four foot pieces each with fourteen claws. We, however, can represent these cards by placing them in a circle outlining the circumference of the table top. It is also quite evocative to arrange the central dancing figures in a roughly spiral way. The full arrangement will be something after the style of Figure 25.

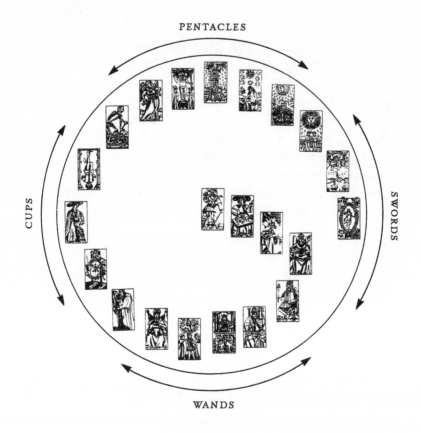

Figure 25

It will save space and also help to create greater realism if we fashion little stands for each of the Trump cards, so that they stand upright. This is most simply done by cutting and folding a slip of thin card to form a V-shaped base, with vertical slots to hold the Tarot card. (See Figure 26.)

In the first instance it will serve to layout the suit cards in straight sequence in clockwise direction from Ace through to King. From this straightforward spread, where all the cards are visible in logical sequence,

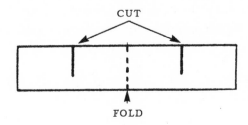

Figure 26

the a-logical sequences and arrangements will have the chance to make themselves apparent to the intuitive and meditative eye.

The four suits represent the four modes of expression of created existence. These four modes have their objective expression at all levels, from the most spiritual to the most material; and also their subjective experience at all levels, from the most interior and mystical to the physical and organic.

There is considerable written material available for the student to gain acquaintance with the dynamics of this fourfold structure. In *The Rose Cross and the Goddess* (now published as *Magic and the Power of the Goddess*) we have built up the same structure starting from the basic principles of nature, and also using musical symbolism. They are familiar, in their subjective aspect, to students of Jungian psychology in the four functions of intuition, intellect, feeling and sensation. W. G. Gray has used the system as the basis for his magical textbooks and indeed did much to pioneer the modern use of it. I have formulated it in elementary terms in *The Practice of Ritual Magic*. And in terms relating to the Tarot specifically they are imaginatively described in Charles Williams' *The Greater Trumps*, though Williams prefers, as do some other authorities and practitioners, to equate Swords with Fire and Wands with Air. This, however, does not affect the general principles of the fourfold magical structure.

An encyclopaedia could be compiled without exhausting the detailed ramifications of the structure that we have laid out. It represents all created existence in all its potential. It is a model of the universe, and thus also a model of the soul of man, which reflects it.

We will pursue one or two possible developments of structure to indicate how insights can be gained in this way.

One of the symbolic functions of this circle is that of time. The turning of the Earth causes the apparent movement of the Sun in the sky, at its zenith in the South, its rising and setting over the horizon in

East and West, and its unseen nadir, below the horizon, in the North. Applying this to our arrangement the Swords take on associations related to Dawn and beginnings of things; the Wands to Noon and the full power of the noon-day brightness; the Cups to Dusk and the receptive twilight time; the Coins to Midnight and the hidden wisdom of the starlit, moonlit hours of the Midnight Sun.

Similarly, by reference to the path of the Earth around the Sun as a function of our time circle, the Dawn of the Year, or the Spring, and all that is associated with it in terms of new life, may be associated with the Sword cards. In like manner the Wands relate to the powers of Summer; the Cups to the powers of Autumn, and the Coins to those of Winter.

These simple allocations of the hours of the day and the seasons of the year to the circle of cards of the suits gives the basis for a deep appreciation of the Elemental forces that go to make up the natural world, and their application to the individual cards themselves.

This application extends also to human life itself, to the dawn and springtime of childhood and youth; to the summer and high noon of young adulthood; to the autumn and dusk of advancing middle years; and to the winter and night-time of old age.

You may tread the circle of cards in the mind's eye, allowing the associations of each time and season to come into consciousness at the appropriate quarter and suit. This can be taken to a greater degree of participation by imagining yourself, like Alice in Wonderland, as very small, or alternatively the cards as very large, and processing about their circle. This indeed is a form of 'pathworking' (see Chapter 4).

You may then become aware of the dancing spiral of the archetypes of the Trumps whirling about the centre, inviting you into the central dance of the inner forces of life, in their infinite complexities and interlocked experiences. And through this whirling dance of the archetypal forces you may discern at the centre the stable zero point, the pole about which all the dance revolves, and about which also the outer circle of Elemental cards is structured, the central Fool. Ultimately you may dance, and merge your being, with the Fool. This is the attainment of a universal consciousness that may be approached and experienced in many ways – just as there are many ways of approaching the centre through the ever changing labyrinthine dance of the archetypal forces that make up the framework of existence.

To return however to our considerations of the circumference of the Elemental cards, we may attain to further realizations by slightly changing their arrangement at each quarter.

There is a certain polar complement between the Swords and Wands on the one hand, and the Cups and Coins on the other. The Swords and Wands with their associations of Dawn and Noon, Spring and Summer, pertain to growth or outer life expression; whilst the Cups and Coins with their associations of Dusk and Midnight, Autumn and Winter, pertain to fruiting and seeding and the inward turning of life expression.

It is interesting to note, in this respect, a traditional Tarot scoring practice that has fallen from modern card game usage. That is that the Aces to Tens rank one way in the Swords and Wands, which have Ten high and Ace low; and the other way in the Cups and Coins, which have Ace high and Ten low. We could express this diagrammatically in Figure 27.

It will be realized that esoterically the numbers 1 to 10 imply an outward turning and conversely 10 to 1 an inward turning of the life forces. On the Tree of Life of the Qabalah, Kether is the 1st Sephirah and Malkuth the 10th; the inner and outer poles of creation respectively.

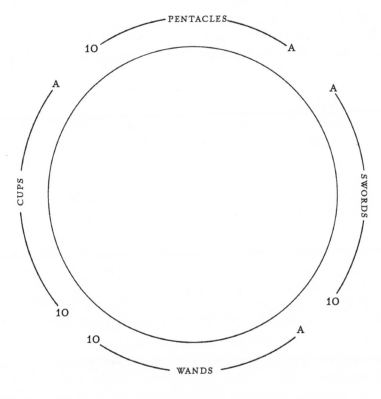

Figure 27

We should note that the Court Cards do not figure in this peculiar method of scoring. They in fact may be seen to occupy a different function esoterically, each one being a mode of operation at different levels of Elemental force.

This is perhaps best expressed by reference to a particular numerical arrangement that was the keystone of Pythagorean number mysticism – the tetractis. This is an arrangement of the numbers 1 to 10 in triangular pattern of four ranks, thus:

1	King
2 3	Queen
4 5 6	Knight
7 8 9 10	Page

Each of these four ranks of numbers can be epitomized by one of the four Court Cards. The King is the fount of all number at unity; the Queen is the principle of duality, and the odd and even principles; the Knight is the threefold expression and the Page the fourfold manifestation of the appropriate Elemental power.

Those familiar with the Qabalistic Tree of Life may also observe a special relationship with the Sephiroth, the King pertaining to the 1st Sephirah, Kether; the Queen to the 3rd Sephirah, Binah; the Knight to the 6th Sephirah, Tiphareth; and the Page to the 10th Sephirah, Malkuth.

Sufficient has been said to provide the discerning Qabalistic student with several avenues of fruitful meditation, and in Figure 28 the layout of the cards on the Tree of Life is shown. It will be observed that the Queen may be placed in the Daath position, mediating between the purely spiritual and the more formative aspects of life expression. In this role she partakes of both the 2nd and 3rd Sephiroth, as Mother of Form in Binah, and Astraea the Star Maiden in Chockmah.

However, one does not have to be a student of the Qabalah or of Pythagorean mathematics to understand the Tarot, even though there are parallels of interpretation, in that the systems, each in their way, describe the same inner reality.

The Tarot is quite capable of demonstrating its own wisdom without recourse to other systems. It is simply a question of actively working with the images, intellectually, intuitively, imaginatively and physically. It is amazing what can be learned simply by persistently laying out the cards and pondering over them. And this is particularly noticeable if one uses packs of different design. Each will prove to have its own ambience of meaning and 'atmosphere'.

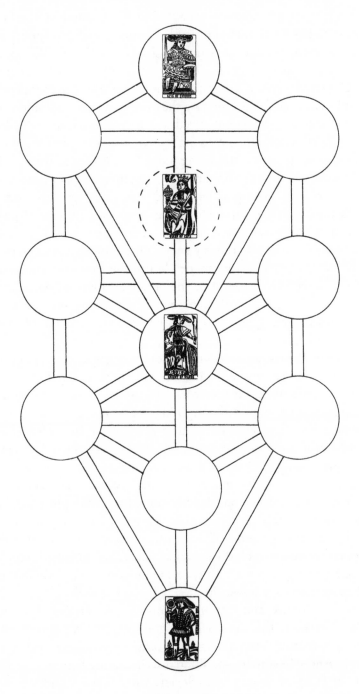

Figure 28

This free approach is demonstrated in the account by the Golden Dawn initiate J.W. Brodie-Innes of his meeting with an Epping Forest gypsy. (This appeared as an article in *The Occult Review* Vol. xxix, No. 2, February 1919, reprinted in *The Sorcerer and his Apprentice*, edited by R.A. Gilbert, Aquarian Press, 1983). Mrs Lee told him, in confidence, the principles she used for interpreting the cards in divination. Brodie-Innes respected this confidence but stated that … 'it was a thoroughly logical and complete system, the four suits representing the four elements, and the four temperaments, and being judged according to their position. The Wands representing fire and the sanguine temperament, a wand card occurring in a bad position would indicate danger from rash and hasty action, anger or quarrelling; the same card in a good position would show noble and generous action, courage, energy and the like.'

He goes on to say, 'Curiously enough the numbers of the pips were interpreted on a system very much akin to the Pythagorean system of numbers, especially in regard to the occult meaning of odd and even numbers. Mrs Lee laid particular stress on the arrangement of the pips on the cards, pointing out its similarity to the arrangement of spots on dice and dominoes.'

However, if we examine a number of Tarot packs we shall find that there is no uniform way of laying out the numbered suit emblems. It seems apparent therefore that Mrs Lee used her own intuition to a great extent in arriving at the meanings, although they were probably based on a relatively rough and ready oral tradition. This is borne out by observation of the card reading technique of one of the older members of my own family who was taught how to read the cards, as a child, by a gypsy. Although individual cards did have a general ambience of meaning, this could be considerably altered according to place in the layout and the effect of surrounding cards. In fact, in practice, cards tended to be read in terms of association and combination in pairs or groups rather than as set individual meanings. This of course is much like life itself, which is ever an infinity of combinations and permutations of similar elements of relatively limited range in themselves.

The imaginative and intuitive approach has certainly been freely indulged by both the cartomancers and the esoteric savants of the nineteenth century, even though the latter might have been loth to admit it. And whilst there are differences in quality between the wilder flights of fancy of some of the Society cartomancers and the deeper philosophic musings of the occult fraternity initiates, each in their way is formulating a workable language. And whilst there may be a difference in aesthetic quality between say fashionable society idioms and the stately forms of a sacred language, they may be equally effective as a means of communication in the appropriate context.

We are dealing with the language of symbols. And if one seeks a language for the elucidation of daily problems of worldly folk then the meanings to be found in any cartomancy book may serve very well, however arbitrary they may seem. If one seeks higher wisdom, then one may do better to go to the classical systems of Pythagorean numerology or Qabalah for a language that can do justice to the concepts involved. The strength of the Tarot is that it can cater for either approach equally well.

As an example, we might cite the traditional titles of the small cards of the Tarot as they have been enshrined in Western occult tradition via the Golden Dawn and their meanings as described in a typical fortune telling book. For instance, a popular fortune telling compendium cites the Five of Cups as a card that 'foreshadows marriage, a happy and triumphant conclusion to a love affair', whilst a respected occult text accords to the same card 'Loss in pleasure. Partial loss. Vain regret.' From the same sources the Seven of Swords is either 'Business success and bright prospects' or 'Unstable effort, uncertainty, partial success.'

It should be plain that different background criteria are being referred to as the rationale for the meanings. In fact the most obvious divergence is whether one regards Swords as symbols of misfortune *per se*, as was probably the case in Renaissance times, or of the Element Air, which is a later esoteric preference.

We should not, from this, jump to the conclusion that the whole thing is subjective and arbitrary nonsense. The fact is that despite these anomalies good practitioners can make the thing work. This is because the inner planes are what might be called ideoplastic – they will conform to many of our preconceptions. So the lesson is that each student should formulate personal interpretations from personal meditation and experience.

This extends even to the numbers, titles, and sequence of the Tarot Trumps. We have seen earlier that the iconography could change over the years. On the original hand-painted Trionphi there were no names or numbers. Therefore there is no documentary evidence as to what their original sequence was, or indeed even if they had a numbered order.

Certainly as soon as they became part of a game of play they would have needed a scoring order and this they had, we know, from the anti-gaming sermon of the Steele manuscript.

However, the numbered order given in that manuscript differs from that of the familiar Marseilles Tarot, and when we look more closely at the historical record we find that there are regional differences in the order.

At the greatest possible count it could be said that there are ten or eleven different orders for the Trumps. However, this can be reduced to three when minor deviations are ignored. Similarly, we may disregard blatant interference with the game for social or political reasons, as when, for instance, in the Papal States, the Emperor, Empress, Pope and Female Pope cards were replaced by four equal ranking Moors.

Following Professor Dummett's analysis we can identify the three basic systems as follows:

Variant A is typified by the Sicilian packs,
Variant B is found in the Steele manuscript,
Variant C is that of the Marseilles Tarot.

Variant A could well be considered a late version. It suffered a certain amount of change during its passage from a probable Florentine origin down through Bologna and Rome to relatively late arrival in Sicily.

Variant B has an early provenance – before 1500 – but of a literary and therefore indirect nature.

Variant C can only be traced with certainty back to the mid-sixteenth century but in the course of time, through the popularity of the Marseilles pack and the industry of the Marseilles manufacturers, has become a standard.

When we place the orders side by side we see, however, that there is a firm general structure that is common to all three. The variations occur mostly as a result of switching the positions of the Cardinal Virtue cards of Strength, Temperance and Justice.

Let us list them, standardising the tides according to our own chosen convention. It will be noted that in none of these lists does the Fool appear, for as the *scusi*, it is not part of the order of Trumps, it has no scoring capacity but simply changes the rules by its presence.

	A	B	C
1	Magician	Magician	Magician
2	Empress	Empress	High Priestess
3	Emperor	Emperor	Empress
4	High Priestess	High Priestess	Emperor
5	Hierophant	Hierophant	Hierophant
6	Temperance	Temperance	Lovers
7	Strength	Lovers	Chariot
8	Justice	Chariot	Justice
9	Lovers	Strength	Hermit
10	Chariot	Wheel	Wheel
11	Wheel	Hermit	Strength
12	Hanged Man	Hanged Man	Hanged Man
13	Hermit	Death	Death
14	Death	Devil	Temperance
15	Devil	Tower	Devil
16	Tower	Star	Tower
17	Star	Moon	Star
18	Moon	Sun	Moon
19	Sun	Last Judgement	Sun
20	World	Justice	Last Judgement
21	Last Judgement	World	World

In these principal Variants the following deviations occur:

Variant A:
+ Hanged Man and Hermit may interchange.
+ Wheel and Chariot may interchange.
+ Lovers may be placed above Temperance and Temperance, Strength and Justice displaced by one.
+ Both Lovers and Chariot may be placed above Temperance, and Temperance, Strength and Justice similarly displaced but the latter two also interchanging.
+ In some cases the Emperor, Empress, High Priestess and Hierophant have been altered for religious reasons, or the Devil replaced by a Ship.

Variant B:
+ Emperor and High Priestess may interchange.
+ Lovers and Chariot may interchange.

Variant C:
+ High Priestess and Empress may interchange.
+ Empress and Emperor may interchange.
+ Chariot and Justice may interchange.
+ Hermit and Strength may interchange.

And when we compare the three Variants one with another, the differences between Variants B and C may be summarized as follows:
+ High Priestess may come before or after Empress and Emperor.
+ Temperance may appear either between Hierophant and Lovers or between Death and Devil.
+ Strength and the Hermit may interchange.
+ Justice may appear either between Chariot and Hermit or between Last Judgement and the World.

The general characteristics of Variant A in comparison with B and C are that:
+ World and Last Judgement are interchanged;
+ and the Cardinal Virtues, Temperance, Strength and Justice remain close together.

All this seems very complicated but we have itemized it at some length in view of the latter day esoteric preoccupation with formulating a one true order. The above should show that this is none too easy and, if one exists, unlikely to be achieved by minor alterations of the Marseilles order. This has been the general esoteric tendency, interchanging Justice and Strength, and possibly the Emperor and the Star, and variously attempting to fit in the Fool at the beginning, the end, or between the Last Judgement and the World.

However, if we examine the general outline of the three principal Variants, as Professor Dummett points out, we see that they fall into three discrete segments if we ignore the Cardinal Virtues. All minor interchanges occur only within the bounds of these segments. They are:

Segment 1: Magician, Empress, Emperor, High Priestess, Hierophant.
Segment 2: Lovers, Chariot, Wheel, Hermit, Hanged Man.
Segment 3: Death, Devil, Tower, Star, Moon, Sun, Last Judgement, World.

This accounts for eighteen cards, the rest being made up by the three Virtues – Temperance, Strength and Justice – plus, as an outsider, the Fool.

So if we wish to conjecture what the possible original sequence may have been, we would do well to confine ourselves within these parameters. We should also bear in mind the change in meaning that has occurred with some of the Trumps, for instance:

the Hermit having originally been Time;
the Lovers having originally been Love;
the Chariot having originally been Victory;
the Hanged Man having originally been a Traitor.

We will then find ourselves presented with four sets of four cards each:

a) 'Powers'	Emperor, Empress, Hierophant, High Priestess.
b) 'Conditions'	Love, Victory, Time, Fortune.
c) 'Malefics'	Traitor, Death, Devil, Tower (of Babel or Hell's Gate).
d) 'Celestial Spheres'	Stars, Moon, Sun, Angelic World or Heaven.

Against each of these sets we can place one of the remaining cards, to represent each set as a whole:

a) Strength – against the Powers.
b) Temperance – against the Conditions.
c) Justice – against the Malefics.
d) World – against the Celestial Spheres.

Oddly, we find that each of these has a correspondence with one of the suits:

Strength to Wands   (one version has a man wielding a club).
Temperance to Cups   (the figure holds two cups).
Justice to Swords   (the figure holds a sword).
World to Coins   (the medallion-like appearance of the World on the earlier cards).

This leaves the Magician with his table of implements as controller, in turn, of these four cards. Thus there is a neat and meaningful symmetry in the arrangement (see Figure 29). The Fool, again, is outside of this arrangement. If one likes, he can be thought to represent the interior, unmanifest side, of the Magician.

Figure 29

We do not claim that this is in fact the original conception. We lay it out simply as an example of the way the cards will arrange themselves if one is willing to adopt a flexible approach and go back to first principles.

This arrangement, if true, reflects a different conception of the suits or four-fold powers of the Tarot than the Elemental or nature based one that we have already outlined.

Instead of Air for Swords we have Evil;
instead of Fire for Wands we have Spiritual and Executive Power;
instead of Water for Cups we have Existential Conditions of life;
instead of Earth for Coins we have Celestial Spheres and their influence.

This, we feel, may well represent a Renaissance view of the universe, magically expressed, and it also accords with the cartomantic fortune tellers' general conception of the cards, which tends to view

Swords as malefic or sorrow bearing;
Wands as organisational;
Cups as emotional;
Coins as financial or matters of material well being.

In this respect Alliette and his like, so despised by Eliphas Lévi and the more philosophical esoteric commentators, may well be closer to the original conception of the Tarot than the savants of the esoteric brotherhoods.

This is not necessarily a condemnation of the latter. Ideas and modes of consciousness move on. And to remain relevant to current needs an ancient wisdom has to grow and develop into a modern wisdom. Hence the changing meanings of some of the cards.

In this context it will be seen that the fortune telling stream of interpretation of the meaning of the cards is a conservative tendency rather than a wildly innovative one, despite appearances to the contrary. And the progress in thinking about the meaning of the cards comes in fact from the esoteric theorists who tend to be thought of, not least of all by themselves, as conservative guardians of ancient secrets.

It is a mistake to consider one generation right and another wrong. Each formulates their own needs and expression of life qualities, and these will be reflected in the Tarot. With changes in the mode of consciousness over a five hundred year period we should expect to find changes and modifications of interpretation. The great strength of the Tarot is its organic vitality, its ability to adapt to the needs of those who go to it. We should, in general terms, seek for expansion of meanings for each card, rather than limitations.

It is similarly limiting to accept later conventions or the assumptions of various esoteric authorities as rigid and inviolable rules. To this end it can be helpful to use, as we have done throughout the illustrations of this book, a set with the names and numbers blanked off. This, combined with the artless crudity of the Marseilles designs, gives a greater freedom for the images to speak.

There are many arrangements that can be made that will afford interesting intuitive insights.

For instance, we could take the Trumps in the conventional Marseilles order and read them off as a treatise of spiritual alchemy. In this layout one has three vortices of four cards, interlinked by pairs. By reference to the layout in Figure 30 the following seed ideas may be used as a fruitful meditation sequence.

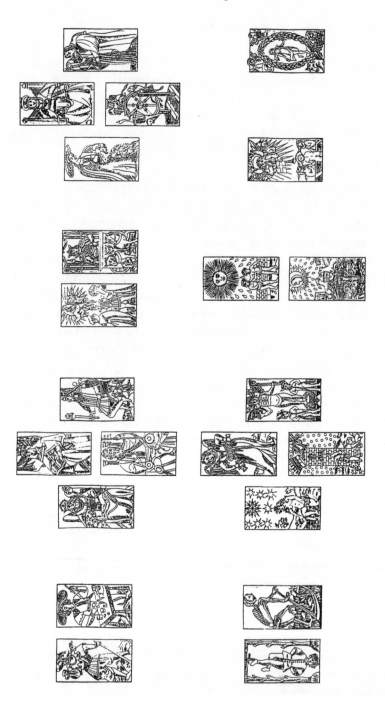

Figure 30

0:            Let the imagination flow freely.

1:            It will form or discover its own structures,

2/3/4/5:   constellating in a four fold manner, Male and Female, Within and Without.

6:            From this dual polarity the flying miraculous creature (Cupid) will be brought forth,

7:            and go forth like a conquering hero in the moving four fold structure, pulled by the steed of wisdom on the wheels of cyclic change.

8/9/10/11:   This produces a further field of archetypal expression:

              Astraea, the Virgin of the Worlds, the holder of the balance and of polarities;

              the Hermit, the light bearer and guardian guide;

              the Turner of the Spheres of expressed creation;

              the Control of driving creative power;

              which brings about:

12:           the principle of sacrifice of the creative spirit into the laws of form expression; and

13:           the principles of time and growth and decay and death.

14/15/16/17: The mixing and tempering of the active principles, leads first to their occlusion, then to the striking down of spiritual force, and the Star is born within the retort that transforms all.

              The waters are poured out and released into:

18:           the Silver of the Philosophers and

19:           the Gold of the Philosophers, which leads to:

20:           the Regeneration of Matter

21:           and its Transformation or Triumphant Expression in balanced four-fold manner.

A similar type of linear arrangement is based on the order of the Trumps given in the Steele manuscript. When I first received a facsimile set of the Visconti-Sforza cards I laid them out in this early order and found the result quite startling. According to this way of looking at them the Trumps came over as a Christian document. (Refer to Variant B above.) Thus, after the Hanged Man (the Crucifixion), comes Death, the Descent into Hell (the Tower), and the portents in the heavens, the eclipse of the sun by the moon so that the stars could be seen by day. (Star, Moon, Sun.) Then the Resurrection (Last Judgement) to be followed in the last days by the universal Judgement (Justice) and the coming of the New Jerusalem (World) ruled by the Redeemer (Fool).

Going back to the beginning of the sequence one can see God the Fabricator or Creator in the figure of the Magician. The next four cards are the dual polarities of archetypal creation. These primal forces are mixed and brought down to a more concrete, complex mode of manifestation by Temperance, with her star spangled robe suggesting Sophia, the Divine Wisdom. From this follows their conjunction in love, forms expressed from impacted polarities, resulting in creation going forth like a maiden in a chariot, from which we derive the intermediate archetypal principles of the life force (Strength), the cycle of events (Wheel), and the principle, or illusion, of time (Hermit).

Another arrangement that can give fruitful results to meditation is based on the triangular formation of the cards suggested by Manly Palmer Hall on the illustration facing page CXXIX of *The Secret Teachings of All Ages*. This has been modified by Daniel Bloxsom to form a layout of secular, sacred and universal paths, between which are axes of balance, activity and inertia. (See Figure 31.)

Hebrew letters are also incorporated in his complete system that present an alternative to the Golden Dawn or Eliphas Lévi attributions, and is just as valid for those who can move with its current of intuitional flow. It is high time we abandoned the idea of a one and only true rigid system of correspondences. The magician of the future has to recognize that we live in a universe based on relative realities. That is, within the limitations of basic building blocks, we structure our own cognitive worlds.

For this reason there seems no harm at all in the various attempts to produce specific Tarot adaptions using Celtic symbols, Tibetan symbols, Egyptian symbols or any other. The Tarot is quite capable of being dressed in a variety of clothes. Just as long as one does not regard any one particular version too seriously. It is one thing to have a favourite; another thing to claim that it is the one and only true version for everybody.

Which brings us to our next arrangement, which is an adaptation again by Daniel Bloxsom, of Peter Balin's arrangement of his Mayan styled cards in *The Flight of the Feathered Serpent*. (See Figure 32.)

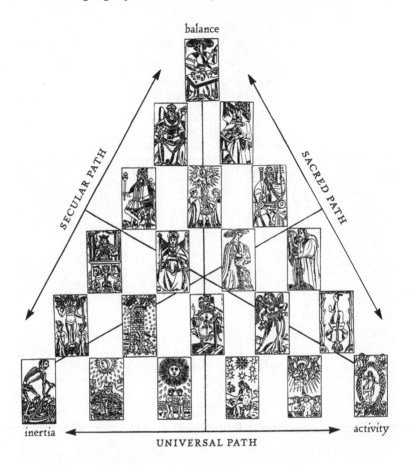

balance

SECULAR PATH

SACRED PATH

inertia

activity

UNIVERSAL PATH

Figure 31

We give no commentary upon these spreads because individual meditation and speculation will prove far more profitable. In these layouts you may find the urge to change about certain of the cards, to disagree with the person who laid them out. This is all to the good. It shows that the images are working for you, that you are finding your own vocabulary, using the language of the cards to formulate the image of your own awareness of inner reality. Your awareness is not necessarily a straight duplication of somebody else's. We are not simply totting up a grocery bill to come up with a simple universal answer. The use of symbolic language is an art not a science.

It is interesting to note how even the most arbitrary changes to the images can be put to use. For instance, the alteration of Pope and Popess to Hierophant and High Priestess by modern esoteric students

93

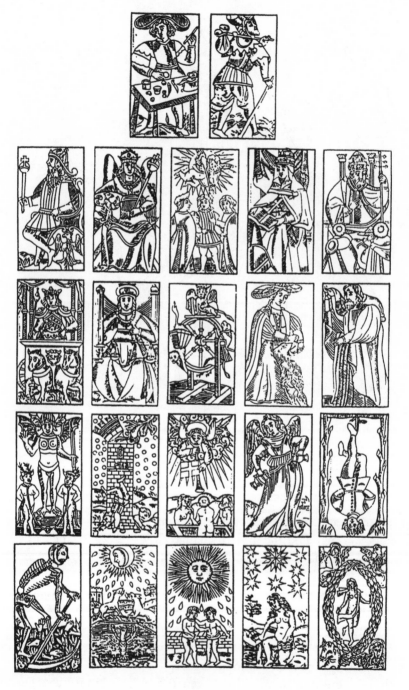

Figure 32

obviously carries considerable changes of overtone to the images without radically changing them. Yet when, in some packs, Jupiter and Juno were substituted, it would still be possible to apply esoteric interpretation to the images chosen. The figure of Jupiter has an eagle, Juno a peacock. The eagle, via the associations of St John, maintains a clear link to the spiritual implications of both Pope and Hierophant. The peacock similarly, with its alchemical associations *(cauda pavonis)* and eyes of Argus in its tail, accords with the more recondite associations of the High Priestess and Female Pope.

When, in the Counter-Reformation, four Moors were substituted for Emperor, Empress, Pope and Popess, this four-fold substitution could well be incorporated into a workable system. After all, much esoteric wisdom came back to Europe through the influence of the Moors.

Even quite whimsical changes such as that of the Devil to a ship can retain associations with the original archetype. The ship may be regarded as Cheiron's ferry across the Styx, or the ship of the Flying Dutchman who consigned himself to hell in his pride and folly, or indeed that of Coleridge's Ancient Mariner.

The Spanish Captain and Bacchus need more ingenuity perhaps, as versions of the Popess and the Pope respectively. But they are indeed almost polar opposites of the original images, and this can tell us something of the function and constitution of the archetypal forces that the Tarot images represent. The actual Tarot cards are like façades, each the façade of a complex multi-dimensional building containing many storeys and many people living within it. The secret of successful work with the Tarot, therefore, is to learn how to get behind the façade to the deep archetypal structure behind.

Tarot Pathworking

PRACTICAL WORK WITH the archetypes of the Tarot is essentially a matter of using the imagination. It may well be that first efforts are barren or subjective, or appear to be. Persistent use will sooner or later demonstrate that through the use of the imagination, a new sense of perception is being developed, that opens upon an objective world or worlds other than the physical.

There are various means of training and using the imagination in this way but essentially they embody the same process. The ancillary symbolism and structural order of the images is far less important than many students appear to think.

Thus there is little point in agonizing over whether Eliphas Lévi's attributions are superior or inferior to those of the Golden Dawn or vice versa. More important is the act of selecting one particular system that comes readily to hand, and that is personally congenial. The practical results that will accrue from putting it into practice will give a basis of personal experience upon which to make one's own street maps of the inner worlds.

The Hermetic Order of the Golden Dawn had a technique along these lines which they called Scrying in the Spirit Vision. The details can be found in Israel Regardie's *The Golden Dawn* but, in our view, the instructions and method are extremely cumbersome, involving the frequent use of coded planetary sigils as a means of checking against memory, mind wandering, psychic interference and other possible blind alleys or side tracks. This may appeal to certain temperaments but is rather like driving a veteran car in preference to a modern one.

In our experience one soon develops an instinct for when one is being side tracked. And even if one does go down the occasional blind alley the experience is usually educative and there are ample opportunities to try again. The chances of getting into serious difficulties are quite remote provided one is not into drugs or on the verge of neurosis. It is spiritual will and intention, rather than formulae taken from a book, that rule the inner planes effectively.

The historical development in the Western Tradition from this Golden Dawn technique is commonly known as 'Pathworking', so called because in its original form it was usually concerned with treading in visualization one of the Paths of the Tree of Life.

This indeed remains an excellent formal training method. Generally speaking one builds up a starting point, a 'composition of place' in one Sephirah, usually in the form of some kind of temple, and proceeds to walk into a picture of the appropriate Tarot Trump. Halfway down the Path one will expect to meet the appropriate Hebrew letter and any personal symbolism or realizations associated with it. And at the further end of the Path at the gateway to the next Sephirah will be found, in similar fashion, the appropriate astrological sign. In fact if one does not find these landmarks of symbolism naturally building up, one puts them there. Magical use of the imagination consists of a skilled blend of deliberately visualizing a formal symbolic structure and spontaneously allowing images to rise.

Which symbols are appropriate to which Path is a matter of reference to various tables of correspondences. My own *A Practical Guide to Qabalistic Symbolism* gives much of this kind of information in considerable detail. To the dismay of the more eclectic student it will be found that there is considerable variation between different esoteric sources as to which are the best attributions.

This apparent confusion does not give occultism a good name in the view of the logically minded outsider, or the beginner, used to the more or less stable structures of the physical plane. However, what may appear as unsupportable intellectual deliquescence to the worldly wise man is a free flowing ocean of delights for those who have developed the capacity to swim therein. And the inner planes, like the sea, have their laws just as inexorable as those of the physical world – but they are different. Not least of all they have a disconcerting fluidity.

All this is demonstrated in the glyph of the Caduceus of Mercury wherein the entwined serpents, as they alternately come together and move apart, demonstrate the alternate rigidity and fluidity of physical, astral, mental, intuitional and spiritual levels of cognition and existence. Physical and mental levels are comparatively rigid; astral and intuitional levels fluid (this is the old alchemical dual principle of *solve* and *coagule*); and at the spiritual level one spreads wings, beyond which are the heads of the Serpents of Wisdom where truths can only be expressed to everyday levels of consciousness in highly poetic or prophetic form.

This should demonstrate the sterility of too much intellectualising about the images and attributions. The Treasure House of Images derives its symbolic wealth from the fluid astral or imaginative level which is best comprehended by the free moving intuition than the categorizing intellect.

Thus an image can have one meaning one day and another meaning in different circumstances. It can be of different significance to different persons. This does not mean that all meanings are arbitrary. Dream images, for instance, can be very powerful and meaningful for the individual dreamer, and demonstrate much wisdom, in certain cases, even for outsiders. But the 'dream meanings' that one reads in a popular fortune telling manual are, for the most part, demonstrably arbitrary and worthless. These untamed images from the deep will not readily be confined in intellectual cages.

However, having said this, it is undoubtedly a help to have some kind of structure to use initially, until experience has given the ability to come to terms with the fluidity of the astral plane. This is the reason for the formal attributions. They should be regarded as a scaffolding rather than a confining structure; a crutch that is, in time, to be dispensed with.

The mention of the term 'astral' brings up the inevitable question as to whether this kind of work is 'astral travelling' or 'astral projection'. We would do well to make a clear distinction between the meaning of these two loosely used phrases. We would say that pathworking is certainly 'astral travelling' but is not necessarily, or even desirably, 'astral projection'. In astral travelling one is always, to a greater or lesser extent, aware of being located in one's own physical body, with its various minor discomforts and distractions. In astral projection one has dissociated consciousness entirely from the physical body.

The latter condition is rare and not particularly to be sought after by the average Western practitioner. It is not necessarily pathological but it is certainly abnormal. All that one normally needs to do of a magical or psychical nature can be effected by astral travelling. It may be that projection, to a greater or lesser extent may take place, and in a deep working there is invariably some small displacement of the etheric vehicle, but one should try to avoid complete loss of consciousness of the body. Failure to maintain this connecting link may simply result in a loss of conscious awareness or memory – to all intents and purposes one has fallen asleep. Or one may become entranced and possibly 'freak out'.

Trance is simply a letting go of the lower vehicles so that they can be controlled by another being, or by a different level of one's own being, usually referred to as the subconscious. Whilst on rare occasions this kind of thing can be helpful, it is not a condition to be encouraged. True magical ability is demonstrated by conscious awareness and functioning on more than one objective level of perception at the same time. Trance, or astral projection, is an abrogation of this principle – a limitation rather than an expansion of consciousness and responsiblity.

The method of systematic visualisation of images was part and parcel of St Ignatius of Loyola's *Spiritual Exercises*, and it should be emphasized that these were spiritual exercises, not mere astral exercises. For St Ignatius they were a preliminary to divine contemplation or spiritual colloquy. A similar higher intention should be the object of the esoteric student. This is not necessarily, as with St Ignatius, a preliminary to affective prayer. The occultist is concerned with working with inner aspects of the creation, and so is not exclusively concerned with contemplation of the Creator, as is the religious mystic.

However, the intention of the dedicated occultist should certainly be aimed rather higher than 'day tripping' in the inner country of the soul. Probably for most beginners the primary higher motivation will be the seeking of higher consciousness or the resolving of particular psychological problems. In this the technique will be found in various workshops of 'transpersonal psychology'. The magically oriented occultist goes on from this stage to an awareness of group dynamics and inner objective realities.

One method that spans the range of possibilities is *The Inner Guide Meditation* of Edwin Steinbrecher. Briefly, this method is to visualize entering a cave – akin to the famous cave of Plato. The way out of the cave is through a passage, led by an animal which is, in effect, a personal totem. One emerges to a scene through which one travels to meet a Tarot archetype, recommended in the first instance to be The Sun.

Ed Steinbrecher uses traditional Golden Dawn attributions to create a link between the Tarot archetypes and the astrological birth chart. He also introduces results of his own researches that categorize people in various ways. Of particular interest is the way that, whether he realizes it or not, the general method is almost a direct reconstruction of the Renaissance natural magic of Marsilio Ficino, who investigated formal meditation upon images to counteract undesirable astrological portents, at about the same time that the Tarot first appeared.

The school founded by Paul Case, Builders of the Adytum (B.O.T.A.), also utilises Tarot images for meditation work, not only in laying out the cards in various permutations and combination, as magic squares and so on according to their accepted number symbolism, but also by techniques of personal identification with certain of the figures as a means of psychological integration.

Melita Denning and Osborne Phillips represent a third American initiative in making these once esoterically reserved techniques available to a wider public. Considerably experienced in the deeper aspects of the Western Mystery Tradition, their book *The Magick of the Tarot* strips the images of much of their more recondite ancillary symbolism and introduces them as dynamics for group and individual dramatic therapy. There is, of course, a very close connection between drama and ritual, between theatrical and magical experience.

However, useful basic structures for imaginative working with the Tarot archetypes can be found from a variety of sources. The simplest is perhaps that of the disciple of Eliphas Lévi, Paul Christian. He simply ranged the Trumps in two files in which one could imagine oneself as a candidate for initiation traversing between them. He chose to present the Trumps in ancient Egyptian guise and in the context of an initiation beneath the sphinx and pyramids. This is no bad method for anyone who is drawn to Egyptian symbolism, and indeed may suggest parallel techniques for those who are attracted to other specialist esoteric packs, from meso-American to Tibetan.

In 1899 a Sufi gloss was given to the images in *The Mystic Rose from the Garden of the King* by Sir Fairfax L. Cartwright, who was at one time a member of the British diplomatic corps in Persia. Here the seeker for wisdom is directed to a triangular tower surrounded by a circular colonnade. The latter shows the cycle of life from birth to death but the ascent of the tower is the way of wisdom. This, we find, is divided into seven stories, with three chambers on each floor that contain within them thinly disguised representations of the Tarot Trumps. (See Figure 33.) The text is reproduced in full in *The Mystical Tower of the Tarot* by John D. Blakeley, Watkins, 1974.

Another important and useful source of imagery is Charles Williams' novel *The Greater Trumps*. Here, the fictional device is used of having the protagonists possessors of a set of sculpted images that are the models for the original cards. These images are kept in a locked curtained room, and when one penetrates to this room one is aware of a low powerful humming and a pale golden light emanating from the figures, that

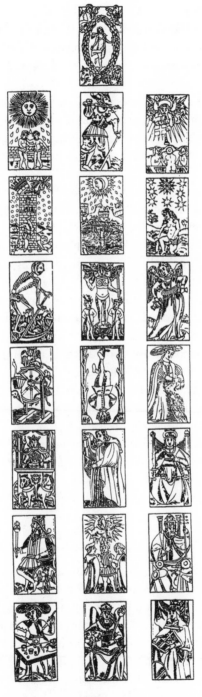

Figure 33

gyrate in dance upon a circular table. The figures are the Tarot Trumps with one figure, the Fool, stationery in the centre, as lord of the dance. However, those who are sufficiently spiritually mature are able to see that the Fool dances with the other figures as well as maintaining the central position.

Charles Williams was a former Rosicrucian initiate and this scenario is in effect a magical composition of place for work with the Tarot archetypes. In fact the inner room represents the inner planes, and the mobile figures the archetypal forces that are behind every set of Tarot cards in existence.

This composition of place was utilized for a working I conducted at Hawkwood College in December 1984. This working is in effect a form of the exercise known as Rising on the Planes, often mentioned in Dion Fortune's writings. It is a simplified pathworking of the central Paths of the Tree of Life from Malkuth to Kether; that is, comprehending the 32nd, 25th and 13th Paths.

It is possible to traverse this journey without meticulous attention to the symbolic detail of all the Paths, although I did bear in mind the appropriate positions of all the Tarot Trumps and managed to give at least a brief mention to most of them in passing. The working was entirely spontaneous apart from this rough ground plan, which of course serves as a useful aide memoire akin to the type of memory system used by Robert Fludd and other antecedent magi. (cf. Frances Yates, *The Art of Memory*, *Theatre of the World*, etc.)

The outline scheme is given in Figure 34 and more specific notes are given at the end of the transcript, which has only been lightly edited to omit repetitious verbiage.

The Pathworking

We are gathered together in a group in an open space before a large wide cave.[1] We enter the cave in the cliff before us. Be aware of the rock and earth under your feet and of the feel of the rock above you and on each side. We are going quite far into this cavern. I will lead the way and R. will bring up the rear; and J. on the right and C. on the left will see that we are all kept together.[2]

As we proceed into the cave we come upon a dark leather curtain which stretches right across the opening. There is just enough light coming in from behind us for us to see our way and the division in the

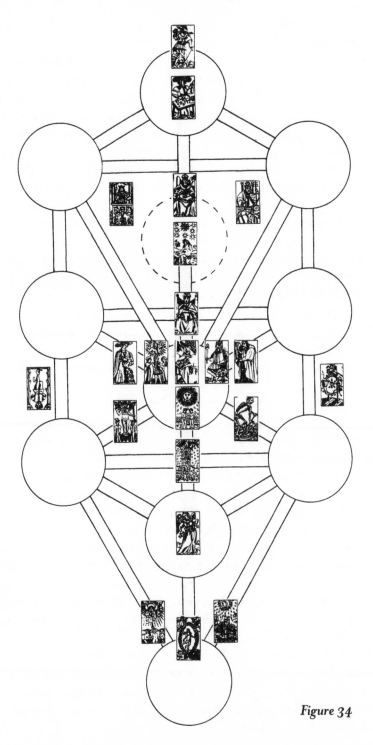

Figure 34

centre of the curtain. This is held up for us by a figure on the inner side, who scrutinizes each one of us as we pass through.

As we come to the other side of the curtain we find that the cave is lit with a certain effulgent light of its own, which is coming from a golden round table upon which the Tarot images move.[3] And we are aware that the Guardian who let us in is in fact the naked hermaphroditic figure of the Tarot Trump of the World, who passes between us to the other side of the table and motions for us to follow.[4]

It is as if we are moving into a dark elliptical wreath, for at this point in the cavern the cave is circumscribed with bay leaves, which we pass through.

We find ourselves going onward and the sense of the confining rock goes from us. In the dark we can see very little but we can sense ourselves approaching two great guardians.[5] The one on the right has all the feeling of Moon force, and one is just aware of a feeling of dark clouds and night sky. And on the other side we feel a figure, barely to be seen, an angel with a long trumpet. We pass between these figures, feeling their presence, and onward into a landscape which gradually becomes lighter.

We find that we are approaching a lake.[6] We are walking on grass now and on a gentle slope downwards. The lake is before us in the very early morning light when there is hardly any sign of the sun but a greenish tinge in the sky. We are aware of the dark indigo purple of the lake before us, and approaching us over the lake, very silently, we see something moving in the darkness. It is a great barge.

There is a figure in the back of it, an angelic figure holding two cups and pouring water from one cup to the other.[7] We are aware that this water is the water of life; and that this great figure is one who guards the boundary between life and death. And that when a new soul is incarnated the waters of life are poured into that soul as from one cup to another.

We are invited onto the barge, and when we are all safely in, it silently glides across the dark waters. As we glide across we are aware of a bright morning star shining in the sky to our right, and to our left the blazing tip of the dawn sun begins to rise over the horizon.[8] We pass onward and see before us a green shore line.

The barge grates onto the shingle of the shore and the Angel with the Two Cups stands protectively to one side to supervise our disembarkation. The sky is getting lighter now and our path is more easily seen. We find we are walking over green downland. We seem to be on an ancient trackway.[9]

We press on for what seems some time over the open land and then, ahead of us, we are aware, in the middle distance, of what seems to be a roadway crossing our path. Unlike the green trackway it seems to be made of stone, of cobbles or even tarmac. And in our path we see there is a tall tower at the crossroads.[10]

At the door of the tower at its foot there are two custodians, who invite us to enter. There is a spiral stairway within. Indeed, the tower seems to be nothing but spiral stairway going up and up, with windows. If we look out of the windows, to one way, to our right as we had been proceeding, we can see in the far distance along the roadway, a tall conical hill. Looking the other way, to the left, there is a great city in the distance.[11]

As we watch from out of the windows, we are aware of a great wind which seems to be gathering force and to be driving along from the green hill, past the tower, toward the city. The force of the wind gets higher and higher, 'til it is howling and screaming around the tower. Suddenly, there is a burst of thunder and lightning, and the whole tower is lit up on the inside with a flash of light.[12] We see ourselves, in that instant, as we really are. That incredible flash of white light shows up everything – our whole souls inwardly. And the effect of that flash, almost like a photographer's flash, is to imprint upon our minds the state of ourselves as we really are, which we can at a later time, at the end of our journey, reflect upon. The naked spirit of truth has struck the tower of our own self-regard and idea of what we are.

We are now aware that the two custodians of the tower are standing at the bottom, ushering us out, and as we proceed, somewhat chastened, but also cleansed somehow, we pass in single file back onward onto the green track that we have been following.

The sun now rises high in the sky before us, and we are climbing.[13] We are on high rolling downs and we see just ahead of us, on the top of a hill that is the highest point for miles around, a circle of stones.

We enter into it, into this great ancient sun temple.[14] There are those here to greet us, custodians of this place. There seem to be many of them. I get the impression of druidic looking figures, in white and bearded. Now I see what it is. The custodians of this place are similar to certain of the Tarot Trumps.[15] There is one that is like the Hermit. He is the figure with the beard whom I took to be a druid. There is another like the Emperor, who is certainly very druidic in appearance but also a king. It is much as if they are priest-kings, the two of them. On the other side there are priestesses. One a priestess of love, and another who has with her a great beast. I would not describe it as a lion but it is certainly a hunting beast, which she holds on a very delicate-looking short rein. And before us we see two upright stones. Between them is the figure of a high priestess. As we stand before her, somewhat awed, she indicates to us, telepathically almost, that we be aware of what is behind us.

We look behind us and to our right side there is an image of death. And behind us and to our left side there is the image of a devilish monster. [16] The high priestess before us smiles a little at our alarm and holds up a mirror, indicating that these two images are parts of ourselves. Then she pulls aside the veil between the pillars and we see a road going forth into the sky.[17]

In the distance we can see a crossroads upon it, with a figure of justice, a female with drawn sword and a balance.[18] We are told, or it is impressed upon us, that to pass that figure we have to be pure in intention.

We each of us step forth, with an act of faith, upon this golden way that leads from the top of the hill towards the figure of justice. Upon reaching it, each one of us in turn stands on one side of the great golden balance, and on the other side of the balance are the figures of death and the devil, and we are aware of vertiginously swinging.

As we do so we look out to one side and see there a female figure in the midst of a complex system of rings and circles. She is indicating to us that she is, in a sense, cosmic time, and that all will in time be healed, and all will be well.[19] And looking the other way we see a figure of a man hanging, upside-down, and he is radiating to us the impression that the realities of the higher worlds are the only realities that are everlasting, and that through the intercession of the higher beings we will be saved and the balance made right. But we are also aware that this is through the principle of sacrifice of higher beings and also the mercy, in a sense, of time, of cosmic time. Very deep mysteries here.

We are now aware that the high priestess who ushered us on to this way is now indicating that we descend from the balance and proceed onward and upward. There is a certain feeling as we do so of great abstraction and even vertigo. We are proceeding over a great abyss and it is like going through clouds.[20] I think the clouds are there for our peace of mind and protection.

Suddenly we find ourselves at a pair of golden gates.[21] The high priestess makes a signal in some way and the gates open and we see behind them the figure of the Empress who is in a beautiful garden. In fact we are entering a vast ornamental garden high above the world we know. It is laid out in geometric patterns it would seem, but there is no sense of rigid formality about it. The Empress greets us and invites us to wander in the gardens. There are fountains and singing birds, butterflies, little creatures looking at us. The first impression I had was of a very formal garden but as one goes on further into it one sees a great riot of individuality and ordered freedom, quite impossible to describe, one just has to observe.

And we are aware of a winding golden way continuing through the garden and we are invited to proceed along it, and we see before us something rather like Mont St Michel or St Michael's Mount, a tall spiralling castle on a high mount. Tall spires brilliant white in the sunlight. We proceed up to the wide double doorway and as we enter we find we are in fact entering the portals of a mighty abbey or cathedral. It is vast. And there are great stained glass windows, quite unlike any stained glass windows one has seen on Earth. One is also aware of the chanting of mighty choirs, with a music one can see, it is in colours.[22]

There is a great multitude in here, a multitude that spreads not only throughout but also up into the heights. There are angels there. There are stone figures, all of which are like a great choral organ sounding forth tremendous symphonic harmonies. And one is aware that somehow those harmonies drive the spheres, drive the stars of the physical universe. That the whole creation below, whether it be stars and planets, cosmoi, galaxies, even atoms and molecules, the rise and fall of nations, in millions and millions of worlds, are all driven by this great orchestrated sound.[23]

And we see that toward the east there is what would correspond to a conductor or organist. It is in fact the mighty figure of the Magician, who is standing at what could be an altar, or alternatively a great organ keyboard. He simply stands there, an incredible figure, there are great spheres of light all around him, rays of light, from which it seems the sound comes as he manipulates the light which fills, translated into harmonies, this great abbey, the great cathedral, this great castle.[24] And one is aware of the scent of incense as well. Every sense that one possesses is aware of this web of harmony.

And then we look past him, up toward the glorious stained glass window in the East, which opens in a blaze of light, and there stands a figure radiant in rags, with feathers in his hair. A figure of utter simplicity and poverty, from whom the most incredible force of love is coming to the meanest and most deprived of all creatures in the universe.[25] For he is making himself at one with them, and raying forth a healing love to the meanest of all that have fallen or are in difficulty throughout the whole cosmos. We pause to open ourselves to this force, this atmosphere.

* * *

You may be aware of beings among us who bring help and healing. It is almost like the coming of the Holy Grail. Whatever one needs, whatever one most desires, can be given to you here by those whose very being is incandescent love.

* * *

We are aware that the whole thing seems to be moving now. We are, it would seem, descending through the clouds.[26] The whole edifice, ringing with sound, vibrant with light, pulsing in every conceivable way with light and love, is coming down toward the stone circle on the hill top.[27] It passes through it, for it is more solid than that.

Down towards the lake.[28] It passes through the surface of the lake, down through it, for it is more solid than the lake, and it takes up within its ambit all the beings of these lower worlds. There are birds, fish, every kind of creature one can think of whose element one has passed through, being taken up into this great influence. And down we come, into the cave. The forms of the great abbey are no longer discernible but the feeling is there, with each one of us. We have in us, and the ability to take away with us, that which has been given us, and has been presented to us in the forms of colour, shape and sound.

The hermaphroditic figure is standing at the curtain and smiling at us, opening it for us to pass back through, leaving the golden table behind us with the Tarot images upon it, which are themselves a map and indicator of the way that we have been and of the realities that we have contacted. We pass into the main body of the cave. R. is the last to come through, and we come out slowly from the mouth of the cave and stand in a group.

Gradually we are aware of consciousness coming back into our everyday present personalities and bodies in this hall. And so I ask you to move yourselves about and make sure that you are fully back with us.

Notes on the Pathworking

1. The way to the stars is into the Earth. Visita Interiora Terrae Rectificando Invenies Occultum Lapidem. See R. J. Stewart, *The Underworld Initiation* for a detailed treatment of this. Steinbrecher

also uses this starting point in *The Inner Guide Meditation* from a more Platonic standpoint.

2. A useful traditional device in a group working to help keep intention and experience unified, but there is no foolproof way of shepherding the more wilful sheep. Generally speaking they come to no harm and their dissipating effect is minimal.

3. This is the induction imagery to be found in Charles Williams' *The Greater Trumps*.

4. In Qabalistic terms this is an invitation to tread the 32nd Path from the Earth Sephirah Malkuth to the inner worlds.

5. These are the guardians of the 29th and 31st Paths on the Tree of Life, whose Tarot Trumps are, in the traditions we are using, the Moon and the Last Judgement respectively.

6. This is the equivalent of the Sephirah Yesod. The Lake also has an important role in Arthurian legend. Refer to my book *The Secret Tradition in Arthurian Legend*.

7. The figure of Temperance, allocated to the 25th Path of the Tree of Life from Yesod to Tiphareth.

8. The gateways to the 28th and 30th Paths, from Yesod to Netzach and Hod, which have as attributions the Tarot Trumps the Star and the Sun in the system we are using.

9. This is the 25th Path from Yesod up to the crossing point of the later 27th Path.

10. The Tarot Trump the Tower, allocated to the 27th Path that runs across the 25th Path, between Hod and Netzach.

11. The Sephirah Netzach and the Sephirah Hod.

12. This is a particular experience, appropriate to this point, of the Lightning Flash, a glyph that can be placed on the Tree of Life to show the descent of Divine Power through the spheres.

13. This is the 25th Path from the 27th Path crossing point to the Sephirah Tiphareth.

14. The Sephirah Tiphareth.

15. These are the Tarot equivalents of the complex of Paths proceeding onward from Tiphareth – Strength, Love, the High Priestess, the Hermit and the Emperor on the 22nd, 17th, 13th, 15th and 20th Paths respectively.

16. The Tarot correspondences of the 24th and 26th Paths that run into Tiphareth from Netzach and Hod.

17. The 13th Path. In this exercise of 'rising on the planes' this is our route of progress.

18. It will be noted that I have not followed the Golden Dawn practice of counterchanging Trumps VIII and XI. Justice seems eminently suited, for our purposes, to the 19th Path balancing the Sephiroth Chesed and Geburah. And Strength seems perfectly adequate representation for the Path between Tiphareth and Geburah.
19. An awareness of the side Paths, the 21st and 23rd, as we swing in this balance point of the Tree, represented by the Tarot images of the Wheel of Fortune and the Hanged Man.
20. Crossing the Abyss by the cloudy or invisible secret Sephirah Daath or Knowledge.
21. The gateway represents the crossing of the 13th Path by the 14th Path beyond the Abyss.
22. At this level there is a general unification of the powers of the higher Paths and the Supernal Sephiroth, the 16th represented by the Pope or Hierophant, the 18th represented by Triumph or the Victory Chariot.
23. This is the function of the *primum mobile* in Kether.
24. An experience of the 12th Path, if distinctions mean much at these unificatory levels. An emanation of Kether.
25. Similarly, the 11th Path as an emanation of the Highest Crown.
26. In a sense, this is a combination of the descending Chariot of Triumph with the mediating powers of the Hierophant.
27. Tiphareth.
28. Yesod.

Conclusion

Not many of those who experienced this working, even if Qabalistic students, recognized the general structure. Most found it to be a profoundly moving experience. In fact one comment was that we seemed to have come back to the wrong place – that the logical outcome was to find oneself transported physically into the glory of Chartres cathedral. Perhaps therefore in the consciousness of those present a little bit of the New Jerusalem was made manifest. It is then up to those so privileged to try to express it in actuality in their everyday lives. This is the magic of planetary, as opposed to individual, healing and regeneration.

Tarot Ritual and Divination

RITUAL IS A MUCH misunderstood term, conjuring images both glamorous and sinister of cowled or naked figures performing unmentionable rites in unspeakable places. This is an indication of the power of the popular novelist's image-making faculty to impose entirely erroneous ideas onto those who know no better.

Ritual is undoubtedly a powerful technique, as is all group work that involves the controlled use of the creative imagination. We have already described the technique of Pathworking or Initiated Symbol Projection as some transpersonal psychologists call it. Ritual is an extension of this by adding simple physical actions or words in a ceremonial form.

Although this is a logical and simple extension it carries considerable power and effectiveness with it. This is because it is an 'earthing' of the group's realizations and intentions in an immediate, formal and balanced way.

Ritual can be constructed in many ways and with various degrees of complexity. It can be made into a gorgeous spectacle by means of robes, ritual accoutrements and regalia. It loses no effectiveness however in being conducted in plain clothes. The reason for this is that it is not only a dramatic spectacle.

A dramatic spectacle, be it the Changing of the Guard or a grand opera, can have a deeply moving effect upon spectators and participants alike. However, the effectiveness of good ritual derives from the imaginative involvement of the participants in a deliberate way. In other words, in ritual, more is going on on the inner levels than on the outer. The outward actions are simply movements in a stately dance, so to speak, that physically key in concerted inner contacts, images and energies.

Similarly, there need be no long speeches. The skilful use of the spoken voice can be powerfully evocative in all group work, and particularly so in ritual. It is, however, not the actor's art that is called for – although some actors have the gift without knowing it and possibly despite their training. Charles Dickens obviously had the gift of being able to captivate the imagination of his audience in readings from his novels. His one-man shows remain a legendary success. It is what might be called the bardic gift, the story teller's art. Yet here again it is not the whole story, because certain actors have a stage presence that can electrify the imagination of an audience. So also a gifted dancer, or political orator. It is what is sometimes called charisma. Some might consider it to be a contact with the Higher Self or with the sub- or superconscious. And although it seems to be a gift rather than an acquirement, we would suggest that it works by using the pictorial imagination with great vividness and in *complete faith as to its power and reality*. This is the faith that will certainly move hearts if it will not move mountains. But when hearts are moved then mountains may soon follow.

By way of illustration of ritual principles we propose to describe a ritual that was devised, using Tarot images, and performed at a weekend workshop. The intention was to involve as many people as possible and give them some experience of taking part in such work, but over-riding this training aim was the intention that it be an effective piece of magical work.

One could conceivably have a Tarot ritual comprising seventy-eight officers, each taking on the role of an individual card. However this would prove impracticably large in most circumstances and we were intent to produce a piece of work that could be contained in a hall of rectangular shape, holding about thirty to forty people sat round in an oval. Therefore, after some deliberation, it was decided to opt for twelve ritual officers altogether.

The first of these would be the magus or hierophant of the working, who would take the Tarot role of the Fool, and control things from the centre. Therefore a small central altar would also be used.

Four officers were chosen to represent the Elemental forces, one placed at each cardinal point. And in keeping with the general ambience of each suit, the most appropriate Court Card would be chosen to designate them.

East: King of Swords
South: Knight of Wands
West: Queen of Cups
North: Princess of Pentacles

Thus two would be male and two female, and each would carry the appropriate magical weapon and represent certain special forces.

The King in the East would represent the outer bounds of the aura of the planet Earth, and would hold a sword to signify his guardian function. As King of Air he represents in a sense the bounds of the Earth's atmosphere, of that which supports terrestrial life.

The Queen in the West would represent the receptive consciousness of the Earth to the cosmic realms, and the influences of outer space allowed past the auric threshold by the King. This receptivity is the significance of the cup that she holds, which in this respect becomes a form of the Grail.

The Knight in the South would represent a lower gateway, and is in a sense an angelic overlord or Elemental King who is guardian and guide of the elements of nature. He would hold a wand as a controller of the etheric realms of the Fire of the Wise, directing the forces of the inner Earth, or barring their way, as appropriate.

The Princess in the North would represent the Planetary Being of the Earth, the great generating Elemental in whom we live, and move and have our being. She would have a pentacle placed for convenience upon a small altar table before her, consisting of a dish of coins, supporting a seven branched candlestick.

The remaining seven officers would represent cosmic powers, the Seven Spirits before the Throne, the Seven Rishis of the Great Bear, the Seven Sisters of the Pleiades, the Seven Rays, or whatever other symbolic expression might be accorded these great powers that are beyond the mundane understanding of man. For our purpose, they would be expressed in Tarot symbolism, each having a three-fold aspect, as follows:

1. Magician – Justice – Devil   (male officer)
2. High Priestess – Hermit – Tower   (female officer)
3. Empress – Wheel – Star   (female officer)
4. Emperor – Strength – Moon   (male officer)
5. Hierophant – Hanged Man – Sun   (male officer)
6. Lovers – Death – Last Judgement   (female officer)
7. Chariot – Temperance – World   (female officer)

The amplified meaning of these images is given below. In each case the general ambiance of the traditional meaning of the card is retained but focused onto the specific purpose of the work in hand. Thus the malefic overtones of the common meanings of some of the cards is over-ridden

113

and all have a more spiritual and cosmic interpretation than would be the case if the same images were being used, say, for a divination about some personal problem in daily life. This flexibility of interpretation and use is one of the great strengths of the Tarot as a magical device and store of symbolism.

First Officer

The Magician: The principle of creating forms from the building blocks of the created elements, to give true forms for the indwelling of spiritual beings.

Justice: The principle of perfect balance, perfect justice, and perfect equilibrium, and the banishment of all that is unbalanced or evil.

The Devil: The principle of taking on responsibility for and abreacting all that is not balanced and true, so that only the true and the good shall be expressed. The expression of the true will of the spirit, the resistance to the abuse of free will.

Second Officer

The High Priestess: The pure ground of divine wisdom that gives peace and knowledge of all levels of created being.

The Hermit: The principle of eternity that shines like a back-cloth behind the illusion of linear time.

The Tower: The principle of opening the will to the higher principles, in all the structures of the creation of the spirit, so that life structures shall be built on the basis of spiritual truth and be towers of inspiration and wisdom rather than of pride and presumption.

Third Officer

The Empress: The spirit of love and co-operation between all beings, in the expression of the family, of groups, of races and of nations, and species, to form a harmonious whole.

The Wheel: The principle of cosmic cycles and the pattern of the dance of life, joyously trodden by all who follow the measures stepped out by the Lord of the Dance.

The Star: The principle of fellowship between the bodies of the starry cosmos, upon all levels of inner and outer space. The love that holds the universe at one, like the apparent pull of gravity that gives spiritual weight to all things by the attraction of like to like in the field of cosmic wisdom.

Fourth Officer

The Emperor: The power of the spirit, the libido of created life, the might that holds the worlds together and all species in the growing and developing splendour.

Strength: The principle of perfect control of the vehicles of form by the indwelling spirit, and of the willing, loving co-operation of the lower forms of life to the expression of the higher.

The Moon: The principle of reflections of cosmic principles and, through the flux and reflux of the higher cycles, of beings of great spiritual magnitude; forming a true outpost for spiritual expression of sacred life.

Fifth Officer

The Hierophant: The brooding love of the power of the spirit acting between the planes, from the highest point of inception to lowest point of expression.

The Hanged Man: The principle of sacrifice of selfless love in all created beings, so that the centre of each life is the good of others rather than the erroneous attempt at protection of the self.

The Sun: The principle of radiation of love and light of a sacred planet, taking its place in the myriad hierarchy of cosmic beings, as a new born child in the stellar universe.

Sixth Officer

The Lovers: The principle of love between individual beings. The loyalties and links that span the ages and the aeons of the cosmos. The microcosm of the whole vast creation in the love between two souls in whatever form of harmonious relationship.

Death: The principle of change, of transmutation and transformation, the resurrection or transfiguration to higher forms of expression by stepping through a luminous veil of transmutation or changing of means of material expression. The death known to a fallen world is a travesty, a distorted shadow, of this process.

The Last Judgement: The call to the new life of all that is past and in error, of all that sleeps in the vale of illusion. The birth into cosmic citizenship.

Seventh Officer

The Chariot: The principle of progress from one demonstration of perfect expression to another, in balanced harmony, drawn by the two-

fold spirit of love, under the four-fold canopy of perfected expression.
The triumphal progress of perfected life.

Temperance: The principle of shared experience, the growing together
in light and in love, as experience is shared and loving friendships opened
and undergone. (Pathworking and ritual is a form of this experience.)

The World: The principle of the perfected Earth. Dancing in a wreath
of victory that was once a crown of thorns, surrounded by the four-fold
balanced cosmic powers.

The threefold nature of each of the seven cosmic-force officers gives a
symbolic link to the story of the three wise men who came, following
a star, to bring gifts to the Christ child. This is particularly relevant to
a work that was being performed in the time of year that runs up to
Advent and Christmas.

However, more is intended than simply an elaborated nativity play.
If each performs their part well, the working can be the vehicle for
higher forces to come into the dark Earth and help raise the planet to
'sacred' status. The general esoteric theory for this conception can be
found in some of the works of Alice Bailey and elsewhere. They have
become, in fact, fairly familiar, accepted principles in the current climate
of esoteric opinion along with much 'New Age' aspiration.

The physical pattern of movement paced out by the seven cosmic
officers is important. Their position in the lodge is in a shallow crescent,
flanking the Eastern officer, the King of Swords. (See Figure 35.)

They are, in turn, called by the Fool to make their journey into the
planetary aura. They start this at the Eastern point, where the Officer of
the East raises his sword in token accolade and salute, and they proceed
in a direct East/West line to the Western officer, who receives them
with an appropriate welcoming gesture, holding her cup. This cup, and
indeed the group as a whole, in effect becomes a Cup of the Grail when
filled with the incoming spiritual energies.

From the Western point, again at the bidding of the Fool, they
proceed anti-clockwise to the Southern point. Here the officer raises his
wand over their heads as they stand facing the central altar, rather in the
manner of the lintel of a trilithon gate, his arms forming the uprights.
And in this brief ceremony of dedicated purpose they are given a taper
by the central officer.

Then, again at the bidding of the Fool, they proceed past the central
altar, this time from South to North. Their taper is lit from the central
altar by the Fool, who is representative of the Will of God in the Earth

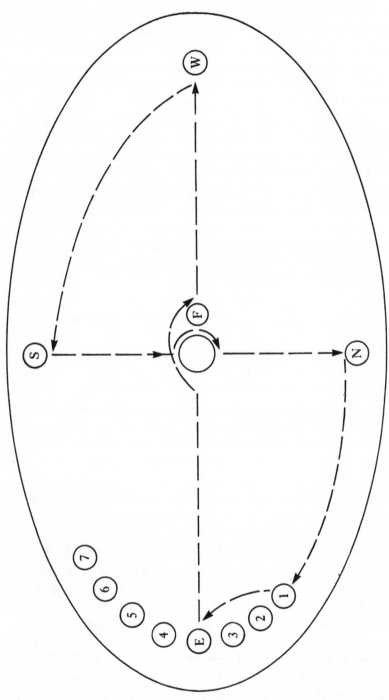

Figure 35

and has control of all forces, however cosmic or spiritual they may be; and who is also Guardian of the one central light of which all other lights are the progeny.

They then light one of the candles of the menorah that is held by the Officer of the North. Having completed their task of candle lighting, the officers return to their original places.

From the ground plan of the ritual it will be seen that a figure of eight pattern has been traced E – W – S – N – E. This is in part a contra-flow to the accustomed time cycle of the four Elemental stations that we have described earlier. However, in dealing with these extra-terrestrial forces, we are concerned not with the limitations of time and the cycles of nature but with the effects of transcending them.

Something of the various ways in which force-flows in ritual occur and may be directed has been described in the opening section of our *Magic and the Power of the Goddess* and is also dealt with in passing in R. J. Stewart's *The Underworld Initiation*.

Once the seven candles have been lit on the menorah, the rite can be fittingly concluded by the Fool leading the Princess of the Earth, the Planetary Being, around the circle of all those present. This traces out an oval path of light, the wreath of victory that is depicted on the Tarot Trump of the World, which also, with the figure of the Fool at its centre, and the Elemental emblems at the Quarters, is in broad terms, the layout of the ritual.

The opportunity can be taken of bringing a gift to each of those present in recognition of the gifts they have helped to bring to the Planetary Being. In this case a glass marble was chosen, which seemed fitting in various ways. Like the Tarot itself it is part of a game, and a children's game at that, which make it particularly appropriate to Christmas. Also its spherical shape make it representative of the world. And its substance, glass, is appropriate in that silicon is among the most common elements on the planet. Indeed it gives pause for thought to consider that besides water and air as common substances that support and sustain life, the earth is abundantly supplied with silicon which, in the form of the silicon chip, has become the basis of a new civilization, world-wide, whose technology utterly surpasses all that has gone before. Finally, the glass marble is, by its attractive colouring, a surrogate jewel, and thus a fitting example of how the Earth itself may transform to the jewel of the Earthly Paradise, in its ideal, unfallen, potential.

Most rituals, in so far that they consist of the spoken word, have a script. In this case, with twelve officers and a fair amount of movement, it was felt that this would prove a distraction. Yet it was too much to expect those participating to learn extensive parts by heart at such short notice.

Therefore it was decided to have no script at all. The bulk of the spoken words were given extemporaneously from the centre by the Officer representing the Fool, with only very simple token affirmative responses required from the other officers such as 'There is'.

Thus, for example:

Fool: Is there one here delegated to represent the Element of Air within this lodge?
Officer of the East: There is.
Fool: Then come to the altar to receive the symbol of your office, the sword.

The whole ritual sequence was conducted in this fashion, from the consecrating of the Elemental tokens of the four Quarter officers, through to the processing and candle lighting of the cosmic-force officers, and to the eventual circulation of the lights and the giving of the gifts.

This had the advantage of simplicity in telling each officer exactly what to do, step by step, and demonstrating to all present the function expressed and intended.

The only script that was used was in fact a set of Tarot Trumps which were laid in the appropriate order on the altar. The central officer simply took each in turn at the appropriate point of the ritual and turned it over when its force had been invoked.

This kind of aide-memoire is useful to have, because in powerful ritual conditions it is not unknown for the conscious mind to be wiped clean of images and concepts by an influx of psychic force. This may be intuitively or spiritually illuminating in the longer term, but can play havoc with the immediate efficient performance of a speech that is committed to memory.

Again the importance of the concerted use of the imagination must be stressed, particularly in relation to the transformations of the cosmic archetypes. Thus effectiveness of the work depended upon the faith and pictorial ability of all present to visualize the transformation of each officer in appropriate form at each particular station.

For example, when the first cosmic officer stood in the East beneath the upraised sword, he was visualized in the form of the Magician, and a brief pictorial description was given by the officiating officer to co-ordinate this. Then when he arrived at the West he was visualized in the form of a figure of Justice, the balance holder. And then in the station of the South, proceeding to the final earthing of the cosmic force, he was seen in the form of the Redeemed Fallen One.

As to results, whatever these may have been in terms of objective realities at various levels, or upon the consciousness of other participants, it certainly, together with the pathworking already described, which was performed at the same weekend, had a powerful and unexpected effect upon the present writer who was the principal celebrant. This was a creative impulse of great and sustained intensity, part of the results of which are to be found in the following section of this book, a set of extended workings based upon the Tarot archetypes, which came through over the course of a period of three weeks.

The effect of these, properly used, should be to open up yet greater depths beyond the surface appearances of the Tarot images. Before proceeding to this, however, it will be appropriate to say something about the art of Tarot divination.

Divination

Although those who practise it may not realize the fact, divination is a ritual magical act.

That is, it is a polar working conducted by two officers, even though they may not be dressed in ritual regalia. By the mutual agreement of their coming together for the purpose, a ritual team is formed, one as the Querent, the other as the Interpreter of the oracle.

The Querent poses the questions of enquiry to the oracle; the Interpreter consults the fall of the cards to interpret the answer. It follows from this that the cards themselves are a form of structured code, or language, between the planes. And also that there is an inner plane presence who is the third pole, or inner communicator, in the ritual structure. (See Figure 36.)

Thus the work should be performed in an attitude of due seriousness if worthwhile results are to be achieved. Both officers should maintain the attitude of seeking guidance from a respected source of knowledge and wisdom.

This does not call for mystagoguic trappings and a portentous atmosphere, which are the accoutrements of superstition rather than of appropriate technique. Quietness, order, freedom from interruption, subdued lighting and perhaps a pinch of incense, provide the correct conditions for successful working. Certainly one must avoid trivialising the operation. It is not a casual chat, still less a form of light entertainment.

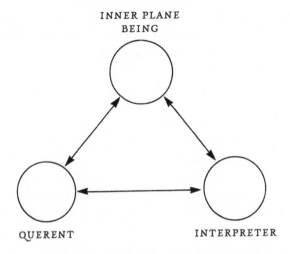

INNER PLANE
BEING

QUERENT   INTERPRETER

Figure 36

It is a serious consultation with a potential guide, philosopher and friend who happens not to be present in a physical body and whose mode of communication is through the coded fall of an agreed system of images.

As with all systems of divination, the Tarot will do as it is done by. Treated with respect it will respond seriously to any enquiry. Treated trivially then trivia will result. Abuse it in any way and it will react accordingly.

The basic pattern of operation is the Querent and Interpreter sitting opposite one another at a table on which the cards can be spread. This is not unlike the picture on the card of the Magician. The table becomes in effect an altar of operation, or put more simply, a focus of attention. (And the original meaning of the word focus is the hearth of a sacred fire.)

It matters not at which quarter of the compass they sit. Generally speaking wisdom is held to come from the East, but in oracular matters it can equally be associated with West or North, as the more passive poles of the magical compass, and indeed the Interpreter could equally well sit in the South, with the Querent in the North, the traditional place in the Lodge of the neophyte, the quarter of greatest symbolic darkness. In practical terms, let the Interpreter select what seems intuitively the most appropriate in the physical circumstances.

Having agreed that it is the Tarot that is to be consulted, and at a particular place and particular time, then the conventions of the method to be used must be decided. This is for the Interpreter to choose, and custom, practice and ease of function are the key factors.

It is a good plan to have the Querent write down the question and state it verbally at the commencement. This clarifies the mind and focuses the intention – two essentials for successful magic.

Then have the Querent shuffle the pack, in a still, reflective frame of mind until he or she intuitively feels it is time to stop. The cards are then put down, and by tradition, cut three times by the Querent, using the left hand (or the right hand if naturally left-handed). The cards are then taken up by the Interpreter for the spread.

The Interpreter should select a spread that is appropriate to the type and nature of the enquiry and its complexity. A short spread that gives good results, and which has been reproduced in many books on the Tarot, is the so-called Celtic method given by A. E. Waite in his *Key to the Tarot*. This uses ten cards. However, there are now many books available on the subject of how to read the Tarot cards and every pack that is sold usually has a booklet of instruction that goes with them. There is no point in our duplicating all or any of these; we seek only to lay down a few basic principles so that the wood may be seen in spite of the trees. Any diviner likely to be worthy of the name will evolve a personal method based on meditation and experience.

Similarly there is little point in our listing out various divinatory meanings for the cards, many of which, from various sources, will be found to be contradictory. The meanings are best derived personally from one's own set of mind and philosophic standpoint. There is no substitute for playing with the cards physically, mulling over them and communing with the ideas behind them over a long period of time.

Of course, if one is using an esoteric pack, certain meanings will be implied by the pictorial symbolism of the cards. If one is content to accept these meanings they will work well enough. However, there is much to be said for working with the old traditional designs, such as the Marseilles Tarot, which do not intrude latter day esoteric sectarian assumptions, and so retain an invaluable flexibility.

In the last analysis it is an excellent and rewarding exercise, and not only for divination, to design and make one's own cards. Whether or not one embarks on such a project, having one's own special pack, dedicated to the purpose, and kept in a private undisturbed place, perhaps wrapped in black silk, will be helpful.

As in all magical procedures, it is not so much a matter of what one does, or even believes, but the way that one does it. Faith, sincerity, dedication, and respect for the inner powers will, with time and application, bring their own tuition and due reward.

Journey to the Centre: Working with the Archetypes

WHATEVER RESULTS the Tarot ritual and pathworking already described may have had upon objective realities at various levels, or upon the consciousness of the participants, it certainly produced an unexpected effect upon the principal celebrant. This was a creative impulse of great intensity for about an hour each morning over a period of some three weeks.

In structure it is a long working through all the Tarot Trumps, the aim of which is to make contact with the spiritual essence or essential self of each participant.

It will prove too long and powerful for use in one session in its entirety. However, it could be built up as a sequence of separate workings for a weekend or one day workshop, or at weekly intervals for a regularly meeting group.

It is therefore split into 'branches' with suggested entry and exit points for those who wish to use it in this way. At exit, simply return consciousness gently to the physical as outlined at the end of the Pathworking chapter. At re-entry, simply build up the immediately preceding imagery as a composition of place.

Once again, the purpose of this sequence is not only to provide material for practical work but also to demonstrate the flexibility and range of the Tarot archetypes. It should be read slowly and reflectively, preferably aloud (the power of the spoken word is little realized nowadays), and with clear pictorial imaginative involvement (the source of inner power), if one is to get the most from it in solitary reading. It may also prove helpful to read it into a tape cassette for later listening in meditative mood. However, best results are likely to be obtained in a small group.

First Branch: (the Fool, The World and The Moon)

We are walking along a country lane. It is summer, the sun is warm upon us, and the birds are singing. The scent of the meadow flowers comes to us across the hedgerows. It is an idyllic country scene.

We come to a bend in the lane, and find before us a little country cottage. It has a thatched roof and dormer windows, and in its neat front garden are traditional country flowers, marigold, forget-me-not, and high hollyhocks standing against the cottage wall at the back. Around the doorway is a pergola arch upon which red and white roses grow. We approach the door and ring the little silver bell that hangs beside it.

After a few moments we hear footsteps within, and the door is opened by an old lady in a flowery patterned dress and with a friendly smile. It seems she has been expecting us, for she beckons us in.

We enter the cottage and find that the old lady is showing us up a stairway. We are conscious of the feeling of great peace within this house and the atmosphere of a lovingly tended home. We emerge on a small landing and see that before us there is a ladder that disappears through a trap doorway in the ceiling. She indicates that we ascend it.

As we put one foot upon the first step she presses something into our hand. It is a card. We look at it, and find it is one of the Tarot Court Cards, the one that is most appropriate to our sex and temperament.

We climb the ladder and find ourselves in a small upper room. There is a circle drawn in the centre of the floor and we sit around it. Behind or to one side of us light filters in through a tiny window, high in the eaves of the cottage. Opposite it, before or on the other side of us, is a door, slightly ajar, that leads to another part of the roof structure of the cottage – but all is completely dark behind it.

We sit in meditation as we realize that we are guests at a place that is sometimes known as the Cottage of Lost Play. Presently, when we have composed our breathing and are sitting comfortably relaxed, we hear from the direction of the ladder beneath a scrambling sound; it sounds like a small animal scrabbling up the rungs. We look toward the opening and a hairy pointed face appears through it; it is a dapple coated dog. It climbs into the room and gazes expectantly at us, its tongue lolling out of its mouth, and a mischievous look on its face.

We have no time to speculate on how it got here or from whence it came, for it is closely followed by someone else climbing the ladder. Through the trap door we see first the head and shoulders and then the rest of a merry looking young man, with yellow hair, and a coat and breeches of many colours. He carries a staff on the end of which hangs a knotted bag. He sits cross legged between us and throws down his bag. It seems full of lumpy objects. His dog sits beside him. The young man looks round at each of us in turn. We are very conscious of the personal contact he makes, with his light blue eyes that are full of merriment, yet which also seem able to see far within the deeps of each one of us.

He speaks. 'Welcome to my mother's house. This is the Cottage of Lost Play and I am the Poor Man who has nowhere to lay his head; the Beggarman who wanders the roads seeking love from strangers; the Fool, because no sensible person would do such a thing; even the Madman, because many would see no sense in what I have to tell them. To the wordly wise I am childish because of my faith in the true and the good, but that is because I am an Innocent. And the innocent, the virgin and the pure are not well regarded in a world of corruption. When the sons and daughters of Earth are young they have innocence. That is why you must become as little children to enter the kingdom of heaven. I am like the pied piper who calls all who are young at heart to follow and join in my dance. For I am the Lord of the Dance and I am the Victor of all Games. Follow me, and I will show you a game that is outside your own space and time.'

He stands, and his dog scurries excitedly round him, jumping up and pawing at his back. He rummages about inside his dark bag and draws out four shining golden objects. He also pours a pile of leaves upon the floor. They look as if they have been picked from a green bay tree but seem big and shiny, with a heavy look, as if they come from a very special tree that perhaps grows in the cottage garden.

'You must help me,' he says, 'to make a circle of leaves around the door. Here are some pins to help you.' He holds out to each of us a packet of shining silver pins that seem to glow with their own light. We set to, surrounding the door that leads further into the attic with an oval wreath of the leaves. The young man himself takes the four shining golden objects and places them at the four corners of the door. Each is a little plaque and on each is a different picture. To the top and the left there is the radiant head of a man, to the top and right, a golden lion, to the bottom right there is a golden eagle, and to the bottom left a golden bull. 'Now,' the young man says, when it is all complete, 'it is time to use your imaginations. For you cannot pass through safely in your ordinary bodies, for you will still be in your own space and time, and will fall through the floor. My mother gave each of you a card when you climbed the steps to this place. Look closely at that card. Then shut your eyes and imagine that you are no longer sitting in your own bodies but are as the figure on the card that you hold in your hand, holding before you a sword, a wand, a cup or a magic medallion. Now open your eyes and follow me.'

We open the eyes of our imagination bodies and find ourselves as has been described. We look towards the door and find that the Fool has gone through.

'Follow me,' comes an echoing cry as if from miles and miles away in a space like a vast cavern. Our movement is as quick as our thought and we find ourselves almost immediately through the oval wreath and the door.

The Fool has gone far into the distance but is still visible as a tiny silver figure receding rapidly from us. There is an echo of laughter all about us, and we find we are drifting in a dark blue void in which there are millions of stars. We have entered into inner space.

The Fool is so far ahead of us that he has now dwindled to a point of light. For a few moments his receding figure can be seen brighter than the background of stars and constellations but it soon becomes indistinguishable from the whole host of the heavens. He could be any one of them now.

We wonder why he has left us, and where we should go.

'Where do you want to go?' says a voice beside us.

To our surprise we realize that the Fool has left his dog, and it is the dog that is speaking to us, his head on one side.

'If you seek to follow my master,' he says, 'then he must be your master too. But you cannot get to where he is until you know who you are. And for that you will need someone to guide you and to open the ways. Are you sure you want to proceed? If not, you may still turn and return through the door. It remains ajar behind you. But if you wish to find your essential self, to discover your true and innermost name, raise the weapon you hold before you.'

Those of us who wish to proceed hold up our suit emblem before us.

'Then I will open the ways,' says the dog, 'but you must be ready to tread them.'

So saying, he raises his snout high into the air and lets forth a long canine howl. We can feel our flesh creep, so eerie does it sound. And then, even more unnerving, there comes, from nowhere it seems, a wilder, answering howl.

At the same time we become aware of a pale radiance gradually growing behind us. There is also a sound of deep and slow movement as of great waters. Turning, we see that the light comes from a great disk of pale-yellow, silvery-white, that hangs in the sky and which we have not seen before. We find that we are standing, not in empty space any more, but on a sandy, pebbled strand, with our feet barely beyond the water-line, for now there is to one side of us, as far as the eye can see, an expanse of calm, heaving, grey-green ocean. And on the other side, under the moon, a pathway leading to distant hills, that first leads between two ancient-looking high and massive crumbling stone towers.

Before the towers, on one side of the Path, stands our guide, the Fool's dog, baying at the moon; and on the other side, a sight to make the blood run cold – a lean grey wolf, with slit eyes and a slavering mouth full of fangs, that also bays beneath the moon.

We wonder if they are going to fight or prevent us going between them along the path. Our thoughts are interrupted however by the sound of slow scraping in the shingle at our feet. It is like pebbles sliding against shells but it is not caused by the slow swell of the sea. It has a different, more rapid and purposive sound. The shingle beneath our feet is heaving up as if some creature were burrowing underneath it, to get to the surface.

A hole appears in the ground before us, and out of it comes a large claw. It snaps in the air blindly. We stand and watch as the claw is followed by a scaly arm, or leg, and another large elongated claw, just like the first one. Then, by a strange looking, fierce bewhiskered grey-green face, and finally, with much heaving and shoving, four other scaly legs and a long scaly body. It is a shell fish, like a gigantic lobster. It rears up on its tail on the path before us, snapping its claws together in a strange and irregular but rhythmic way.

As it does so, we see, all about us along the shore, more piles of sand and shingle appearing, followed by pairs of claws and similar creatures. Even in the sea, craw-fish heads and claws are appearing over the waves and snapping in the air, taking up the rhythm of their leader.

We wonder if they are going to dance, rather after the fashion of the lobster quadrille in *Alice in Wonderland*. We see that all the lobsters have advanced from the beach onto the path and the surrounding grass and have formed up in lines and curves and circles in odd geometric patterns, snapping their claws in time and shaking their scaly armour to give a rhythmic rattle to their swaying dance as they gyrate up and down and around the baying dog and wolf and the two towers.

The moon hangs in the sky, much bigger than any moon seen on Earth, but it begins, like the ordinary moon seen from the Earth sometimes does, to grow a halo round itself, like a veil of silver mist. As its silvery light shines onto and into the mist, so there appear delicate rainbow colours within and around it. And behind the veil of mist it seems almost as if there is a face on the disk of the moon; a broad, gravely smiling almost loving face.

Then, from the configuration of circles of silvery rainbow light around the moon and the straight rays of similar rainbow colours spreading starlike from it, where the lines and rings intersect, there appear great coruscating silver drops in the sky, which become bigger and bigger, and then drop like dew to the ground beneath. Whereupon the lobsters break the formation of their dance with outstretched claws and seek to catch them as they fall.

We realize that we have to catch some of this moon dew too. Whether we individually hold a sword, a wand, a cup or a talismanic medal, we use it to catch some of the drops. We do this by sighting a large and beautiful drop of the precious moon liquid that is falling towards us, and placing our Tarot emblem in its path. In normal circumstances one would expect a great splash but here it does not happen. Rather it is a splash of light as, with a high pitched ring, like a little silver bell, we see that our emblem has been decorated and transformed.

If we have a cup or a disk the impact of the moon drop has made a pattern upon it as if it were inset with hundreds and thousands of little diamond gems, and in a most beautiful complex six-fold pattern, just like a magnified picture of a snowflake seen on Earth.

If we have a wand or a sword we point it toward a falling drop and with a similar silvery ring, instead of shattering and splashing, the drop transforms to a similar coruscation of light, in crystal fire, about the end of the wand or sword.

We look at these beautiful objects, and see also that the lobsters have filled their claws with liquid light and are streaming in an excited column along the pathway between the two towers toward the distant purple hills. The silver liquid in their upheld claws seems like flaming torches in the distance and the whole concourse is like a great triumphal procession.

We wonder if we should follow, and look towards our dog. We see that the wolf is racing off, his fur blazing like silver frost, to take the head of the procession. Our dog is standing on his hind legs looking expectantly up at the moon, which no longer drops dew as the mist about its face clears. Now that we can see the face more clearly, it has a strangely familiar look. It seems almost like the Fool's.

As this thought crosses our minds the Moon's face gives a slow smile. The dog jumps up and down like a furry ball in excitement, as the last remaining clouds of the moon mist form into a bright straight moonbeam. The dog leaps upon it, as if it were a solid path, and races up along it towards the moon's disk.

As it does so, the face on the moon slowly fades but in its place there remains a shape left on its surface that has the rough appearance of a man walking with a bundle on his shoulder and followed by a dog. *Exit-point One*

Second Branch: (the Last Judgement and The Sun)

The last of the lobster procession has departed and we stand alone on the desolate moor before the two dark crumbling towers.

We start to walk along the path between the two towers, after the procession of lobsters, whose lights can be seen twinkling along the path before us over the moor and hills.

Before us, however, between the two towers, there remains, slanting down to the path, a single ray of moonlight.

As we enter the slanting beam everything suddenly changes. There is a ringing trumpet call, and the moonbeam turns into a golden upward path at the top of which can be seen, not the moon disk, but a glorious angel, in red and gold and silver, whose wings span the heavens. It is he who is blowing the horn. Three great blasts he blows, and then, smiling, looks down towards us and beckons.

Needing no second bidding we hurry up the golden hill, which is like a bridge, for it has a parapet each side over which we can see. We pause to look, for far below us we can hear the sounds of cheering and great merriment. And there, far into the distance can be seen the whole torchlight procession of lobsters, who are looking up and waving. But the procession seems to have grown in size and diversity for it is not just composed of lobsters. It contains every creature one can imagine – bears, horses, dogs, cats, lions, lambs, giraffes, monkeys, all proceeding in a long column toward the distant hills. Whilst immediately below us, light is coming from the previously dark towers. Soon they are transformed into large bright structures as perhaps once they had been when first they were built. Light shines from their windows, and on their battlements crowds of richly dressed men and women wave excitedly up towards us, whilst others scatter from the towers, dancing and singing with joy, making their way to the end of the golden pathway bridge, following in our footsteps.

Full of exhilaration we look back up to the smiling angel, who stands resting on his long trumpet, from which there hangs a long unfurling banner, upon which we see a combination of the designs the moon-drops have made upon our emblems. It has a beautiful complex snowflake pattern in gold, and in the centre a flower of red.

We continue up the hill, with the sound of excitement, music and revelry below, as the crowds from the towers follow behind us.

When we arrive at the top we cautiously approach the angel, because he is of great size, and there is all about him a blaze of light that has sound within it as well, so that as we step into the radiance around him we also hear choirs singing beautiful melodies, and orchestras and organs playing, and harps, and there are other winged beings floating around and about the aura of the angel. But so great is his radiance it is difficult to see what they are, whether birds, or other angels, or cherubs.

We are encouraged to approach the angel however by the reappearance of our dog, who is cavorting excitedly before the angel's feet, in and out of his flowing draperies, and around the stem of the golden trumpet and the furls of the banner which fall to the ground.

We find we barely come up to the knee of the angel, who stretches above our heads like a mountain. 'Who is he?' we ask, through the background of music that surrounds the angel when we stand close to him.

'Behold the great Transforming Angel,' says the dog, 'who changes things; all things; people and creatures; to help them grow. He has been changing you all of your life; otherwise you would not even be babies; you would not grow from the seed in the egg in the womb of your mother. He is one of the great principalities and powers who rule the world – from the inside – from where we are now. Here, as in a seed, are the patterns held of all the things that grow, and also the strength and power that makes them grow.'

He bids us look over the parapet again. Looking down from this great height the ground below is spread out like a map. We see the long road leading from the sea toward the distant mountains, and all the creatures with their lights moving along it. Looking toward the mountains we see what at first appears to be a great city. But on closer gaze we realize it to be a number of towers similar to the ones at the beginning of the path. These other towers are, however, newly constructed, and in pairs at distances along the roadway. We see that they are inhabited, or being built, not by humans but by animals, many of whom have been in the procession of evolving life forms, one of which we saw commencing with the lobsters.

The dog explains that they are building worlds like our own outer world. That each of those pairs of towers has a round ball in outer space called a planet, orbiting some far distant sun from our own. And there they are building their own civilizations. And when their planet has lived out its useful life as a ground for their civilization they hear the trumpet call of the Transforming Angel and ascend to where we now stand.

At this point we discover that the first rank of people from the towers immediately below us have reached the top of the golden bridge. We are startled to find that although they looked like beings such as ourselves from a distance, it is plain to see that they are far different. They are much taller and thinner and their faces are yellow. They have pointed ears, dark hair that stands up straight into a point behind, and their eyes are green. Wherever they come from it is not our Earth.

We are therefore urged to move on lest we find ourselves caught up with them and their destiny, and at risk of being drawn into their ambit, either into the heaven worlds away from our own mission, or back into another planet somewhere in some different space and time. We are bidden by our dog to close our eyes and to think of the sun, a golden sphere before us, feeling its warmth upon our hands and face. And when we so feel it to open our eyes again.

When we do so, we find that the great angel and the milling throng has gone, but hanging in a clear blue sky before us is a golden sun. It has a face just like the Moon had earlier, big, broad and smiling, and with a distinct resemblance to the Fool with rippling flames and a heat haze passing over its surface continually; so that it is difficult to make out its features exactly.

Before us is a sward of bright green turf before a garden wall, over the top of which tall sunflowers nod their heads. And in a circle on the grass before us are lots of small animals gambolling and playing – white mice, guinea pigs, rabbits.

'This is the pet's garden,' explains the dog, 'or part of it. In other parts we could find cats, dogs, or ponies. Any animal so closely associated with humankind that it has been given a personal name.'

He says we can, if we wish, go to any of these other parts of the garden. They are all similar to this, with green sward, wall and sunflowers before the Sun, but with different types of animals. There, if we call the appropriate name, reacquaintance can be made with some once loved animal.

There are children's gardens up here too, we are told. Those who leave the outside world prematurely, by illness or by accident, so that they can finish growing up.

One may also see dreaming worldlings, who are only visiting, for comfort and refreshment. These, however, are like vapoury ghosts and look as if they are asleep, which, indeed, in the outer world is what they are. They may not remember their visit, except perhaps in confused remembrance of dream, but we are special visitors, we are having a waking dream, or induced vision, and so will remember all of what we see in these Summerlands of Between the Worlds.

But with this realization comes the remembrance that we are on a dedicated mission, and not seeking rest or fulfilment of curiosity. Yet at times of need we may indeed return here, to this happy land of individualizing animals and children.

For a little while longer we are allowed to bask in the rays of this inner Sun and to make contact with any who reside here. We do this by calling their name and thinking of them with love as standing in the sun before us.

Then we must pass on our way.

Exit-point Two

Third Branch: (The Star and Temperance)

We turn to the Fool's dog who opens and guards the ways, to be directed in the next stage of our journey to the profounder depths, or more extended heights, of the inner worlds.

He tells us we must seek the Star Maiden, who is to be found where land and waters meet. This is a similar location and condition to where we first saw the inner Moon but is on a higher level. However, we take a sighting on where land and water meet by looking below us. We look intently at the ground on which we stand, and as we look we see it become transparent, and we can see land and sea and shore line far beneath. We follow the dog as he starts to run towards a point below which the line of land and water meet. Then, raising our eyes, we find we are on the shore of a calm clear lake at our own level, with rushes and water plants at its margin. We stand on the grassy bank and look out over the water.

To our surprise we find that stars appear to be forming in and upon the still water. It is as if the night sky were being reflected in the water of the lake, but above us the sky remains the bright blue of the day.

We notice that the stars seem to form a pattern. It is rather like the kind of star map where lines are drawn to represent the shapes of constellations. Only whilst on star maps the figured drawings often do not seem to relate very closely to the actual pattern of the stars, in this case, although there are no lines drawn, the actual pattern of the stars in the water very clearly shows an outline. It is of a maiden kneeling. She is holding two vases of water. One of these she pours out into the waters of the lake itself. The other, because the figure is so close to the shoreline, she appears to be pouring onto the land by the lakeside.

Also reflected in the water is a ring of bright stars around her head. There are seven, bigger and brighter than any star we have ever seen.

Parts of a landscape can be seen behind her, outlined in the stars. It is of low rolling hills, with a tree that has clusters of star blossoms and leaves and fruit all at once. There are star birds within it too, and shining butterflies, outlined in the different silvery blue, green, red, purple and yellow colours of starlight.

We wonder if the starry country laid out in the lake is under the water or in the skies overhead, and if so, why we cannot see it in the sky above.

'It is neither under nor over the water,' says a deep flutey voice behind us, and turning, we see a large white swan standing on the bank, regarding us with a hard round eye.

It walks past us and with a light splash slides onto the waters of the lake. The outgoing circle of ripples causes the pattern of stars in the water to bob up and down for a little, but as the waters still, there remain the star images in the lake, plainly to be seen, of the tree and birds and butterflies and the maiden pouring water from her vases.

'Neither under nor over the water,' repeats the swan, floating in the water before us, at the feet of the image of the star maiden, 'but *on* the water. That is where reflections are.'

We wonder why we cannot see the real stars that the reflections come from, for the sky above is the bright clear azure of the day.

'Because you do not have eyes that can see what is real,' says the swan, in answer to our unarticulated question. 'You come from a world of illusions. On a spinning ball whose whirling movement spins out a thread of weaving patterns you take to be the real. You only see in reflecting surfaces. You are children of the mirror. But there is much to be learned from the starry lake, and passing to the other side of the looking glass.'

And so saying the swan turns, and instead of swimming away, plunges down into the water. As we watch we see her, now an outline of stars within the picture, receding into the distance toward the centre of the lake. We wonder whether we are expected to follow her but, as we watch, a star in the lake seems to be growing bigger. It is the great star over the maiden's head that begins to grow in size and brightness, to such an extent that the other stars in the water become quite pale by comparison.

And it begins to come, beneath the water, towards us. Soon it is like a glowing ball just beneath the surface of the waters at our feet. We are aware of nothing else within the waters until, with a splash, it rises out of the water before us and we see that, bobbing on the ripples it has made on the surface of the lake, it has become a little boat. It is white in colour and shaped in the form of a swan. Its prow is built up high like a swan's neck and it has a beautifully sculptured swan's head at its top. The rest of the boat curves round like a swan's body but with the normal shape of the wings removed, to reveal the bottom of a boat. It is swept round to a stern that is similar in shape to the tail feathers of a swan, and at the back of the boat, on a little seat, there sits a tall figure with blue and silver draperies, and wings.

The boat comes to the shore before us and, following the dog's lead, we step into it. Being a magical boat, despite its small size it can contain any number of people. We sit facing the stern looking back toward the angel, who we see holds two cups, as did the image of the star maiden in the lake.

Smiling serenely the angel raises one cup on high and begins to tilt it so that the contents pour out. It is like a firework display. From the cup there falls a stream of coloured lights, sparks, and flaming shapes; some whirling like catherine wheels, some shooting off brilliant points of light, some spouting forth golden rain, and in every conceivable shape and colour. The angel catches the flow of fiery liquid shapes in the other cup and holds it forth for us to look at. When we look into the rim of the cup it is like looking out of a hole let into a huge expanse of sky. As far as the eye can see, there are revolving, spinning balls of different sizes and colours floating in space, some of them orbiting round each other. It is like the making of a host of whole worlds and suns and planets.

Then, in another breathtaking sight, the angel extends its brilliant wings, like a butterfly's, and gently fanning them, propels us across the lake.

As we proceed we are struck by more wonders. We no longer seem to be floating on the surface of a lake with reflections of the stars in the waters. Out on the lake the stars are real, and we are proceeding through bright indigo darkness with the stars all about us and on every side and above us, as well as below the boat.

And we listen too, for from the stars about us there comes a beautiful singing, like a harmonious choir, that contains all kinds of wondrous sounds, as if from instruments yet unknown that we have never heard on Earth.

And then a great brightness appears on the horizon – if it can be conceived that the space between the stars can have a horizon. A golden glow appears behind us, in the direction in which we are proceeding, and we turn in our seats to regard it. It grows in intensity and lights up the airy waters about the boat so that the stars begin to fade, and it is as if we are now proceeding across a mirror of golden glass. Then we realize that our craft has stopped.

The angel has ceased to propel us and, smiling, indicates that we alight. In that smile there is a blessing also, although no words are expressed. As we have noticed before, the beings in these higher worlds, including our dog, are telepathic. They can read our thoughts and put their own into our heads, and can do this so gently that one might quite easily think the thoughts are not theirs but our own. This can be a mixed blessing and requires vigilance over our own states of mind.

The boat has beached upon the edge of golden yellow sands, which seem to stretch for miles ahead as far as the eye can see. The scene is lit by bright golden light which seems to have no source, and we feel the thoughts of the angel, within our heads, responding to our barely formulated question as to why we can see no sun in the sky.

We do not need a sun to give us light. Light was created before there was any sun or moon, or even fire upon the Earth. A sun is but a vehicle of the outward expression of light. A moon of its quiet reflection.

The angel now rears up to a great height, and gazing down upon us, laughs with joy as once again it pours streams of coloured fire and light from one cup to another. Then it up-turns the lower cup so that it pours into the swan boat. There is a sizzling, hissing sound, and the boat rears up out of the water, transformed back into a swan, which, beating its massive wings, soars up and away, back over the way that we have come. And we see, perched upon its back, between the beating pinions, the figure of the Star Maiden, shining like silver. And the swan and the maiden disappear into the distance, to become no more than a tiny

point of radiance like a bright silver star. The form of the angel slowly disappears, dissolving before our eyes until nothing remains to be seen in the shimmering air. But a thought comes into our minds: 'Because you cannot see a friend it does not mean that you are alone.'
Exit-point Three.

Fourth Branch: (Death, the Tower and the Devil)

We stand and recall the dedicated purpose of our journey which is to find our own true names and the expression of our own essential self. We follow the dog, who begins padding along what seems to be a footpath that is hardly ever used. The landscape about us is flat and hard-packed sand.

A realization comes to us that we are entering the Dangerous Wastes and that we should pause and perform a little ceremony of dedication. We stand in a circle and each putting our left hand over our heart we raise our jewelled Tarot emblem. We find that the uplifted magical weapons are bathed in sunlight, and at the same time a golden warmth enters into our hearts and radiates from us. Nothing but love for all seems to exist for us, coming to us and flowing through us.

Immediately upon having done this simple act we feel as if a rapid wind has departed from us suddenly, and a certain darkness we had not hitherto observed has lifted from us.

Somehow, things seem lighter and brighter than they had been before, less glaring and harsh. An overshadowing darkness has left us. We remember how angels' thoughts can come into our heads and realize that other spirits' thoughts may do likewise. In the one case we will be impelled to the true and the good, and in the other to quarrelsomeness and distrust, or spite, lack of charity and lies. But our free will remains our own. The pictures or thoughts that come into our heads may be another's, just as any circumstance in outer life may not flow from our own initiative, but it is what we do about those pictures, thoughts or circumstances that counts. It is another's will that we be tempted; our own will if we succumb.

We continue on our way, and see something shimmering in the distance before us. It is either a spot in the desert where water wells up and brings life to all around it, an oasis; or else it is a mirage, that will lead us astray with its empty promise and illusion. Although in this desert, we begin to realize, there may be mirages that do not disappear on approach, and these can be the worst kind.

The place we see in the distance is indeed beautiful. It is a tall ivory tower, each window gay with colours, and at its top is a shining golden dome with a high point. The tower rises out of the desert emptiness like a giant pillar or a lighthouse, and about its foot are shady trees and gardens laid out around the rocky promontory upon which the tower is based.

As we approach the sun begins to go down, or that is what on Earth we would have assumed, for there has not been any sun to be seen in this sky. Anyhow, gradually the sky grows darker and the air colder as we proceed. It seems to us that we have been travelling long and that night will shortly fall.

The tower appears yet more beautiful in the twilight. A tall, slender, graceful, purple silhouette against the crimson coloured sky behind it. Welcoming lights begin to shine in the high windows and in the gardens at its base, fires seem to be lit, and the savour of herbs and spices and appetizing smells, even incense-like bonfire smoke drifts towards us on the desert air.

Nonetheless, we hesitate before going further, recalling the warnings that we have received. But as we stop we hear a noise. It is like a steady drumming in the far distance behind us. Although it is not loud, it is powerful, and the ground begins to shake slightly beneath our feet as it approaches.

Above the deep drumming we also hear a high pitched kind of singing, whistling noise, quite soft, but very eerie. And then, somewhat to our alarm, in the ground all around us, cracks begin to appear. The sand is running down into some of them, and the cracks spread out in a regular pattern like the tracing of a web.

The ground beneath our feet shakes yet more violently and a large crack opens beside us. In it we see livid red earth and dry bones, what looks to be a human arm, a rib cage, and a foot and leg. With a crackling noise other fissures open, and in all of them we see lying under the surface, nothing but dry bones and skulls.

We decide we have no option but to run to the tower. As we run we find ourselves in effect performing a bizarre and ungainly travesty of a dance as we strive not to put a foot into any of the cracks that open up around us. But it takes our minds from the sinister drumming noise which has become louder and louder, a dull throbbing persistently beating inside the brain. The whistling noise has become a high pitched shriek and it seems as if something is pursuing us.

As we reach the welcoming trees about the tower it seems that it is almost upon us. We turn to face it, and see that the drumming noise has been the beat of the hooves of galloping horses. A dozen or more great black beasts race towards us as if to run us down, but sheer off at the last second, unwilling, it seems, to enter the grove of trees and bushes. As the horses wheel past at full gallop, whinnying fiercely, showing long yellow teeth and the whites of rolling eyes, we see the riders on their backs. Each is clad in robes of flowing black that stream in ragged tatters behind. They carry long scythes which they whirl beside their charging steeds to cut down anything that comes their way. And from beneath each dark cowl of this hooded band there peers, not a face, but a skull, with grinning teeth and vacant sockets for the eyes, each lit up with a putrid luminous green. And from the bony hands that grip the scythes, and the bony feet in the stirrups we see that each one of them is a skeleton.

They wheel back into the surrounding darkness and the ground gradually ceases to shiver and crack. The sound of their hoof beats and swinging scythe blades recedes into the night, and we realize the air about us is very cold. The tower, with its bright lights and appetizing smells, certainly seems more inviting than the cold dark desert with its bones and fissures underfoot, and galloping bands of skeleton reapers.

We make our way toward the tower and mount the winding row of shallow steps that spiral round its base. As we approach the wooden door we hear sounds of music and great festivity going on within. Beside the door is an iron ring on the end of a chain. As soon as we touch this there comes a loud jangling noise from within the tower walls.

The door is thrown open and in the light that streams out from it there stands a tall and gauntly beautiful lady in a long jewelled dress of red and gold. Her eyes light up as she sees us and she extends her arms in a gesture of welcome. She ushers us in and closes the door behind us.

We find ourselves in a narrow hallway, hung in rich red velvet with golden facings. The hall swings up immediately into a curving staircase, thickly carpeted, for the tower is quite narrow, rather like a lighthouse. We are also struck by the warmth of the place. After the cold night air it seems almost oppressive and makes it hard to breathe. The air is scented, with a sweet sugary smell. At a distance from the tower this had seemed enticing and inviting but close to, in the thick of it, it seems slightly sickly and oppressive.

A tall man appears and stands behind the lady. He too is richly dressed, in a tight fitting coat of black, with silver and pearl buttons, and a wide starched collar that protrudes like wings on either side, and that is cut so high that he has to hold his head forward and up in an unnatural and uncomfortable way. He peers at us in an oddly eager fashion, without taking his eyes from us, and beckoning continually, he shuffles backwards before us up the stair well while the tall lady advances behind us. And so we ascend the spiral stair, towards the sound of shouting and singing and raucous jollity.

The tall man stops outside a tall narrow door hung with curtains. The noise from behind is intense. A hectic party is obviously in progress. He swings the curtains back upon their rod – and instantly there is silence.

We are ushered into a strange scene. The room is full of people but everyone has stopped stock still and is silent at our entry, staring fixedly at us. It is as if each one of them had suddenly turned into a statue. But they are living all right. Their hot flushed faces are plainly not of stone, and they breathe heavily from the exertions of barely a second before.

The tall man and woman walk forward with us to a clear space in the centre of the room. We look around at the circle of heavily breathing, staring faces about us. A riotous party has been taking place. There are bits of cake, half eaten sandwiches and cocktail delicacies all over the floor, some trodden into the carpet. Tables around the edge of the room have their cloths half pulled off, their contents spilled around them. And by the state of their disarray and attitude some of those present have been interrupted in pursuits other than drink or food.

The tall woman addresses us. 'We welcome you to join our celebration,' she says, 'to welcome you and receive your gifts.'

We realize that the gifts she means are the jewelled Tarot emblems that we carry before us, and we feel great reluctance to part with them.

'I know they were given to you by someone you regard a friend,' says the woman, smiling, 'but not to keep for ever!'

'To exchange, to barter, for something better,' says the tall man, coming forward holding out his hands for them, 'so you may join our privileged company, where everyone can do as they like.'

We look around at the company. They do not look exactly happy – but rather desperate and degraded.

We realize that not only do we not wish to join them, but that we are firmly determined to keep our emblems given us by the Fool and his mother. They represent our personal integrity.

'Do not forget we may be bigger and stronger than you,' adds the woman, with a note of menace.

'We are the King and Queen of this Tower,' says the man, 'and you are our prisoners.'

We instinctively gather into an outward facing circle, to protect ourselves.

'Children of Night and Delight,' cries the Queen, 'tear them down!'

The figures about us in the room immediately take on life and movement, and slowly gather in a circle about us, a vicious or a mocking gleam in every eye.

'Fear not!' comes the clear voice, in our minds, of the Fool's dog. 'Raise your emblems before you, that were given you in wisdom and power and love!'

We raise them before us and the jewelled stars give off a diamond radiance that obliterates all the hatefulness about us.

'Begone all phantasms!' comes the clear voice of the dog, 'Show yourselves as you are.'

There is a rumbling and crumbling noise that grows louder and louder, culminating in an awareness of falling objects all around us. We ourselves do not experience any falling sensation and the falling objects do not harm us. When all is silent the dog tells us to lower our emblems, for our adversaries now stand in the light of truth without illusion.

As we do so the diamond radiance fades and we find we are standing on the ground in a pile of crumbled stone and rubble. It is as if we were in the midst of a decayed ancient city that has been overcome by a great catastrophe and been left to the wild beasts and the elements for countless years.

But we are not alone. We stand in what seems to have been a courtyard or open room. The remains of broken pillars are all around, with mossy boulders and crumbled masonry scattered on the ground. On the far side of the space is a massive block of grey stone and plaster; it looks rather like a stage in some broken down old theatre. And upon this block or stage is sitting, cross legged, a huge revolting creature.

It could well seem very frightening because of its size and monstrous appearance. Its head is like a goat, with long curling horns. And although it has the body of a man, its legs have scales, which turn into bedraggled feathers and clawed feet, like a bird. And at its feet, with chains around their necks that fasten them to the block below, are the King and Queen of the tower – one on each side. Although now, instead of seeming rich and powerful and dangerous, beside the great beast they are small, powerless and pitiful.

'Now see what you have done!' screams the Queen at us. But her voice is a weak thin shriek that is almost lost in the air.

'You will be sorry for this!' shouts the King, only it comes as a wheezing high pitched croak. He turns towards the towering figure above him, pointing a scrawny finger towards us. 'Devour them!' he cries.

But the great figure, far from doing as it is bidden, cries in a loud and petulant voice, cracked with self conceit, '*I* do as *I* will!' which it repeats over and over again. Its voice is not that of a giant, or what one might expect from so large a creature, but is a chorus of high pitched voices that are just like the raised voices of the revelling rabble within the tower.

As it chants its monotonous sing-song it strikes the mock king and queen repeatedly with a greasy bladder on a stick that it holds in one hand. In a way it seems to be a spiteful travesty of the Fool. The blows are not hard enough to injure but enough to bowl the King and Queen over and knock the breath from them.

The monster grunts, sniffs and looks around. We feel that it has sensed our presence but is probably very short sighted. Then it catches sight of us and hisses and growls, muttering to itself with its many voices. We feel it is probably also fairly slow witted, even if cunning and malevolent. Then it focuses its gaze and attention on us.

'Come!' it says in its creaking voice, 'Give! Obey!'

It stands towering high above us and we realize that it is particularly desirous of the emblems we carry. It opens its bat like wings that have been concealed behind its back, a parody of one of the mighty and beautiful angels. Beating its pinions with a shattering clatter it rises into the air above us, its claws extended downwards, to grab our treasures or us.

'Come!' we hear the voice of the dog clearly in our heads. 'Straight forward! Fear naught! Remain true!'

He rushes straight towards the hovering monster and underneath it. We follow behind, straight to the block upon which it has been standing. There we find a dark and narrow little door that has been beneath its feet, between the chained King and Queen.

We are momentarily conscious of the stench of the monster, like rotting meat and blocked drains, and then we are through into clean air with the fresh smell of earth. We pass between narrow earthen walls in single file behind our faithful guide.

Presently we find ourselves in a relatively spacious chamber underground, a cave in the earth and rock. We stand and look about us. We realize that this is the place that the beast was trying to guard; trying to prevent people finding. It wants them to go back to death and the desert, or else to become, like itself, slave of the proud tower. But it is only like a waking bad dream.

Its only power is if you are afraid of it, or fall to its crude temptations. It has many voices and many names. One of them is Legion. Another is the Dweller on the Threshold or the Shadow. But if we let the light shine within us it loses all its tawdry glamour. Now we are safely past it we can proceed to the next stage of our journey, from the desert margins of creation toward the very heart of things.

Exit-point Four

Fifth Branch: (The Wheel of Fortune)

We proceed down the narrow passage and as we do so it gets gradually wider until, after a while, we find it is fairly comfortable to walk. The path slopes quite steeply downwards but although it is not steep enough to be called a staircase natural shelves in the rock beneath our feet make our descent easier; and the path seems to be ever curving so that we can not see very far in front or behind. This gives us the chance to examine the walls and narrow ceiling and floor of the passageway. We find that the jewels on our magical weapons give off a cool clear light which enables us to see where we are going without stumbling. We see that we are going through solid rock, which changes in colour and texture from time to time as if we are descending through different strata. Sometimes veins of other brightly coloured rocks run through the duller rock of the floor, walls and ceiling. Occasionally there are isolated pockets of crystalline rocks, that seem like strange flowers or gems embedded in the surrounding rock. Then we realize they are in fact gems.

It is like going through a gigantic treasure box surrounded by what appear to be emeralds, rubies, sapphires, and diamonds gleaming in greens, and reds and blues and starlight crystal fire about us – in clusters, or singly, like stars in the night sky. And like the stars in the night sky, as we go deeper and deeper, so do the gems glitter and glisten with their own light – not simply reflecting the light that we carry. And as we go deeper still, little living flames can be seen flickering about them, and the way becomes light enough for us not to need to rely on the light from the emblems we carry.

Even the solid rock of the roof and floor of the cave begins to glow with its own quiet light and then becomes almost transparent, as if it were, although still solid rock, also like a mountain mist, swirling and thickening and clearing unexpectedly, making strange shapes about us. We begin to think we can see movement in the rock all about us, like figures moving through the mist, and all going in the same direction as ourselves.

And sure enough, on either side of us, as we travel on, we begin to see little men, with long beards and pointed caps and bells on their pointed shoes, marching beside us beyond the walls of the rock. Most of them carry sacks on their backs or the tools one might expect to see in a blacksmith's shop. Hammers, tongs, little portable anvils.

It also seems to be getting warmer and we begin to hear a dull low roaring noise, and what sounds like the tapping of hundreds of tiny hammers. The path now slopes down less steeply. In fact it has levelled out and the walls of the rock have become so clear that it is as if we can see through clear pink mist at a wide circular clearing in which sit, as far as the eye can see, hundreds of the little gnomes. Each is sitting cross legged, with a little golden anvil before him, beating away with hammer and tongs, fashioning the most beautiful gems and jewels that ever eye has seen.

We think for a moment of how the monstrous beast, and those who are enslaved by it, would envy and covet these treasures. Yet these gems are too pure for them. Even if they could, by some impossible chance, lay their hands for a second upon them, the treasures would fade into the appearance of old leaves, or dust and ashes, in their grasping hands. They are allowed to have and to hold certain low quality gems and precious metals in the outer world, as an act of mercy and training, but it is their own debasing greed that stops them from valuing anything much better than dirt. And the really precious things seem to them to have no value.

We walk slowly through the ranks of labouring gnomes, admiring the beautiful gems that they fashion. And we realize that the little folk are in fact seated in circles around a central rim from which shines an incandescent light. At the same time, we become aware of a gradual sensation of movement, and realize that we are slowly revolving around this centre, as if on a great carousel.

We wonder why we feel as if we are going round, and the thoughts of the dog answer us. He tells us that everything that exists is always going round. That it is called the Great Dance, and all created systems, from little atoms to mighty galaxies, do it. We do not notice it normally, but as we get near a centre so we begin to realize we are spinning and to feel the movement. The centre itself, of course, is still. Paradoxically, although obviously, there are many centres besides the One Great Centre of All. And if we go to one centre, even if it is the centre within ourselves, we are not far off all centres, for they all have the quality of stillness, that some people who have experienced these things would call eternity. As to whether we will see the One Great Centre depends on each one of us, and whether we really want to. The One Great Centre is at the same time very far and very near. If you do not know how to look for it, it is a universe away. But if you do know how to look, it is very near. We have, in each one of us, a replica of this universal centre. It is called the heart.

We now advance towards this centre to which we have come. As we approach, a shaft of white light powers up from the ground before us, and we realize we are standing near the brink of an enormous precipice, a circular well that plunges into untold depths below. And from it is blazing a light so bright that, like the light of the sun, it is almost impossible to gaze upon. We are at the top of what might perhaps be called a volcano of light, or one could think of it as a fountain – a light fountain. We gaze in awe at the jets of coloured light that can be discerned within the overall whiteness, and our eyes follow the pulsing jets downward, into the depths of the light well. And as our eyes grow used to the brightness, we begin to see movement and shapes down there.

It seems as if we are looking at a great wheel, with another wheel within that, going another way. And another one still. Wheels within wheels. Indeed, as we gaze, we begin to see the outline of what looks like a giant gyroscope. That is, a circular wheel turning between two rings that hold it as in a simple cage. There are children's toys made like them, like spinning tops that will stand secure and still, kept so by the speed and force of their spinning.

In this cage all the rings are in motion. In a slow stately movement like the turning of the Earth or the stars. And as well as being three rings, they are also disks, for the material of which they are made extends from the rim to the centre of each disk, and so the three disks turn and interpenetrate each other all the time. And when they do so they cause currents of light to form at their points of interchange. So we are looking down not only onto a great, slowly turning sphere of light, but within that sphere, great rays of light are traced out in a pattern of huge figures of eight, each having as their centre the common point of the centre of the sphere. We count six of these great double lobes, or solid figures of eight, and each one is a different colour. As well as this the sphere is forming bands of light within itself, also of different colours. We can count seven of these, spheres within spheres, all inside the great spinning sphere made up of three turning rings. We are gazing upon the most magnificent many coloured jewel that it is possible to imagine, its colours ever changing.

'Would you like to see it closer?' asks a gruff but kindly voice beside us. We look round to see that one of the gnomes, who seems to be a chief or senior one, has approached us. He has a very long grey beard that reaches almost to his toes, and a brown leathery face wrinkled into a broad grave smile.

We say that we do so wish.

'These are the Wheels of Fortune,' says the gnome, 'and I will summon the Lady who spins them, to tell her you are here.'

He takes a horn from his side and gives three mighty blasts that echo and re-echo. As the last note dies away, as if formed from the vibration of the notes in the air, there appears before us, standing over the abyss, a fair lady dressed in sky blue, with long golden hair.

She smiles at us and beckons us to approach. As she does so a pathway of brilliant light forms before our feet, and taking our courage in both hands, and not looking down at the incandescent depths below us, we step onto the narrow bridge, towards the lady, whose radiant smile of welcome dispels all fears.

We stand at the centre before her, looking up, for she is twice the size of an ordinary human being, and many times as beautiful.

'Have you come to gaze in wonder at my beautiful spinning wheels?' she says. 'Or do you seek to pass through the Gates of Space and Time?'

The dog speaks for us. 'We look for the One Great Centre to find our real names and our essential selves. And then to return to take them back to the outer world.'

'All ways lead to the One Great Centre,' smiles the lady, 'and all lesser centres have a gate through which one can pass in the twinkling of an eye. Or there is the longer way around the Paths of the Spheres that takes millions of years. Let me show you a central secret Path that will not long delay you.'

As she says this we begin slowly to descend. We pass between cylindrical walls of brilliant light, then there is a slight, almost undetectable bump and a feeling of gentle vibration.

'We enter the North Pole of my spheres,' says the lady. And as we descend, so the vibrating feeling encloses us, and we can no longer see the white light-walls of the shaft but find we are in a gigantic sphere.

It is a world of rainbow colours and of sound as well, and even scents and tastes and feelings. It is like being inside a piece of music. Each sound has a colour and a shape so that we not only hear it but see it as well. And there is no discordant noise or ugly shape. All is melody and rich harmony. Melodies appear like strings of beautiful necklaces of light, and harmonies appear like deep pools of merging colour into which the eye as well as the ear can sink in delight.

'This is the heaven of the spheres,' says the lady. 'All the sounds and sights you see and hear are angels making patterns. This is a place of patterns. If you could copy these patterns in the outer life you lead, then your little world would be harmonious too. But the angels do not think of the patterns they weave. They simply sing for joy straight from the heart, and being full of love and joy the beauty and harmony follows. It is really very simple.'

And as we continue our journey toward the centre and gently come to rest we see we are at the meeting place of twelve great corridors of light and echoing sound, that swing off through the sphere, each of which has its own dominant shade of colour and different range and tone of harmonies. If we look down the corridors of each one we can see great figures appearing in the distance. Some of them are animals. We notice a golden lion in one, a mighty bull in another, and in another a curly-horned ram. Others are people, a man pouring water from a pot, and a pair of twins. They are in fact the signs we associate with the constellations of the zodiac. We are in the centre of a great jewel that is the perfect pattern of our cosmos and we pause to regard the wonders that can be seen, and to imbue our souls with the essential harmony and beauty and serene peace of the centre of a perfect pattern.
Exit-point Five

Sixth Branch: (The Hanged Man and Strength)

We now look to the floor upon which we ourselves stand and see that it is like a shining glass window or perhaps a crystal ball, and bright and clear within it is the image of a man who is upside-down.

That is, his head is closest to the floor at our feet, so in a sense he might be said to be the same way up as ourselves. But past his head we can see that he is hanging. Hanging by his feet from a wooden frame that straddles a deep precipitous chasm.

Whether this is a kind of distorting mirror we cannot be sure, but it seems as if the man is very long and tall; that his feet are miles and miles away, so small and distant are they. But his head and smiling face are right at our feet and a golden glow seems to emanate from it and from out of the mirror towards us so that it is like standing in the warmth of a radiating fire.

'This is the mirror centre,' says the lady, 'it looks like a window but in fact it is a door. There are many kinds of door to many kinds of places. Some doors are for going through, and others are best kept shut – at least for a time. But where there is a door there is always a choice. So it is for you to choose whether you wish to go through.'

We wonder how it can be that a mirror reflects something that is not there.

'It reflects something that is very much there, and here,' says the lady in reply to our thoughts. 'Remember we are at the centre of things, and so a mirror image will be in the same place as that which it reflects.'

We stare down at the figure of the man in the floor beneath us, and see that he has varicoloured clothes, and his hands are held behind his back. He gazes upon us, smiling.

'He seems to recognize you,' says the lady, 'so if you want to go through the door just wish.'

We look into the man's face, and feel that he is a friend. Someone we can trust. And we wish we were through the door.

As we do so the hanging man's arms come from behind his back and up and out through the mirror floor. As they do so, showers of golden coins fall round and about us. But we have no time to stop and pick them up for we are seized in strong, protective hands and pulled through the floor. There is a confusing topsy-turvy dizzy moment when we know not whether we are up or down as we pass through the mirror surface and then we are plainly on the other side with the man, hanging upside-down in an abyss whose depths seem bottomless. We have no time to feel frightened, for doubling himself up from the waist, the man, still holding us, places us at the top of the chasm on firm ground. Then with masterly agility, he unhooks his foot from the hanging loop of rope, and leaps from over the yawning gap to stand before us. We see now, however, that he is of normal size, and he has a strong resemblance to the Fool, though there is a radiance about his face that makes it difficult to be certain.

But there is no doubt from the actions of the dog, who throws himself upon his master in a paroxysm of twisting and curling and tail wagging and turning round and round and jumping up and down, until at length he ceases his cavortings and sits by us, his head on one side and his ears cocked, looking up at his master attentively.

We want to ask many questions about how we got here and where we are but the radiant-headed man smiles gently and we realize these things are beyond our understanding, at least until we have completed our Journey and can see things in a true perspective.

In a sense, the twisting and turning of our minds has no more chance of understanding the universe than the capering of the dog. When our minds, like the dog, are still, the man raises his arm and points into the distance.

'Before you is a hill,' he says. 'Climb that and you will find the way to clearer understanding.'

We turn and see, over rolling countryside, a round green hill in the middle distance.

When we turn back to ask more questions we find we are alone. Of the man and the gaping chasm and the scaffold over its depths there is now no sign. There is no sign of life in the deserted landscape either, but it has a friendly and welcoming feel.

We make our way towards the hill. It seems to take us a long time, perhaps because of the quality of stillness about the place. But eventually we see that after only two or three more undulations of the rolling downs we shall reach it.

As we draw closer we notice what appear to be white markings on the side of the hill. At first we cannot make out what they are, but suddenly it becomes apparent. Carved in the side of the hill is the unmistakable figure of a lion, a great white lion with long curling tail and huge shaggy mane. And at the top of the hill can be seen a ring of standing stones.

When we reach the foot of the hill we find it does not seem so small. Certainly it is perfectly round, but whilst this looked pretty from afar, when we arrive we find that this means that the sides at the bottom are almost sheer. And from this point we can see nothing of the lion carving or of the standing stones at the top.

We realize that there is nothing else for it but a hard climb, calling for determination and faith – or remembrance of what we have seen from afar. Fortunately the grass is quite long so we can hang on to it to help us to climb.

The grass is quite slippery to stand on or to hold, but it grows in tussocks, which we find we can use like stepping stones. And so we scramble on and up, sometimes giving each other a helping hand.

After a time the going gets easier. As we come round the vertical curve of the hill we begin to see the lower markings of the lion cut into the turf, the end of the tail, and the feet; although it is more difficult to see that it is in fact a lion now that we are so close to it.

Gradually the rest of the carved figure comes into view and we find ourselves standing along the underbelly of the huge figure. The grass is cut away in a long curve to either side of us, and before us is the bare chalk of the figure.

The chalk is very white, and looks very polished and slippery. Apart from this it also seems very special, and we do not feel we should walk on it. So we make our way sideways beneath the white carved figure. The going is not so hard, for we are no longer climbing, but we have to take care not to slip. Having climbed so high up so steep a slope, to lose faith and tumble could mean a nasty fall.

We come to the beginning of the front legs and realize that we shall have to go back down again, the whole length of its front leg and then up its other one, and then all the way round its head, but there is nothing else for it if we are to avoid clambering over the figure.

'There is another way,' says a voice.

We look round, wondering where it can be coming from, and see, high above us, the head of a maiden. Her head is all we can see because of the curve of the hill.

'You are wise not to tread on the lion,' she calls in a gentle voice, 'for this is holy ground. But if you show due reverence and respect for that which is beneath your feet, you may be allowed the short way up. Remove your shoes and leave them behind. Then you may come straight to where I am.'

We sit on the grassy tussocks and remove our shoes, and barefoot, start up across the chalk of the carved lion. Although it had seemed as if it might be as slippery as ice, to our bare feet it is warm and gives a reassuring feel. The slight vulnerability we felt on abandoning our shoes gives way to a sense of freedom and sure-footedness.

We climb the decreasing slope to the top of the lion's back and find ourselves face to face with the maiden who had called to us. She is very beautiful, with long yellow hair with many-coloured flowers plaited in a wreath to make a little ringlet crown. Her dress is patterned with flowers, and she has more flowers in chains all around her neck and waist, spilling onto the ground about her feet and onto the chalk surface of the lion. We see too that the grass of the upland above the lion is no longer lush dark green tussocks of coarse-bladed grass but rich short turf, covered with varicoloured flowers, not only buttercups and daisies but all imaginable kinds of little rock plants. The grass is of different quality up here, just as the fur on the various parts of the body of a lion, long and shaggy around its mane but short and smooth on the top of its head. Indeed, we realize that the chalk figure is not just a decoration but shows what the hill itself really is. And as if by way of demonstration, the maiden waves the end of her long skirt over a patch of ground in front of us in which there is a fissure in the soil, like the cracks that appear on a long dry summer. And as she does so, 'Huff! Huff! Huff!' there are three rumbling snorts, and from the cracks in the ground, three puffs of smoke arise, accompanied by a shower of sparks.

'Lion's breath!' the maiden cries. 'It may seem hot enough to be a dragon's. Indeed some people do call it a dragon, but to those who know it, it is a friendly lion – although that does not mean that it is not wild! He could burn us all to cinders, or shake us off his back, or swallow us all, if he had a mind to. He is very strong.'

And she swirls her dress about in a few wild steps of dance, the strings of flowers whirling into spiralling shapes about her. As she does so, between her bare feet, the ground shakes and trembles and shoots forth jets of smoke and fire. It is like standing on a volcano.

The maiden stamps her feet rhythmically so that a pattern of puffs of different coloured smoke hang in the air about us. She laughs with infectious gaiety as she whirls about us, and the drumming of her bare feet on the turf draws us into imitating her dance, whirling and spinning and spiralling. The maiden is dancing so rapidly now that the whirling of her skirts, and the ropes of flowers she has, become blurred to our sight, so it appears as if she herself might be somehow made entirely of flowers.

'The grass and the flowers and the trees and the moss and all things that grow, dance on the back of the lion,' she sings. 'Let us dance the dance of the life of the lion.'

And we do, proceeding in wild spiral dance, led by the dancing flower maiden. And so doing, we approach the stone circle that stands on the top of the hill.

Here we encircle a flat stone that stands before a trilithon gate and there are impelled to stand quiet and still before the quiet majesty of the stones, while the maiden dances off back down the hill waving a joyous farewell with the swirling garlands about her head.

We remain standing before the entrance to the stone circle contemplating its great age and ancient purpose.

Exit-point Six

Seventh Branch: (The Hermit, the Lovers, the Chariot)

We regard the low stone beside the trilithon gateway before us. It has a shallow depression in its top and beside it a silver bowl of water. We each take the bowl in turn and pour a little of the water onto the stone. There is a low rumbling sound as we do so, and then as the last one of us puts back the bowl upon the stone, a deep roll of thunder, a flash of lightning, and a deep strong voice cries 'Who comes?'

We see a tall figure standing in the pylon gateway who gazes sternly upon us. He is as lean as he is tall, and has a long white beard, a white robe and long white hair with a tonsure shaven on the top. In one hand he has a long thick staff, intricately carved with twining serpents, and in his other hand he holds aloft a flickering lantern.

'Who comes to the Circle of the Stones of the Eternal?' he asks again. 'If you seek to enter, utter the password.'

'That which is truly reflected is as that which is upright,' replies the dog on our behalf.

'Enter, little ones of the flickering light of time,' says the old man, standing aside. And as each of us crosses the threshold of the grey stones he scrutinizes us most carefully, holding his lantern to illuminate our faces. We see that the candle inside it is minutely divided with marks to record the passing of time.

'The light in my lantern is time itself,' the old man says, walking gravely before us, 'which ever burns itself away.'

'When this little candle is all burned away then time itself will be no more, and will give way to the brighter light of eternity.'

As he speaks, he leads us through a maze of standing stones. They seem to be in some sort of order but there are so many that it is difficult to see what it may be. It is rather like walking through the mechanism of a stone clock. But in the centre there is a clear circular space in the midst of a pattern of dark blue coloured stones. And in the very midst of all is a low rounded stone, with a smooth flat top of light pinkish grey. And upon that a yet smaller stone of pure white, cut into a perfect but ever changing shape, that sometimes seems to be a cube, at other times a pyramid. Sometimes an eight-fold diamond shape, and at other times more complicated, with lots of sides of triangles or pentagons. Indeed it is a shape-shifting Platonic solid, whose planes are ever equidistant from its centre.

'So you seek to enter the realm that has no time,' he says, 'that is called the Land of the Ever Young and also the Land of Great Wisdom.'

He raises his serpent staff high above the white stone, and in the lantern light the serpents carved upon it seem to wriggle and to hiss, and two wings grow out from either side of the top of the staff and beat rapidly, whilst the very top, shaped like a pine cone, glows as if it were very hot.

'Open the Gates of Time!' the old man cries, 'And let eternal love come in!'

He thrusts downward with the bottom of his staff, which is sharpened to a spike, a spike that wriggles and squirms like a sting. It strikes the white stone and as it does so the stone takes on the appearance of an egg. The staff cracks and smashes a hole into its shell, and it falls into a thousand fragments onto the stone beneath, its yoke wetting the stone and pouring away into the ground. But from the egg, hovering in the air before us, is a young boy. He seems no more than four or five years old, and he glows brighter than the old man's lantern, with a warm ruddy kind of colour. It is as if he came from the midst of invisible flames. He hovers on bright wings before us in the air, holding a bow and arrow.

Smiling at us, he stretches the bow string tight, and shoots an arrow high into the air. It rises like an ascending rocket, leaving a rainbow trail of sparks and coloured vapour.

'Quickly, quickly! Over the rainbow bridge!' cries the old man. And he hustles us onto the central stone where a cloud of the coloured vapour from the arrow has descended. We find it is like solid ground and that we can stand on it.

'On you go!' cries the old man. 'Out of the stones of time.'

Led by the dog we race up the rainbow path. It is like climbing the green hill all over again, except that this time it is like going up a narrow bridge rising high into the sky. Looking down we can see the rolling countryside far beneath us, the green hill with the carved lion upon it, the flower maiden still dancing round it, puffs of smoke and fire coming from beneath her feet. And at the top of the hill, now far, far below us, the circles of stones within stones, in a complex pattern, but looking no bigger that a button, so great is our height. And still the old man's voice urges us on. 'Go! Go! Out of the circle of the stones of time!' But now his voice is no longer that of an old man, it is a childish treble that calls after us – or so it appears at this height.

Gradually the steepness of the rainbow path of the arrow decreases until we reach the top of its arc. As we pass the zenith we find that as we go down we go faster and faster, until our speed has become so great that everything about us is nothing but a blur. And then it all becomes so fast that we no longer even have any sensation of falling. We appear to be floating in some state of suspended animation.

'How do you like my chariot?' comes a clear laughing voice.

We look around and find that we are sitting on something flat and square and solid, with a beautiful complex pattern on it. It seems rather like a magic carpet, for it flies swiftly and silently. At the rear of it stands a young woman with a flowing dress and golden reins in her hands. These stretch over our heads to where we can see before us a team of four beautiful horses, with silvery backs, and huge golden wings held upright, for they do not seem to need them to fly, but gallop merrily through the air as if it were their natural element.

'I am the Spirit of Victory,' says the maiden, 'and these are my four great steeds. You have been shot far from the Earth by the arrow of Love. And now we are travelling faster than the speed of light. When you travel as fast as this all kinds of things happen that otherwise would be impossible. No-one behind us can see us. And we approach people who are in front of us so fast that we are past them before they see us coming. And of course once we are past them they cannot see us anyway. And so we are invisible. And of course if you travel fast enough you are always in the same place. All straight lines join up together at infinity and turn into circles because everything is curved. And if you go round a circle fast enough you are always in every part at once. So we are always wherever we want to be, and that is wherever the heart is. If we slowed down you would find yourselves not so far from where you want to go. I know you seek your true names and your essential selves and they are in the direction of Love's arrow which is where the winged horses are taking us. Straight to the heart of the empire. And look below, for there it is.'

Looking down we see that the horses pulling us have begun to circle, and gradually we are spiralling down onto a flat plain that lies beyond a range of mountains over which we have just passed. The mountains are a beautiful dark blue and lit with tiny diamond lights.

'See the Celestial Mountains, or the Mountains of the Stars,' says the lady. 'The stars you see in the outer heavens are in those mountains. And those mountains are indeed your night sky. This is where the arrow of Love and the chariot of Victory bring you. To the land of the Emperor Beyond the Stars. You see his palace below you and all who are assembled to welcome you.'

We look down and see that there is a space marked out for us towards which the horses circle round and round, getting lower and lower. Marked out on the ground is a system of circles, one within the other, and coloured like a rainbow. In fact it is, in one sense, like a target for the arrow of Love; in another it is similar to a plan diagram of the spheres, at whose centre we found the mirror gate of the Hanged Man.

All about the circle are ranged people who have come out to see us. As we descend we realize that the great square is the central square of the palace. The palace itself is huge, like four palaces in fact, ranged on each side of the square. Its tall white and golden spires and turrets reach towards the sky and it seems that a glorious army is come out to meet us. As we come to rest on the shimmering rainbow circle, right at its centre, there is a burst of triumphal music.

On each side of the square about us are ranged winged angel soldiers in different coloured uniforms, and as one, they raise their spears and banners in salute to us. They stand rank upon rank before us clad in gold and yellow. Those to our right are dressed in the reds of fire. Behind us they are all in purple and blue. And to our left the ranks are in shades of green.

The yellow clad angels, for that is what they appear to be, for they have wings arched behind them, are armed with bows and arrows, like the child who so wondrously guided us here from out of the stone circle.

The red ones have long slender spears with flames at the tip, for controlling monsters and giants.

The blue angels have nets and tridents, and are so equipped for seeking the seas for monsters who lurk in the dark depths.

And the emerald angels have mirror like shields, which are not only for defence, for any attacker seeing his own reflection will be stunned by it, or even turned to salt or stone.

However, we are led to understand that there are no such enemies to be fought against here, but that these angelic powers are for helping to keep the law in the troublesome mists and waters of the lands of time, at the further side of the Starry Mountains from which we have come.

Finally we say farewell and give our thanks to the winged horses of the chariot of Victory. Upon each is a cloth of a different colour, yellow gold, crimson red, dark purple blue, and emerald green. And the horses' names are embroidered upon each cloth, and each one is named after a wind. The one in gold and yellow is called Oriens, after the East Wind. The one in red Meridies, after the South Wind. The one in blue Occidens after the West Wind. And the one in emerald Septentrio after the North Wind.

And we stand for a few moments communing with their mighty forces that coincide with the army of angels with banners that guard our own and the higher worlds.
Exit–point Seven

Eighth Branch: (The Emperor and the Hierophant)

'Now that you have seen his servants,' says the Lady of Victory, 'you should present yourselves to the Emperor. If you turn round and lift your eyes you will see that he is standing there before you.'

We turn but can see no-one.

'Look further,' she says, 'toward the far mountains.'

We do so. The palace is in a plain in a wide valley. When we approached it we crossed a dark blue range of mountains studded with stars. With our backs to these mountains we now look to the further side of the valley and to the mountains that rise there.

These are of a different colour, mostly reds, from scarlet to crimson. They are also studded with coloured points of light, like radiant gems. They rise to an enormous height, and are dominated by a huge promontory that is lighter coloured, like pink granite. From this there descend frozen streams, or glaciers, that merge on the lower reaches into stretches of snow. The summit of the promontory is also covered in snow, and about it have been built what appears to be a miraculously high wall of gold, regularly carved into turrets of fantastic shape, with coloured inlays, like slabs of precious stone.

The golden wall round the top of the mountain looks something like a crown, and indeed as we look more closely we see that it *is* in fact a crown. And the huge mountain is like a head, and what looked like pink granite cliffs is in fact a face. We can see the eyes and nose; and that which we took for ice and snow is white hair and a beard.

It seems like a gigantic carving but as we watch we see it move. And what we thought was going to be an avalanche turns out to be a smile. We are gazing, not at a mountain range, but at the head and shoulders of an ancient man, with long beard, red gem-studded robe, and a jewelled crown upon his snow-white head.

'We are at the gate of the World of Giants,' says the Lady of Victory.

'Greetings and welcome,' cries a huge voice. It is deep and awesome as thunder, and rolls echoing round the valley.

'You will have to believe your ears and trust your eyes,' it says, and

breaks into a chuckle that is like an erupting volcano. 'Fear not, my little ones, you are coming to me.'

We see, suddenly, travelling with enormous speed towards us, a gigantic hand. And before we know what is happening we are plucked from where we stand and are rushed through the air within its gentle grasp.

We are dropped lightly onto the crimson coloured surface of the emperor's robe, and gaze in wonder at the panoramic view that we see from his shoulder.

Below us, like a tiny model, is the four square palace with the troops drawn up on all sides of the rainbow circle. There stands the lady with her triumphal car, like a tiny dot before us. And across the valley is the far mountain range, dark blue with glittering stars.

'There stands the universe,' says the great voice above us, and as it speaks, it rumbles right through us for we stand on the very shoulder of the body from which the great voice speaks.

'As you can see, it's not quite as big as me. But it is as big as it needs to be. It is. Just as I am I. And although I created it, if it belongs to anyone it belongs to those who are within it. That is who it was made for. But I see you wonder for what purpose it was made. And whom it serves. Those are very big questions. Far too big for me!' The giant chuckles, and beneath our feet it is like a minor earthquake.

'The answers to questions like that you will have to discover for yourselves. They are to be found only in the Gardens of the Blessed. And you may learn your true names there too, and find your essential selves. You also wonder why I am so much bigger than you,' he continues. 'That is just because I know more. I know all the laws that govern the universe and how to keep them going, and every hair or scale or feather on every animal, fish or fowl that walks or swims or flies or crawls or burrows throughout all of that which you call time and space. That is why I seem bigger than you. But when you find what you have come to seek, that knowledge is so great that you may well find yourselves as big as me. And that, I may say, is a considerable responsibility.'

As he says this he stands up. It is like going up in a fast lift. As if the ground beneath us shot upward into the sky. Except that there does not seem to be any sky. Just a great light blue turquoise light all round us as far as the eye can see.

And far, far below us, if we strain to see over a fold in the crimson cloak that seems like a giant earthwork, we can see, as if laid out on a table, the little mound of twinkling indigo blue that is the entire universe.

'Fear not where you are going,' says the Emperor. 'You see little for the moment only because your eyes are short sighted and the light is so clear that it dazzles you. I have a close companion very much like unto myself, who will look after you and lead you to the garden. Seek for his coming. Look for a star.'

We stand wondering if we shall see another huge face before us like a mountain. But then, high in the air we see what looks to be a moving star, that is gradually growing bigger. As we watch the star at first a tiny point of diamond light, grows brighter and larger, and we see that it is plainly descending.

As it does so it begins to take on shape and we see that it seems to be a great building descending through the sky. It has a three-fold structure. In the centre is a dome, from the top of which the star light comes, and on either side of the foursquare building there is a tall tower rising, pointing upward like a pillar with a spire. The whole building, its central hall and side towers, is of stone of brilliant white.

It ceases its descent and hovers in the air before us some distance off. Faintly we can hear music coming from within it, and a spicy pinewood smell like incense seems to drift across to us. The two doors of its central tower are flung wide open, and the sound of music rolls towards us and the scent of all kinds of woods and flowers and hedgerows.

As we watch, it seems that a radiance and a vapour surrounds the building and extends to where we ourselves are standing. It is like a vibrant lake of silvery purple mist. Then a figure comes to the open doors. We can see his outline dark against the light that blazes from within. He slowly walks towards us, across the lake of light, as if along the bright path of reflected light that shines from the radiant doorway.

As he approaches we see he wears the rough dress of a shepherd and that he has a tall staff, curved at the top like a shepherd's crook. Our dog leaps forward to meet him, running round and round him joyously like a shepherd's dog. The young man stops before us and smiles.

'Welcome to my house,' he says. Smiling, he beckons us to join him on the silvery walkway of light across the shimmering lake. We walk together towards the doorway of light.

'I should warn you it is not so much a house,' he says, 'in the usual sense of the word. It is not meant to be lived in. It is more in the nature of a gate keeper's lodge. A place for passing through.'

We approach the double doors. The singing of mighty choirs and the scent of incense swamps us as we enter the blaze of light. It is like a brilliantly lit cathedral, with an undefinable sense of Christmas in the air. As we pass through the door we pass also through the brilliant light that hangs like a curtain before it, radiating its illuminating power to the world outside. Inside the door we see before us a mighty pillar that soars upward high above us, and extends outwards like a bowl or a chalice at the top. It could almost be a huge baptismal font.

'This,' says the young man, 'is really a magic fountain. But a fountain that is blocked. And if you go close to it you will see who it is who has blocked it.'

We approach and see that it is made up of thousands of grey bricks, or stones like bricks. And as we look closer we see that each one has a name on it. And we each discover a grey stone that is deeply inscribed with our own full name.

'Do not marvel at finding your own name amongst all the thousands there,' says the young man. 'There is no such thing as chance. Whatever you truly seek you will find. Each stone stands as a record of all who are blocking the flow of the magic fountain. You can remove your own grey stone from the channel if you will, but you will find it is stuck tight until you can replace it with something better. That is, with a stone of gold and crystal that bears your true inward name, that expresses your own essential self. Then this model of a dark tower will become a shining bright pillar, and a model of the true goodness of all whose names appear in it. The gold and crystal stones will not block the fountain's flow because it is a fountain of light. Light spurts from the source of all being, and jetting high into the air becomes clear crystal water that dissolves all evil it touches. It transforms all that is sick and ailing or neglected into beauty and health. And that will form into a lake with a beautiful garden surrounding it. And from the garden four great rivers will flow into your dark world, and into the other dark worlds in the Mountains of the Stars, to transform them into a place of wonder.

'But as I said, where we now stand is only at the gateway to the Lands of Wonder. If you seek to find the gold and crystal stones with your true names on I would ask first to entrust your jewelled emblems to me that were given you at the start of your journey. But that must be something for you to decide, on the grounds of whether you feel you can trust me. And that is a wisdom of the heart. Does it warm within you when you think of giving me your treasures?'

And then we pause long and consider whether or not we should give our emblems to the young man who stands smiling before us, who stands offering a key to us in exchange, if we so decide.

Exit-point Eight

Ninth Branch: (The High Priestess)

The young man gently takes from us the sparkling emblem that we offer to him, and in return he gives us a little gold or silver key.

'Find the lock that will take those keys,' he says, 'and your mission will be all but complete. But in times of trial or testing, remember me.'

It is our dog who leads us on into the building. He scampers, with his nose down to the ground, round the tall dark font. And as we go past it, clasping our keys; we notice how the dark stones that bear our names have begun to grow a little lighter in colour, a little more translucent, even to glow very dimly.

Past the font we find we are passing through a great hall. It is, in proportion, like a church, but is festooned with coloured lights and all manner of decorations. All around the sides of the hall it seems that there are merry groups of people full of chatter and laughter. From high above us light streams down onto the scene below through windows of many coloured glass. These show scenes that seem to be associated with Christmas. A star guiding three wise men. Shepherds in the fields at night talking to angels. A baby in a manger surrounded by an ox and an ass and other animals. A fir tree laden with presents, with a fairy on the top. A jolly red cloaked Santa Claus laden with gifts from the North Pole, reindeer pulling his sleigh. The same merry figure walking the snowy roof tops and nimbly descending the chimneys through glowing hearth fires to leave his gifts by the bedsides of sleeping children.

Our dog, however, with nose to ground, hurries on, and we follow him. He leads us to a wide circular maze, outlined on the floor with patterned tiles. It is equal in extent to the dome in the roof high above it.

It is not a puzzle maze. There is only one path for us to follow. But it goes round and round, and back and forth, until every patch of ground within the circle has been covered. And at last, after a short final straight bit, we find ourselves at the centre.

It is a tradition with such mazes that the distance through the maze is the same as the height from its centre to the high point in the roof. We look up and marvel at the height of the pitch of the dome above us. We admire the bright and beautiful pictures painted on the inside of the dome. It is of the starry sky, with angels pushing the stars round as if they were movable lamps. We also see mighty constellations depicted; those that surround the Northern Pole. The Great Bear, the Swan, the throne of Cepheus the king, and the curling, coiling Dragon. And we realize that the point of the dome is the North Pole of the heavens, about which all the stars turn throughout the night, all the way down to the zodiacal creatures at its rim.

Looking down, at our feet we see embedded in the floor in the very centre of the maze is a little picture in shining mosaic. It is of a naked figure, surrounded by a wreath of holly and mistletoe, dancing in a night sky, holding in each hand a spiral wand, one of gold and the other of silver. It is difficult to see if the figure is male or female but around the wreath are emblems of a lion, an eagle, a bull and an angel. We look closer and see that each of the spirals has throughout its length a number of tiny keyholes.

We each take the key that the young shepherd has given us, to see if it will fit one of the keyholes. Soon each of us finds we have found a keyhole that will receive our key. If we have a gold key it will fit into a silver keyhole. If we have a silver key it will fit a gold keyhole. Then, having fitted them, together we turn them, for none will work unless they are turned together. Each is like the facet of a combination lock.

As the keys turn a strange thing happens. The whole floor of the maze starts to turn, not round and round, but over onto its back, so that we find ourselves, upside-down, under the floor.

Only we soon forget that we are upside down because above our heads is another great dome, exactly the same in shape and size as the one before, but with different pictures painted on it.

The pictures around the rim, of the Zodiac, are the same, although, because we view them from another side, they now seem to go round the other way. But the paintings on the rest of the dome, although they are of stars, are not the familiar ones of the upper dome. They are those of the terrestrial Southern hemisphere. They are mostly sea pictures. Of Argo, the great ship that bore the heroes in search of the Golden Fleece, of Cetus the great whale, and other sea monsters, and high above shines a Lighthouse Altar and the Southern Cross, near the Centaur, who by tradition invented all the signs of the constellations.

We realize we now have to tread our way back out of the maze, not forgetting to take our keys. The dog, his nose to the ground, leads us along the circuitous way. We find that the exit to the maze is at the far side from the way we came in. In other words if it had been the westernmost point of the circle we had entered we now leave it at the eastern side.

We now pass through another part of the building. It would correspond to the choir if we were in a church. High seats tower on either side of us, except that one can hardly call them seats. Each is rather a niche that is occupied by a model of an angelic figure, every one with a stringed instrument or a horn of some kind, and they play a slow and stately solemn music in contrast to the merry noise of the upper side of the building. It is like a great mechanical organ, with figures, played by some unknown mighty hand.

At the far end we come to a shallow flight of long low steps that lead upward to a throne. We are aware of a powerful presence seated upon that throne, for we feel the power of her eyes upon us as we approach. We tread instinctively in time to the stately music of the model angels high on either side of us.

Behind the throne is a rich tapestry that shows all manner of fruits of the earth. And this theme is continued upwards by the soaring pillars and stained glass windows that show, glowing in the coloured glass, pictures of every bird and beast that can be imagined. There are indeed birds and beasts represented there that were never seen on earth, and some that are heard about only in legend, such as centaurs, unicorns, amphisbaenas, phoenixes, basilisks, winged serpents and many more besides.

We stop at the foot of the steps before the throne, and look up to the grave beautiful woman who gazes down at us with eyes that seem to see through to the very core of our being. It is the kind of look from which no secrets are hid. She sees all that we are and have ever been.

She is fair of skin, with great violet eyes, and wears a glittering silver crown upon her head, and a long cloak of blue and silver which falls about her feet. Behind her head and shoulders, as part of her throne, there is carved a golden sunburst, an image of the rays of some far off sun behind or beyond our sun, that shines with a sparkling coruscated light. And at her feet, partly concealed by the folds of her robe, that billows like waves of the sea, is a large silver crescent moon that shines with its own deep silver light. And one of her silver shoes is resting upon it.

Her eyes are the more powerful because she wears a veil that hides the lower part of her face, although it is made of such diaphanous silk that we can see that she is smiling. Upon her lap she holds a large book, with thick black covers, and with one hand she holds a marker between the pages. Slowly she opens it and gazes long upon the page that she has marked.

'I see that you aspire to much,' she says at length, 'but that you have the power to pass the secret gates, which brings a high responsibility –

and not a little danger. The danger that comes to all who seek to fly so high. For the higher you fly, the more dreadful may be your fall. You have been given great opportunity but to those who are given much, much is expected in return. To complete the quest that you have commenced you now must face your greatest test. If you will – pass beyond my veil.'

She indicates the tapestry of living things behind her, and rises to her feet and stands to one side of it.

'I should warn you that to pass this way demands your deepest dedication. Are you willing, in order to do the greatest good, that you yourselves may even cease to be? For it is said that no-one who has passed beyond my veil has ever returned to tell the tale of what was to be found there. You may refuse, with honour, at this stage, if you choose. Pause and reflect, consider deeply, before you seek to lift my veil.'
Exit-point Nine

Tenth Branch: (Justice)

We stand before the figure of the high priestess.

'The way is before you,' she says, and with a regal gesture that is also supremely gentle, she pulls the throne aside, and behind it is revealed a narrow gap within the veil through which she motions we should pass.

As we start to mount the steps the angelic trumpeters above and behind us blow a mighty fanfare that stirs the blood and gives us courage to go forward in faith and meet whatever is to be found beyond the veil.

There is utter silence as we come through the other side of the curtain. We find ourselves in a world devoid of sight or sound. Nothing can be seen before us but a shining silver mist.

It is like being in the middle of a vast grey-silver ball, except that the inside of the ball seems to be an infinite distance away. We are, it seems, in the middle of nowhere. We turn to look behind us and discover that the veil through which we have come is veil no more, but black, hard, shiny, solid rock. In fact we stand on a perilously narrow ledge, on a blank rock face, with nothing extending before us but the empty air.

It looks almost as if we may have been tricked or trapped.

Even our dog seems at a loss. He shakes his head thoughtfully, and although he tries to put a brave face on things, his tail sinks a little between his legs.

Logically we ought to be on the far side of the building that was the young man's house or porter's gate. Except that we would be upside-down because we turned topsy-turvy under the dome. However, neither logic nor common sense seem to work here very well.

Our main hope seems to be the good faith of the young man who sent us here and whether we were right to have faith in him.

We close our eyes and think of him as vividly as we can. We recall his smile and his face. His robe and his shepherd's crook. And we invoke his aid.

But a stern woman's voice, that echoes like a giant's, startles us.

'Who is this that disturbs the silence?'

Opening our eyes we see the voice comes from a great figure of a woman who appears to be floating in the air, far out from the rock face, over the abyss.

She is similar in some ways to the lady through whose veil we have but recently stepped. She sits on a throne at the top of shallow steps but her robes are a dull silvery grey, shot with dark crimson and scarlet. A helmet of iridescent metal is upon her head, and in one hand she holds a set of golden scales that swing gently up and down, first to one side and then the other, on their narrow balance beam. In the other hand she holds aloft, point upward, a sharp and naked sword.

The Fool's dog answers for us. 'We have come in good faith to seek our real names and our essential selves.'

The woman bursts into a peal of laughter that has a hard mocking edge to it.

'And what do you think you will find out here? Do you realize where it is that you have come to?'

She pauses, and we make no answer.

'To the place where you will find nothing. Nothing. You are on the outside of all things.'

She pauses again while we consider this, and then continues.

'And if you find that difficult to understand,' she says, 'it is because there is nothing to understand. What you call reality is behind you. In the lands of illusion. Behind that dark rock face in the world of dreams.'

She swings her sword round and round in a circle of fire. Sparks and flames leap from it, sizzling off in all directions.

'My place is to stand guard outside that realm of illusion', she says, 'and to turn back all presumptuous wanderers. I stand at the gulf of emptiness between what is real and what is not. Only behind me and beyond me, on the far outside of nothingness is the real world, where no evil dwells. You who strive to emerge from the cosmic egg have only emerged from the yoke. You are into the white, and the limits of what you see all about you is the inside of the shell. Only when the chick is ready to hatch, can that shell be broken. And that will not be for aeons – millions and millions and millions of years. That is to say, if the egg does not become addled first, with internal corruption, and have to be destroyed.'

'But we were sent here, by one who gave us a key,' says our dog, 'and who told us that this was the way.'

The woman receives this in silence, considering it and looking at us searchingly. Then she continues in a slightly more conciliatory tone.

'You may try to go further, if you are ready. And as to that you must satisfy *me*. For I may not suffer anything unworthy to go beyond this place.'

She lowers her sword, holding it straight out before her, its point directly towards us.

'You have to tread a path as straight and narrow as the blade of my sword,' she says. 'If you are not straight enough in your intentions and desires you will fall from the perilous bridge and be lost, floating forever in nothingness through all eternity, for that is the penalty of overweening spiritual pride – utter permanent aloneness.'

And as she speaks the sword, in a marvellous manner, extends itself, and grows so that its point reaches the edge of the ledge where we stand.

'And know also,' she continues, 'that even should you reach the cross hilt of my sword, you will then be weighed within my scales to see if you are worthy.'

We wonder if her words are just meant to frighten us and to test our faith. And we decide we must concentrate on living up to the faith in us of the one who sent us here. Would he have done so if he thought we could not succeed? He believed in us. Now we must believe in him. If we keep thinking of that, and of him, perhaps that will keep us upright and straight along the narrow way.

And with these thoughts in our hearts we each step firmly and quickly across the narrow bridge, which seems quite broad once we are on it, surrounded by a golden light as if in a radiant protective cloud that saves us from looking down and falling prey to our own negative thoughts and fears. And we find ourselves standing at the sword's golden hilt, which is like a crossroads, in the centre of which we stand. The seated figure of Justice towers high above us.

'You have dared much to reach the greater test,' she cries, 'now you must be weighed within my scales.'

She brings the swinging balances close to us. They are huge, each pan like a cauldron of shining brass. And a white fluffy feather comes floating down from on high and settles gently into one of the pans. It hardly deflects it downwards, so light is it.

'Behold, a feather from the Dove of Peace that laid the egg,' the voice of Justice cries. 'It carries no weight of evil within it. If any of you weigh more than that, then your side of the balance will go crashing down and you will be spilled into the emptiness of the everlasting nothingness.'

We hesitate before this seeming impossible test.

'You were proud enough to present yourselves,' comes the woman's stern voice. 'Is your hesitation now one of fear or of true humility? Or a new-found vision of your own unworthiness in the scales of reality?'

We console ourselves with the thought that if we are doomed to perdition it were best if we faced our doom together. In any case, we have a feeling that, in this world between the worlds and maybe in the worlds of reality, a united group may weigh more favourably than a lone proud individual. So believing we leap into the near side pan of the balance.

There is a sickening swinging for a few moments, and then slowly but surely we start to dip. Down and down we go, as we far outweigh the beautiful feather in the opposite pan. Our pan begins to tilt to a steep angle as it nears the bottom of its traverse.

It seems that our fate is sealed. But we send a last call of faith and love to the young shepherd. We shut our eyes tight, and visualise that we are all hands together, thinking of him. To our mind's eye, this time he does not appear like a young man, but as a boy, golden haired and smiling, and with his shepherd's crook green and bursting forth with spring shoots and flowers. And we begin to feel the pan stop in its slow descent, hover still, and then begin to go up again.

Hardly daring, we open our eyes. To our surprise and delight we see that as well as the feather in the opposite pan of the scales, there is the young shepherd boy, weighing down the other side to make a perfect balance. He is smiling and waving and shouting great joy and encouragement to us. And the pans of the balance softly settle, gently swaying level and we are filled with joy and relief.

As the scales settle to rest in perfect balance so they become transformed. They flatten out into platforms, upon one of which we stand, and the chains upon which the pans have swung become solid, and form coiled golden springs out of themselves like frost forming on a window. The cross beam becomes fixed and solid, as we see it to be a golden lintel across two golden gates of finely traced scroll work.

The great stern figure of she who had held the scales and sword slowly disappears. It is as if she evaporates like morning mist. And so we stand outside a pair of golden gates, and with us is the young shepherd boy holding his flowering crook, covered in little white flowers, whilst sitting upon his shoulder is a pure white dove.

The gates seem firmly locked. And there is nothing above, below, or behind them to be seen. It is as if we and they are floating in space.

The young shepherd boy smiles and, taking the gently cooing dove he casts it into the air. It makes several long swoops around us, and we see that it holds in its beak a tiny branch of wood, with grey-green leaves and fruit upon it; an olive branch.

As it swoops around us the dove appears to be growing in size. The second time round it seems as if it has grown to the size and bulk of a peacock, although still in the form of a dove. And after the third or fourth gyration it is more the size of a large hawk or an eagle. But still it wheels about us, round and round and above and below, until it is difficult to tell how big it is, for as it grows so its circles of flight grow greater, so that it is further away.

Finally, at what seems to be the bounds of the sphere in which we are confined, the silvery-grey sky which stretches as far as the eye can see, it must have become of enormous size, but still it wheels and then, as it reaches the confines of the sky, a thunderous cracking sound begins.

We gaze up and around us in awe as the silver sky remains glassy and opaque no more, but rapidly is spread with jagged cracks, black against the silver. With loud rumbling cracks, like ice floes breaking up or the start of an avalanche, or a bridge or a building starting to fall, light begins to shine through. Light so bright that it seems like lightning, particularly when a forked crack grows larger and wider and a jagged stream of light bursts through it. And all in all it seems as if the sky were falling in all around us, with the thunder and lightning of the most tremendous storm.

We look across to the shepherd boy and see that, far from being alarmed, he is not only smiling, but capering with joy, his staff held high in the air, and he looks across to us and cries: 'We are nearly home!'

And at that cry the gates swing open. With a last roar the sky disintegrates and falls away. A pure golden light like that of the rising sun at dawn shines through the open gates toward us, causing our faces to shine like gold as we look upon it.

Exit-point Ten

Eleventh Branch: (The Empress and the Magician)

On the other side of the gates we see a golden yellow path, with gleaming bricks within it, and on either side of the path, as far as the eye can see, the most beautiful and perfect gardens. They are formal and in intricately laid out patterns near the path and become rolling parkland beyond. In the parkland and among the trees animals roam. Deer, bears, dogs, sheep, creatures one has never seen before, even dinosaurs. And none of them interfere with or chase the others, even those one would suppose to be enemies.

As we walk forward in wonder through the gates the shepherd boy kneels on the path before us and prises up some of the stones. Smiling, he presses one of them into the hands of each one of us. Each stone seems to glow with a light of its own that comes from deep within it. And on it is our own name, deeply carved. But as we look, other names appear below it and so on deep into the centre of the stone, until, far into the heart of the stone, in strange characters that we could not in our ordinary minds have deciphered, is a final name that when we look upon it causes our hearts to burn within us. It is as though we had at last met someone, or received a message from someone, who loves us and knows us far better and more deeply than anyone else has known us before. Indeed, better than we have ever known ourselves. It is like finding a long lost possession that has been lost so long ago that is has been almost forgotten entirely, and the refinding of which brings back memories of great joy of wonderful times past, and at the same time the realization now that it has been found, of wonderful times to come.

'Paving stones on the way to the one true centre,' says the young shepherd boy, smiling broadly. 'The record of your own true names. You see that you have many, for many are the ways that you may have been named in different times and climes but in the centre of all is your own true name, of which all the others are outward forms. They are yours to keep for they belong to no-one else, unless we include the Great Magician who made them, for he owns all in the end. And he will be overjoyed that you have found them. First, however, we must meet the Lady of the Garden, who rules over all the flowers and plants and birds and beasts within this place, and over the fishes in the lakes and pools. This is a garden that goes on for ever. No-one I know has ever come to the end of it yet. And the entrance, as you have discovered, is not easily achieved. But were the whole world to enter in those gates the garden would be large enough for all of them. There are no limits to the space that is needed here. Each one can be alone in the midst of a personal horizon if they so wish to be, because this is the Garden of the Heart's Desire. Anything that you wish for is yours. You may have heard the story of the Holy Grail, that brings to those who see it the food that they most desire in all the world. The Grail is just a little cup containing the essence of this whole great garden.'

We walk slowly along the golden path, and as we walk so a crowd gathers about us, of animals that have been wandering and grazing. There is a great stag with huge spreading antlers. And sheep and goats. And little squirrels and rabbits and hares and mice. A grand tawny lion with shaggy mane. A beautiful slinking leopard or cheetah. A lynx like a great cat with prominent ears. And on the animals' backs there ride birds. Little sparrows and coloured finches, some of them perched on the branching antlers of the stag. And on the lion's back there is a sleepy looking barn owl, blinking wisely. And flocks of bluebirds and swallows whirl about our heads.

Soon the path leads by a lake, and as we walk so we see that fish are swimming alongside us, of all shapes and sizes, some putting their heads out of the water, and smiling in fishy ways. One or two bigger ones even wave their fins, or leap right out of the water, their scales shining rainbow colours in the air.

Presently we come round a curve in the lake and find a rustic bridge that leads across to an island. The shepherd boy leads the way and all the animals follow.

The island is a riot of flowers and growing things. It is almost like climbing into a flower basket. Little paths lead through the clumps of blossoms so that none of the animals or we ourselves need tread on them, and the flowers are swaying gently to and fro in unison and singing, and each of the blossoms has a little face. With their singing they give off a beautiful scent that varies with the notes of the tune they sing so that it is a melody of perfume as well as of sound, coming from the glorious variegated colours of the blossoms.

Then we notice a deeper strain to the song as if others were joining in, and we realize that the animals about us are singing too. The stag and the lion and the other big creatures in deep bass voices. And the birds are singing their hearts out as well although much higher up the scale. We are now all ranged round a little mound of rocks, piled up in the centre of the island.

The rocks themselves that comprise the little hill are clumps of crystal that glow and change their colour and brightness in unison with the song. The smaller creatures, the rabbits, the stoats, the weasels, the squirrels, the mice, even butterflies and humming birds, and multicoloured insects, sit between the stones of the hillock looking up towards its top where, upon a throne of pure white marble, a most beautiful young woman sits. Her hair is yellow and her skin fair and she wears a circlet of multicoloured flowers as a crown, each of which has its own little face and joins in the song. Her dress, which flows down to her bare feet, is of green and decorated with patterns of leaves and plants and flowers, and she holds a golden sceptre in one hand, and in the other a heart shaped mirror that flashes with a dazzling light whenever it catches the sun.

She smiles upon us all and slowly raises her golden sceptre. The song of the flowers and the animals and birds comes to a natural close and we stand facing her in a pure and golden silence.

'You are now near the centre of all things,' she says. 'A part of you will stay here, now that you know of us, but you still have much to do on the outer side of things. All parting is only a seeming so. You will see me, if you develop the eyes to see, in all the flowers and growing things of nature. In all the fish, the animals and birds. For I am the queen and empress of all living things. And then one day, and it will be the last long day, you may return here, if you wish, for ever.'

'I see from the gold and crystal stones you carry that you have gained already most of what you need to know. Your True Names are the key to your Essential Selves. If you will exchange your stone for the jewelled mirror that I offer you, your own Essential Selves will be revealed to you if you take them away in your hearts and learn to gaze at the truth in them.'

We each advance and proffer her our stone and receive a jewelled mirror. As soon as we have done so there is a deep rumbling from the rocks below that rapidly grows louder and louder, and then with a great splashing sound a huge fountain jets up from behind her throne and shoots high into the air far above our heads, and the spray begins to fall like gentle rain.

As we look up we see that the softly falling spray is as a veil before the diamond bright sun that hangs high in the sky above us, and that a most glorious rainbow is forming about it. In fact it is a full rainbow. A full circular rainbow, and a triple one as well. Three full circular rainbows in the spray of the fountain.

Then the rainbow itself begins to take on form and we see the figure of the shepherd boy, who is capering and dancing and waving to us.

'Come up into the heart of the rainbow,' he cries.

The dog, with a bark of joy, leaps into the air and runs straight up towards him as if on invisible wings. Before we have time to doubt our ability to do so, we do the same, and run to join the shepherd boy. It is like running through a funnel of rainbow coloured light. The falling waters of the fountain are like mist upon our faces, tingling and refreshing. We run so easily that we might well be running downhill instead of steeply up.

The boy is silhouetted against the diamond white disk of the sun.

'Come along,' he cries, 'up toward the sun!' and he leads us in a merry dance, on upward toward the diamond disk behind him.

'The sun behind all suns!' he cries.

We seem to be going ever faster. It is the attraction of the diamond sun, which pulls all things towards it. And the nearer we go the stronger the pull. As we approach it faster and faster so indeed it grows larger and larger and brighter and brighter, until we strike what must be its surface.

As we do so the boy gives a great cry of laughter that echoes like joyous thunder all about us, and he suddenly appears like a giant before us.

'Had you forgotten you were in the land of giants?' he cries, laughing. And he merrily juggles a multitude of coloured spheres in the air before him.

'See my worlds. My ideas for worlds. Each one more beautiful than the last,' he cries. 'If you were standing inside one I expect you would call it a universe.'

He snaps his fingers in the air and they stream off up and into the far distance, glinting in the light like a stream of soap bubbles.

'I am a magician you see, as well as a juggler,' he cries. 'Come and see my table.'

He points a finger at us and beckons, and we find ourselves wafted into the air before him to look down on the surface of a square table below.

'Now we must see about getting you home,' he says. 'Look down at the top of the table.'

As we do so it lights up, like an illuminated screen or a clear window. It is in fact a window in space because there we can see our own sun and its system of planets whirling and turning around it. As we watch the vision grows closer, past the outer planets to our own blue Earth and then down through its atmosphere.

Soon we see directly below us the roof of the building wherein our physical bodies now sit.

'It is time for you to return, with the things you have won in the inner worlds,' he says, from behind us. 'But remember we are never very far away. You see how easily I can see you when I want to. And you can see me too, with the power of love in your hearts and by building our pictures in your minds. Keep the windows of your inner perceptions clear. And cherish the things you have been given on your journey here. Your own true names, and the mirror of your own essential selves. Keep hold of them in your minds' eye and you will never be lost or alone, no matter what trials and tribulations may seem to come upon you when you are in the dark worlds, where people are still learning to see. And for your part it is up to you to give me a name by what you see of me.'

And before our eyes he turns into the Emperor we had seen before the Mountains of the Stars, and into the bearded old man we had seen as the priest of the stones, and the man with his head hanging down into the abyss, and then into the Fool we first met.

And beside him there appears the young woman from the island below, with her flowered dress, and they put their arms in love round one another, and look down upon us. And she also takes on all the different forms, of the veiled lady on the throne, the stern lady with the scales and the sword, the maiden on the victory chariot, the young girl with the lion.

And the dog appears beneath their feet, and he has grown to giant size, even greater than the lion.

'Farewell!' the three of them cry, and we find ourselves sinking downwards into the table. And as we look back toward them we see behind the young man and young woman and their dog a great white tower building. And although it is in shape like the evil tower in the desert on our journey upwards, we realize that that was but a shabby imitation of this one in its purity and power.

We turn our eyes down to the table again and see the roof of the building in which we physically sit coming up, as it seems, towards us. And gently we come back inside our physical bodies and our own heads, and even the imagination bodies we had made are gone.

Final Exit-point

Although the sequence of workings we have given in the Journey to the Centre was taken using the cards in a relatively loose order, there will be discerned behind it a structuring that aligns with the basic principles of the Tree of Life. It is, in effect, a progress up the 32nd, 25th and 13th Paths but without confining the Trumps rigidly to the Paths assigned in *A Practical Guide to Qabalistic Symbolism* or similar works.

The whole sequence might be mapped out as follows:

1st Branch: The Fool and the World – the inner side ofMalkuth. The Cottage of Lost Play is a term borrowed from early Tolkien but the mysterious cottage concept is found in fairytale and fantasy novels. The Moon marks the start of the 32nd Path.

2nd Branch: The Last Judgement and the Sun represent the approaches to the lower side of Yesod; the Summerlands of the Spiritualists in some respects.

3rd Branch: The Star and Temperance – a journey across the magic mirror lake of Yesod.

4th Branch: Death, the Tower and the Devil – the testing 25th Path, the Tower being the crossing point of the 27th Path after which the work becomes deeper.

5th Branch: The Wheel. The 25th Path beyond the testing point toward the Sphere of Tiphareth.

6th Branch: The Hanged Man and Strength. Into the central mysteries of Tiphareth.

7th Branch: The Hermit, the Lovers and the Chariot. Passing out of Tiphareth into the higher spiritual air of the lower reaches of the 13th Path.

8th Branch: The Emperor and the Hierophant. Could be equated with the crossing point between Chesed and Geburah of the 19th Path.

9th Branch: The High Priestess – approaching the mysteries of the 'hidden Sephirah' Daath.

10th Branch: Justice. The abyss. The Daath sphere.

11th Branch: The Empress and the Magician. Passing the crossing point of the 14th Path towards the topmost sphere of Kether but returning to Malkuth (which is symbolically closely linked to Kether) rather than passing on into the Uncreate Realities of the Limitless Light beyond.

This is a similar structure to the shorter Path working given earlier but the different way in which certain of the images have been used should exemplify the flexibility of approach that is recommended. Thus the Tower in one instance is a place of self-revelation, in the other a temptation and trap.

Extensions beyond these could be taken. The Hermit, for instance, could well be Gandalf, or Merlin, or any great prophet, magician or seer. The maiden on the lion hill has many resemblances to the goddess to be found behind the nature forces. A whole inner universe is to be discovered through these Tarot figures – we should not try to confine them too closely to our own preconceptions.

It says something for the inventive genius of whoever selected the series of Tarot images that they knew what to use and what to leave out – which is the acid test of any creative structure.

Thus its apparent imbalances or omissions, which have led to endless controversies about 'Where does the Fool go?', 'Should Strength and Justice be interchanged?' or 'Where is the fourth Cardinal Virtue?' is in fact the mechanism that gives the whole structure its dynamism.

It is therefore arguable that this makes it a superior system to, say, the Mantegna Tarot, an attempted improvement on the scheme where a by no means unintelligent and unperceptive mind has endeavoured to 'fill out' the gaps in the Tarot images by introducing others to give a complete intellectually rounded system, with a full complement of Conditions of Man, Apollo and the Muses, Liberal Arts, Cosmic Principles and Celestial Spheres in a 50 Trump system. Unfortunately this very act tends to render the whole thing static. It has lost its mainspring or its pendulum in some strange fashion.

The Mystical Tree of the Tarot

THERE IS MORE THAN one way of working with the Tarot Trump images and the Tree of Life, one of which we have outlined in the last chapter. This was a following of the symbolic Serpent of Wisdom as it trailed up the Paths between the Spheres of the Tree from Malkuth – the outer world – to the mystical heights of the Supernal Triad. Originally this particular presentation of imagery came to me very powerfully in the form of a children's story, which is one reason why I have taken liberties with the presentation of some of the archetypal images. There is, I should say, in my view nothing wrong with putting one's own interpretations upon the images, and there are of course nowadays many different varieties of Tarot pack to suit all tastes. Although most are based upon the traditional images.

In this tale a couple of children experiment with their grandmother's Tarot cards, encounter the Fool, and with his dog go on a harum scarum adventure through the inner worlds in search of their True Names, or spiritual essence.

The book more or less wrote itself and in retrospect it was in some respects an early experiment halfway between creative fantasy and channelled material. I was aware however that there was little prospect of it being published at the time and so consigned it to a bottom drawer. There it remained until it seemed worthwhile resurrecting for this book with the children stripped out of it to present a more conventional series of pathworkings with a lighter touch than is often the case.

However I think it lost a certain amount by this slaughter of the innocents and was later pleased to see it produced in its original fictional form under the title *To the Heart of the Rainbow* by Skylight Press, which committed readers may be interested to consult and compare. In other words, it was my version of a standard Rosicrucian device of a *ludibrium* – an amusing tale that has an inner meaning which when read with openness and imagination may serve as a powerful key to intuitive understanding of the Western Mystery Tradition.

Needless to say, that is not the only way of approaching the conventional attributions of the Tarot Trumps to the Paths of the Tree of Life. What follows is an altogether more radical approach, placing mystical rather than psychological interpretations onto the images, and also having the advantage of being shorter and thus capable of working in its entirety at a sitting. It is none the less powerful for all that, and might perhaps be best attempted after having taken the more piecemeal approach of the last chapter.

We start by imaginatively creating a sacred inner space. In terms of the Tree of Life this can be located at Tiphareth, the central sphere of harmony and balance. Above us are the spiritual worlds, below us are the worlds of form, and we can fix our position by reference to two Tarot images that are upon a level with us. On one side is that of the Hanged Man and on the other that of the Wheel of Fortune, which are allocated to the vertical Paths on either side of Tiphareth, connecting upper and lower worlds.

However, let us look to the centre of our sacred space. We see there the brickwork of a circular well that we can look down. Far below us is the surface of the water, that corresponds to the Sephirah Yesod, and further below that the ultimate floor of the well, the Sephirah Malkuth, for we are gazing down the equivalent of the 25th and 32nd Paths.

Let us not bother too much with Qabalistic terms however, but concentrate our faculties of sight upon fish that swim within those waters below. They seem quite contented and to have all they need. And although some of them may rise to disturb the surface from time to time they are unable to pass through it. Indeed they can have no conception that there *is* anything beyond it. Their consciousness is limited to their own aquatic world, bounded by the circular wall of the well around them and the rock of the bottommost depth.

Let us pause for a moment to reflect how this is an image of the condition of those who are unaware of the existence the higher worlds – of any reality beyond that of their immediate physical environment. The ability to rise from one element to another is one of the aims and gifts of initiation.

So having established where we are in terms of consciousness let us now look back to the Tarot images that are upon a level with us. As we do so, with the intention of turning our gaze upward, rather than downward, we see that both of them undergo a simple transformation. By the process of turning!

The Hanged Man, turning upside down, now appears as a figure right side up, the radiant figure of an archetypal guardian and initiator who stands between pylon gates that before seemed to have been a gallows. And the Wheel of Fortune, which is operated by the goddess Fortuna (usually left off contemporary cards), also turns, and in turning transforms from a vulgar fairground image into the turning sphere of the stars, or Wheel of Arianrhod, and then into a Round Table, which we may now see as being placed as a cover over the well shaft to the lower worlds. In this transformation of the Wheel we may perhaps call to mind the magical motto *Deo Non Fortuna*, as it transmutes from an image of the crude play of so-called good or evil fortune to form the intricate movements of the patterns of the will of God.

This turning about of the two images upon a level with us is a signal that we are about to be concerned with a journey into higher consciousness, and so we become aware of two guides who have appeared before us. Their images are associated with two Paths that rise from Tiphareth. One is that of the Hermit, a wise old man, sometimes winged, with staff and lantern. The other is that of Justice, a female figure, sometimes blindfold to indicate impartiality, bearing balance and sword.

These two will lead us on our way. And as it involves an over sea journey, over higher waters, the Hermit takes on also the archetypal function of the Ferryman – named in some mythologies as Chairon, in others as Barinthus. He will be the pilot at the stern of our boat.

The figure of Justice, although seeming quite a conventional image, also has deeper aspects, as Astraea, the Virgin of the Stars (and in the constellation Virgo holds the balance of Libra), for she is ultimately the epitome of cosmic law who will make all things straight in the latter days. She will be the figurehead at the prow of the boat in our spiritual journey.

But where is the boat in which we are to travel? The answer comes as we look up into the sky above the ocean which we now find laps at our feet as we stand on its strand, between two modes of consciousness, shore and sea. We see the full moon shining clear and high before us in the light of which, walking across the high blue background of stars is the great figure of the goddess Isis, whose usual representation in the Tarot pack is the High Priestess, ruling over the 13th Path that leads up to the Supernal heights.

It is she who will provide the Moon Boat – which is a very ancient symbol of initiatory journeying, and as it appears in the shallows before us, a simple barque, like a silver crescent moon, we embark upon it, with Justice and Hermit, (or Astraea/Virgo and Berinthus/Chairon), before and behind us.

One other presence is needed, however, before we can cast off. And that is, in a sense, the guardian who watches over the boundary of the Solar Logoidal jurisdiction. Without her blessing we cannot pass. On the Tree of Life she is commonly called Strength, and stands on the transverse Path above Tiphareth, in the form of a maiden and a lion.

What is the source of her strength, and upon whom or what does she exert it? That source is shown by a symbol that is sometimes depicted above her head, and also in the chain of flowers that winds around herself and the lion in a figure of eight conformation. The emblem of Eternity. For her authority is a cosmic one (emphasised by her name of Una) that transcends the laws of limitation of the Solar Logos. That great overseeing consciousness is represented by the Lion, who in alchemy is sometimes depicted as swallowing the sun. Leo, (containing the original marker star of the zodiac, Regulus the King, at its heart), is also a major constellation which marks the point when the sun begins its annual descent. At this stage of our journey we may see lion and maiden at either side of the gates of a harbour entrance as we make out into open sea, in cosmic terms receiving permission to pass on out of the Ring-Pass-Not of our Solar system.

As we continue our voyage in the Moon Boat we will, as we progress, find a certain cosmic expansion of power and significance in the two guides who journey with us. This is the influence of those powers that on the Tree of Life are represented by the two Paths that depend from Chokmah (Divine Wisdom) on the one hand, and the two that depend from Binah (Divine Understanding) on the other.

The one pair, represented by the Tarot images of Emperor and High Priest, overshadow the figure of the Ferryman, express the powers of supreme kingship and of ultimate priesthood. In other words, the Ferryman takes on the aspect and function of a Priest King, which in Biblical terms has been expressed as a combination of *melech* (king) and *zadok* (priest), or Melchizedek.

The other pair, that overshadow the figure of Astraea, are great feminine powers that are somewhat obscured in the iconography of modern Tarot, although the truth shines easily through the forms of the Lovers and the Chariot. The important figure on the Tarot Card of the

Lovers is the Goddess of Love herself, whilst the rider in the chariot is none other than Winged Victory – another form of the goddess of love, as hinted by the title of the Sephirah Netzach whose planetary attribution is Venus, a goddess who is classically portrayed as being victor over the strife of Mars. Thus the figure at the prow of our boat is the feminine embodiment of divine Love as well as of Law.

With the realisation of this we may feel the moon boat beneath us leave the surface of the waters as we rise up into another element entirely which we might regard as the cosmic aethyrs. This is perhaps the equivalent of Daath upon the Tree of Life, as we pass to the possibilities of a higher level of Knowledge altogether, that of direct cognition of the Supernal World.

The bounds of this are represented by a pair of golden gates, and we may well see in them a higher analogue of the Una and the Lion that guarded the harbour gates from which we began our journey.

And so we disembark upon a higher terrain and enter into a virtual Garden of Eden or Paradisal Garden, which is ruled over by a figure depicted as the Empress in the Tarot, associated with the transverse Path that conjoins the spheres of Divine Wisdom and Understanding.

She appears in similar vein to us, and also similar in some respects to traditional presentations of a faery queen, enthroned between two trees before a flowing fountain, which may be a reflection of this almighty figure before us, who is indeed the closest we can approach to a vision of the feminine side of God, the Great Mother, who holds a mirror out before us, inviting us to gaze within.

We may look hard and long for it can reveal to us our entire past – in this life, in this world, in past lives and in other worlds, ever since we were first created as eternal spirits. The Spiritual Experience of Binah is called the Vision of Sorrow, which in its deepest aspect is a vision of all experience in the worlds of Form. Whatever we discern in that mirror might be regarded as a form of higher clairvoyance, or "spiritual reflection", and is part of that process that was succinctly written above the gates of the Delphic Oracle – *Know Thyself.*

It is hardly likely that we shall do this at one sitting but once having gained these heights of perception we should, by divine grace, be able to recall the experience and continue to gaze and to learn.

Having gazed our fill we are now directed to proceed further into the Garden where at a consecrated spot, or *tenemos*, we come into a presence which is represented in the Tarot by the Magician or Juggler, a thinly disguised form of the great being known as Hermes, not only a god of magic and learning and travellers and trade but also as Hermes Trismegistus, the founder of the Hermetic tradition, the Mystery system of the west. And this in turn is but a cloak by means of which we can look upon the masculine side of God, the progenitor of all, the ultimate Great Magician.

He stands before a cubical altar, which we realise to be the Cube of Space and holds out toward each of us our own individual cube for contemplation. It consists of $7 \times 7 \times 7$ smaller cubes, each cube representing an aspect of ourselves, but the ultimate one in the very centre contains the basic name or formula of our origin in the cosmos or Mind of God – the name behind all our subsequent magical or given names. These cubes, or Vision of God Face to Face, Qabalistically speaking, represent our cosmic past as compared to our past in the worlds of form that were discernible in the mirror of the Goddess.

This aspect of the search for our own true being can also be followed up by later contemplation. (As a magical aside, emphasising the basic importance of number in the formation of the worlds, we might regard the number of cubes in a $7 \times 7 \times 7$ cube, (or 7 cubed), to be 343. And here is a guide to the central cube or our own being. On entering keep 3 cubes above you, and 3 cubes below you, 3 to the left and 3 to the right, and press on inward until you have 3 cubes behind you and 3 before you, and there you are, four square in the centre!)

And in contemplating such mind games as this we find our attention raised to yet another figure, that of the Heavenly Androgyne, whose outer equivalent is Trump Zero, the Fool of the Tarot, a youthful figure of indeterminate gender, carrying a rose, which, as in the climax to Dante's *Paradiso*, is an emblem of heavenly reality as closely as can be expressed in form terms, as well as being, of course, at the heart of the Mysteries of the Rose Cross. Who bears a bag in a staff over his shoulder which contains the *infinite possibilities* of the Mind of God. We may also choose to see, if we wish, the accompanying dog as a representative of unconditional devotion (which is the prime spiritual quality) or the traditional functions of guardian (Cerberus) or opener of ways (Anubis) which are to be discovered at all levels.

This young androgynous figure of the Godhead may naturally be difficult to hold on to, but we now see it transform into a more conventional archangelic figure. One who stands pouring the waters of life from an infinite source into an infinitely capacious container, framed within a rainbow, the Bow of Promise, traditional sign of the Divine Covenant between Creator and Creation. And we realise that this figure is the equivalent of the Tarot image of Temperance, which in terms of the Tree of Life is associated with the interior of the well beneath us.

This has major consequences, for it represents God made manifest in the realms of Form, which is no less than a foreshadowing of the events of the Last Days.

As we realise this, the starry Round Table cover of the well blows off, for the well beneath is disintegrating and falling, but it is falling *upwards*. It has all the time been an inverted tower, represented as such in the Tarot, now struck by spiritual lightning. Thus the male and female figures who have been confined within it are seen also falling upwards, back to the heaven world of the Creator and their origins in cosmos. Similarly, the human figures to be seen in the cards that represent Death and the Devil are also seen to be released, and returning heavenward. Released from confinement in form and confinement in illusion respectively. All this is a representation of 'the freeing of the spirits in prison' that is brought about by direct intervention of the Godhead.

And in a representation of the final Revelation of the Last Days, so the physical spheres that are most closely familiar to us are also called back, 'falling' into the only one true reality. These are the Sun, the Moon, the Earth (represented in the Tarot as the Last Judgement, or final days of the planet) and its ideal pattern, Venus, the morning and evening star, represented by the Tarot card of the Star.

As a final Epiphany we see the Androgyne with the Rose finally transform into an image represented in the Tarot as the World or Universe – the androgynous figure within a triumphal wreath, holding the Sun in one hand and the Moon in the other, standing upon the Earth and with the Star above, whilst at the four quarters are four Holy Living Creatures at each corner – Lion, Angel, Eagle, Bull – which have their Elemental and Stellar and Apostolic and Biblical equivalents – as Fire, Air, Water and Earth; as Regulus in Leo, Fomalhaut in Aquarius, Antares in Scorpio, Andromeda in Taurus; Mark, Matthew, Luke and John; and as the four rivers running out of Eden. In terms of Qabalistic mysticism this could well be equated with the concept of the Shekinah – the presence of God in Malkuth – or in Christian terms, the Holy Spirit.

There is thus a whole cosmogony and theogony to be found within the Tarot, which is why it is so intimately associated with the heart of the Western Mystery Tradition.

The interpretations described above have been worked in a ritual context with powerful results but should not be regarded as exclusive. There are many ways of approaching the symbolism of the Tarot, in theoretical and practical, mystical or magical terms, and a considerable modern literature has developed, some excellent and original, some derivative or fanciful. Given some ability to separate the wheat from the chaff (the prime virtues of Discretion and Discrimination) it can be an inexhaustible school of knowledge and wisdom in which one is ever learning.

❁ 8 ❁

Images and Number in the Lesser Arcana

WE HAVE SO FAR confined most of our attention to the system of Tarot Trumps or Greater Arcanum, but we should not neglect the numbered suit and court cards which make up the Lesser Arcanum.* In the annals of scholarly research the Lesser Arcanum pre-dates the Greater, being based upon the packs of playing cards that entered western Europe in about the 1370s from the Far East via Egypt and Venice, and which were widespread some fifty years before the first known Trumps.

The earliest examples contained four suits consisting of ten numbered cards from 1 to 10 along with three court cards – King (*malik*), Viceroy (*na'ib malik*) and Under-Deputy (*thani na'ib*) – which were however represented by abstract designs as Muslim law forbade the depiction of human figures.

The earliest suit emblems were Wands, Cups, Swords and Coins, and so they remained in Italy and Spain, but popular playing card packs soon transposed these into leaves, acorns, hearts and shells (in Germany), or shields, acorns, roses and shells (in Switzerland), or the familiar spades, clubs, hearts and diamonds (in France) that we inherit in Britain and America. The original suits were however retained in the Tarot, which became a game in its own right.

However, when it comes to the meaning of the cards, Arthur Edward Waite, who was responsible for the first completely pictorial versions of the Lesser Arcana in *The Pictorial Key to the Tarot* (1911), claimed simply to have followed the lead of popular fortune tellers for the meanings. Nonetheless there is more than a hint of an esoteric numerological

---

* Dictionary definition: a secret, a mystery, a secret remedy or elixir; *singular* Arcanum, *plural* Arcana, *adjective* Arcane or rare. *Derived* from the Latin *arcanus* – *arca* – a chest – as in the ancient Hebrew ark of the covenant which contained the Tables of the Law, and the floating chest of Noah's ark that preserved Earthly life during the deluge.

symbolism behind them and, as I tentatively pointed out in *A Practical Guide to Qabalistic Symbolism* (1965), one based upon the Tree of Life of the Qabalah.

It will be worth recapitulating the gist of this here. The suit of Wands is indicative of the First or Power Aspect of Divine creation. That of Cups the Second or Love Aspect. That of Disks, Coins or Pentacles of the Third Aspect of Wisdom or Active Intelligence. Whilst Swords represent the much misunderstood Fourth Aspect which may be called the Destroyer or Disintegrator. This last is subsumed in the First Aspect in the *Treatise on the Seven Rays* of Alice Bailey but is accorded a separate category in some of the lesser known teaching of Dion Fortune which I summarised in paragraph 25, page 72 of the first volume of *A Practical Guide to Qabalistic Symbolism* as follows:

> Esoterically speaking God manifests in Four Aspects as opposed to the Three Aspects or Persons of the exoteric church. These Four Aspects are the Father, Son, Holy Spirit and the Destroyer or Disintegrator. The Aspect of the Father is the Power Aspect or the Spiritual Will. The Aspect of the Son is Love, that is, complete understanding of the needs of all, not sweet sentimentality. The Aspect of the Holy Spirit is Wisdom, Active Intelligence or Illumination. The Fourth Aspect is the Withdrawer of Life from the death of form and ultimately of all manifest life to the Unmanifest.

What we have, in effect, in the esoteric significance of the numbered suit cards, is the action of each of the four Divine Aspects expressed in the conditions of each of the ten Sephiroth of the Tree of Life. This seems to me to be more illuminating than the esoteric allocation of the Four Elements, although the latter has much to be said for it.

Wands

The **Ace of Wands** stands for the Fount of **Divine Power**, Will or Strength in Kether. In Chokmah it is represented by the **2 of Wands**, the Lord of **Dominion**, and this dominion is placed on a firm footing when the powers of Will manifest through the third Sephirah Binah and the first Triangle of Manifestation is formed, thus the **3 of Wands** is **Established Strength**.

Chesed, the fourth Sephirah is concerned with the true imprint of divine creation in the lower worlds, hence its association with rulership and the title of the **4 of Wands** is Lord of **Perfected Work**. The function of the 5th Sephirah Geburah being the preservation of balance and eradication of excrescences naturally gives rise to the **5 of Wands** being called Lord of **Strife**. The establishment of the Powers of Will in the 6th Sephirah Tiphareth, the central sphere of the whole Tree and marking completion of the Second Triad makes the **6 of Wands** the Lord of **Victory**.

The harmony of Tiphareth is overset to establish manifestation on the denser levels, manifesting in the sphere of the 7th Sephirah Netzach with the **7 of Wands** as Lord of **Valour**. In the 8th Sephirah, mind is formed and this flashing method of communication gives rise to the title of the **8 of Wands** as Lord of **Swiftness**. The Third Triad is then completed in the 9th Sephirah Yesod, called the Foundation, and hence the **9 of Wands** is Lord of **Great Strength**.

In the 10th Sephirah, Malkuth, comes the full crucifixion of the spirit in dense matter and hence the title of the **10 of Wands**, strange as it may seem in a blueprint of divine perfection, is Lord of **Oppression**.

Cups

The **Ace of Cups** stands for the divine Fount of **Love** in the 1st Sephirah Kether and thus in the 2nd Sephirah Chokmah, its reflection, the **2 of Cups** is appropriately called the Lord of **Love**. As a result of this union a third is produced in the Sephirah Binah along with creation of the First Divine Triad and so the **3 of Cups** is the Lord of **Abundance**.

From here the pure Love of God seeks manifestation and comes into form in the 4th Sephirah Chesed, represented by the **4 of Cups**, the Lord of **Blended Pleasure**. This activity of the spirit conforming the principles of form to its use gives a certain unbalance which has to be corrected and so we have in the 5th Sephirah Geburah the **5 of Cups**, Lord of **Loss in Pleasure**. But inevitably a harmonious outcome is attained, represented by the 6th Sephirah Tiphareth and completion of the Second Triad and the **6 of Cups** as Lord of **Joy**.

Proceeding more deeply into form, Love in the 7th Sephirah Netzach is a transitory phase, for the function of Netzach is the diversification of unity and acts as a prism which splits one light source into seven, which presents a complex situation, so that the **7 of Cups** is known as the Lord of **Illusory Success** or glamour. Whilst love manifesting in the sphere of mental analysis and diversity, the 8th Sephirah Hod, is represented by the **8 of Cups** as Lord of **Abandoned Success.** The Third Triad of Love is completed by the formation of the 9th Sephirah Yesod when love is expressed by the **9 of Wands** as Lord of **Material Happiness.**

This naturally is finally expressed in the 10th Sephirah Malkuth as the **10 of Cups** signifying **Perfected Success.**

Coins, Disks or Pentacles

The third Divine Aspect is represented as fount of **Active Intelligence** or Wisdom by the **Ace of Coins** in its first appearance in the 1st Sephirah Kether. In the 2nd Sephirah Chokmah the **2 of Coins** is Lord of **Harmonious Change**, which indeed is the principle behind all form evolution, expressed in aim and principle in the 3rd Sephirah Binah with the **3 of Coins** as Lord of **Material Works.**

Moving on from the First Triad of Active Intelligence into the realms of form, we find more detailed aspects of it in the 4th Sephirah Chesed as the **4 of Coins** as the Lord of **Earthly Power.** Close concern with the causes of unbalance and the remedial action needed in the 5th Sephirah Geburah gives the title for the **5 of Coins**, Lord of **Material Trouble**. But achievement of balance is consolidated in the 6th Sephirah Tiphareth represented by the **6 of Coins**, Lord of **Material Success.**

From this point of stability representing the completion of the Second Triad we pass to the 7th Sephirah Netzach which is one concerned with action within form manifestation which gives us the **7 of Coins** and Lord of **Success Unfulfilled.** However this situation is brought toward completion in the 8th Sephirah Hod which is represented by the **8 of Coins** as Lord of **Prudence**, for it is the function of mind to weigh up possibilities before committing to action, which once done completes the Third Triad of Active Intelligence in the 9th Sephirah, Yesod, with the **9 of Coins** as Lord of **Material Gain.**

The final concretion of this in Earth gives the reward in the 10th Sephirah Malkuth – the Kingdom – and the **10 of Coins**, Lord of **Wealth.**

Swords

The suit of Swords refers to the action of the Disintegrator Aspect, and as its direction is thus towards withdrawal from existence in form, it is perhaps better for us to examine the cards in reverse order.

The withdrawal of life forces from the dense form inevitably produces the ruin of that particular form, so the **10 of Swords** in the 10th Sephirah of Malkuth is appropriately Lord of **Ruin**. This should not be considered as evil but a necessary precursor of new life, and it is part of a continuing function in the whole natural world as well as the affairs of humankind.

Similar considerations apply in the 9th Sephirah Yesod where the **9 of Swords** is considered the Lord of **Despair and Cruelty**. This, like the 9 of Spades of modern fortune tellers has the reputation of being the great malefic of all the cards and (as dramatically displayed in the opera *Carmen*) stands for death. As the forces of destruction or withdrawal acting in Yesod means the complete break up of the roots of personality when applied to man, the applicability of the title of this card will be obvious. The **8 of Swords** as Lord of **Shortened Force** stands for the withdrawal of force on the level of mind in Hod, the 8th Sephirah, and the disruption of the form-giving forces in Netzach, the 7th Sephirah, provide the reason for **7 of Swords** being Lord of **Unstable Effort.**

Moving up from the Third to the Second Triad of the forces of withdrawal and disruption we find in Tiphareth, the 6th Sephirah, a realisation of the true principle behind sacrifice, or giving up one thing for another, in Lord of **Earned Success** for the **6 of Swords**. In the 5th Sephirah Geburah, which has its distinctly destructive aspects, we find the **5 of Swords** as Lord of **Defeat**, for nothing can stand against the destructive might of the cosmic destroyer when an evolutionary phase is complete. In the 4th Sephirah Chesed we find the withdrawing of the resources of being, represented in the **4 of Swords** as Lord of **Rest from Strife.**

Passing on to the First or Supernal Triad, the **3 of Swords**, as Lord of **Sorrow**, relates to the 3rd Sephirah Binah. Divine sorrow is a deep mystery and has much to do with the attitude of free spirit becoming bound in form as much as being withdrawn from it. In the 2nd Sephirah Chokmah we have a similar situation to what we found in Chesed but at a higher level. Enriched with the experiences of manifest life, the **2 of Swords** is the Lord of **Peace Restored**. The **Ace of Swords**, in the 1st Sephirah Kether, the Crown of Creation, represents a final return to the uncreate realities of the cosmos as well as being the **Root of the Taker of Life** back to whence it came or **Release from Form.**

So much for a Qabalistic analysis of the signification of the cards of the Lesser Arcanum. This is an intuitive approach to their meanings which has much to be said for it, for those who are familiar with the dynamics of the Tree of Life and working with abstract concepts. It is also possible however to present them in a more approachable manner, by means of pictures demonstrating the dynamics of each card in human life. This has been the approach of A.E. Waite who, with the talents of the artist Pamela Coleman Smith, produced a complete set of pictorial cards.

This is very much in line with the magical tradition of 'memory theatres' whereby the pictorial imagination is used to remember images and sequences. Actually there is a great deal more to be gained if the serious student, rather than relying on the imagination of A. E. Waite or anybody else, evokes and imagines his or her own imagery for each card. Indeed in my training of my more advanced esoteric students I set them the task of designing and drawing their own complete set of Tarot from their personal meditations on the principles involved.

In illustration of this type of approach it may be helpful to exemplify it with a description of the meanings of the cards as visualised by A. E. Waite along with another version, published almost a hundred years later, issued by the Society of the Inner Light. Although described as the Dion Fortune Tarot, in fact the designs were the work of David Williams, a later Warden of the Society of the Inner Light.

Waite/SIL comparison of numbered suit designs

Wands

2 Dominion
AEW: a man standing between two wands looking from his battlements out to sea and holding a globe in his hand, while to his left is a lily, rose and cross emblem.
SIL: a heraldic lion, crowned and holding sceptre and sword, seated on crown over the Earth in which a black monster is grasping the continent of Africa.

3 Established Strength
AEW: a man standing on a cliff top with three wands, his back turned to us, gazing at ships passing over the sea.

SIL: a classical temple building showing secret lines of construction, with emphasis on squares, circles and a bold triangle as main feature.

4 Perfected Work

AEW: a garland suspended on four wands, with a castle and maidens, with more garlands in the background.
SIL: a potter working at completing a pot on his wheel with four green staves growing in a pot behind him.

5 Strife

AEW: five youths having a mêlée with staves.
SIL: a cavalry battle scene with five spears prominent in front.

6 Victory

AEW: a horseman, laurel wreathed, as is the stave he carries, accompanied on foot by five others with staves held high.
SIL: a knight victorious in combat against another, a maiden in distress in the background. Sign of a hexagram to the fore, made up of six laths.

7 Valour

AEW: a young man apparently on the edge of a cliff defending himself against the assaults of six others whose staves are only visible at the bottom of the card.
SIL: a First World War army officer standing defiant before a union flag at a break in a barbed wire fence.

8 Swiftness

AEW: eight wands flying through the air, open country in the background.
SIL: eight red aircraft shooting through the sky on a flying display.

9 Great Strength

AEW: a man standing guard before a palisade – the number of staves, his own and those of the palisade, are nine in number.
SIL: Figure of the giant Atlas holding up the world, on one knee between two pillars, one white one black. Cross hatching in front of four red and five blue lines.

10 Oppression

AEW: a man staggering under the weight of a bundle of ten wands which he is carrying.

SIL: bearded man holding two children from William Blake etching, kneeling behind ten vertical bars as if imprisoned or excluded.

Cups

2 Love
AEW: a caduceus surmounted by a winged lion's head, while below a youth and maiden pledge each other in a garden.
SIL: image from Greek icon of Virgin Mary and child Jesus.

3 Abundance
AEW: three maidens pledging each other with upraised cups in a garden.
SIL: three tumbling cups with coloured balls spilling from them.

4 Blended Pleasure [Pleasure in SIL version]
AEW: a young man seated under a tree looking at three cups on the ground before him while an angelic hand in mid air offers him another.
SIL: a geisha girl (although she appears to have a male torso) with four cups and bowl of fruit.

5 Loss in Pleasure
AEW: a cloaked male figure confronting three other overthrown cups while two upright ones stand behind him.
SIL: prostitute with skeleton head and arms, with man approaching from high lit up buildings. An illuminated sign says WHAT YOU SEE IS NOT WHAT YOU GET, and another AIDS KILLS. Five cups overturned and spilling contents.

6 Joy
AEW: two children with flower-filled cups in a garden.
SIL: naked dancing male figure between six cups, similar to William Blake's Orc.

7 Illusory Success
AEW: a man confronted by seven chalices with fantastic visions arising out of them: a man's head, a veiled radiant figure, a serpent, a castle on a pinnacle, a pile of treasure, a laurel wreath, and a winged serpent-dragon.
SIL: Large inverted cup spills rainbow colours on confused mass of

figures (theatrical, artistic, film star, religious) with newspaper headline at back saying PACK OF LIES.

8 Abandoned Success
AEW: three cups on five, lined up in the foreground, with a man walking disconsolately away between bleak rocks by sea or river in the moonlight.
SIL: beached, wrecked sailing ship on the strand beside a ruined temple. Eight overturned cups spilling contents on ground.

9 Material Happiness
AEW: a stout replete man with folded arms sitting before a high curtained table, arc-shaped shelf supporting nine cups.
SIL: jolly Dickensian scene of a family celebrating in outline of house and nine cups all round.

10 Perfected Success
AEW: ten cups in a rainbow, with a man and woman arm in arm hailing it, while two children dance by them.
SIL: the Holy Family of Joseph, Mary and Jesus with donkey surrounded by ten cups.

Swords

2 Peace Restored
AEW: a seated blindfolded woman, her back to the sea and rocks, a horned moon above, balancing a diagonally held sword on each shoulder, her arms crossed on her breast to hold them so.
SIL: allegorical figures of Sun and Moon embracing.

3 Sorrow
AEW: three swords piercing a heart; rain and clouds in the background.
SIL: stone figure of Virgin Mary with heart pierced by three swords.

4 Rest from Strife
AEW: a knight laid on a tomb in an attitude of prayer, possibly deceased, one sword depicted in bas relief on side of bier below him, and three others, depicted point downward, on wall behind.
SIL: Christ-like figure parting the clouds, looking down on a presumably contentious crowd round a hill, now looking up in wonder.

5 Defeat

AEW: the sea in the background and two defeated figures walking away, their swords left lying on the ground. Their victor carries two swords on his shoulder and holds another with its point to the ground.

SIL: Samson bringing down the pillars of the temple.

6 Earned Success

AEW: all the swords are point downward in a punt, in which a man ferries a woman and child across a river.

SIL: an angel wielding swords drives off demonic figures while looking down on scales weighing souls.

7 Unstable Effort

AEW: a man stealing off with five swords, two others left behind, and an armed camp in the background.

SIL: network of linked swords before an atomic explosion.

8 Shortened Force

AEW: all the swords stuck in the ground beside a bound and blindfolded woman.

SIL: Adam and Eve with apple and serpent in the Garden of Eden.

9 Despair and Cruelty

AEW: a woman sitting up in bed, grief stricken, with nine swords, horizontally placed, dominating the background.

SIL: nine bleeding swords in formation of calvary cross with Blakean figure running off in despair.

10 Ruin

AEW: a dead man transfixed to the ground by ten swords in his back.

SIL: ruined city seen from above, with ten red swords in foreground.

Coins

{AEW tends to show discs with pentagrams depicted on each one; SIL tends toward coins.}

2 Harmonious Change

AEW: a lemniscate figure round the discs being held by a dancing man

in high crowned hat. Ships on wavy sea in the background.
SIL: diagram of alchemical distillation process.

3 Material Works

AEW: a mason working upon a design of three discs at a double doorway, watched by monk and an overseer who holds the plan.
SIL: a tall stepped pyramid.

4 Earthly Power

AEW: a seated king holding one disc, another on his head and one under each foot, a city in the background.
SIL: landscape with Sphinx and Egyptian pyramids.

5 Earthly Trouble

AEW: two beggars passing in the snow before a lighted window on which five discs are inscribed.
SIL: theatrical tragic mask with five Roman coins.

6 Material Success

AEW: a merchant, scales in one hand, giving money to one of two kneeling beggars. The discs are shown overhead.
SIL: warrior goddess seated before castle, with eagle and cornucopia, possibly on triumphal chariot.

7 Success Unfulfilled

AEW: a man leaning on a staff gazing into a bush in which are six discs, with one on the ground.
SIL: Don Quixote charging a windmill.

8 Prudence

AEW: a mason carving discs, working on one of them, another at his feet, and the others hung up in display.
SIL: a lady with group of maidens in a forest, contemplating sleeping man guarded by dog. Greek gold coins all round.

9 Material Gain

AEW: nine discs embedded in prolific grapevines, a garden and manor in the background. A woman stands in the midst with a bird on her wrist.
SIL: nine golden spheres in golden flame-like leaves of plant.

10 Wealth

AEW: a man and woman at the gate of a manor house and grounds, accompanied by a child who looks at a bearded ancient man sitting caressing two dogs. His robe is heavily embroidered with mystic signs and bunches of grapes. The ten discs are superimposed on the whole picture and suggest by their positioning the Tree of Life.

SIL: Ten piles of gold coins.

It is not necessary, of course, to go for this full pictorial method. The oldest tradition of designs for the numbered cards was for them to be abstract designs – and in this there is plenty of scope for hidden symbolism. From my own researches into comparative sources, as in the final section of *A Practical Guide to Qabalistic Symbolism*, I found little that was consistent between one set of designs and another. Generally speaking with the esoteric packs (as in my own *Gareth Knight Tarot*) the attempt was made to suggest the meaning by the positioning and ancillary decoration of the symbols on the cards. The principle here, generally speaking and in my opinion, is the simpler the better. Aleister Crowley produced a set of cards to go with his book *The Book of Thoth* in 1943 painted by the very talented artist Lady Frieda Harris, but they are so loaded with symbolism that, although no doubt a guide to his personal followers, they tend to be a distraction for students less committed to his personal teaching.

We suggest it is far better to produce a complete set of cards of your own, working off your own resources. Or, as is our personal approach, to use one of the old 'non-esoteric' packs, using your own imagination when contemplating them, untarnished or influenced by any one else's esoteric notions.

The Court Cards

We cannot, however, leave our contemplation of the Lesser Arcanum of the Tarot without some consideration of the Court cards. An interesting element in this is that originally they appear to have been all male figures. The Queen made her way into the company only at a comparatively late date. And oddly enough one finds the same kind of situation with regard to the pieces of the game of chess. There is a certain similarity between the chess pieces and the court playing cards. Each has a King, a Queen and a Knight, and we would suggest that there is a strong connection between the Page and the chess Bishop, in that the former often has the divinatory meaning of a message, and the Bishop (generally called the Strider on the continent) is a wide ranging piece quite capable of delivering unexpected messages to an opponent with its sweeping diagonal movement. This leave the chess Castle or Rook, which I would tend to regard as equivalent to the Ace. If this sounds a little far fetched there nonetheless does seem to be some kind of subliminal connection between cards and chess – a most common example being found in the adventures of Lewis Carroll's Alice. *Alice in Wonderland* finds herself in great adventures with a pack of cards, while *Alice through the Looking Glass* finds herself involved in a strange game of chess. More esoterically, there was the little researched notion of so called Rosicrucian chess, experimented with in the Golden Dawn – with four sets of Egyptian god figures circling round the board – to say nothing of the ancient Celtic tradition of the Gwyddbwll.

In esoteric terms I have rather favoured, in my contemplations of the Lesser Arcana, placing the Court Cards not at the head of the numbered cards, but at intervals in between. Thus as a mnemonic for a popular course on Tarot that I once floated I helped students recall meanings of the numbered cards by recourse to telling a story based upon Waite's pictures. We give an example of this method in Chapter 10, where it will be seen that we start with the Page and four cards (the 10, 9, 8 & 7) then come to the Knight and three cards (the 6, 5 and 4), then the Queen and two cards (the 3 and 2), and finally the King standing before the Ace. As well as being a simple memory device it does have an esoteric underpinning. The lowly Page being part of the lower spheres of the Tree of Life representing the physical body and Personality, the Knight being custodian of the three cards representing the Higher Self, with the Queen and King and Ace representing the Supernal levels.

The Fourfold Structure of the Greater Arcana

RATHER THAN simply learning off 'meanings' as is the practice in many elementary books of instruction, the Tarot is best approached by coming to a first hand acquaintance with the archetypal powers behind each card. It is a method we devised some twenty-five years ago to form a practical correspondence course that was road tested with a group of students and supplemented by a series of esoteric workshops. What follows is taken from the cassette tape recording of the original course, providing a step by step guide line for students who may wish to come to terms with the Tarot images in this way.

First sort your Tarot pack into two piles, one containing the Trumps and the other the Suit cards.

Take up the pile of Trumps and sort them into numerical order, and make an ordered pile of them, face upwards, with Trump XXI (The World) on the bottom and Trump 0 (The Fool) facing you on the top.

Take the Fool and place him facing you at the top of the table. You should now have, also facing you, on the top of the rest of the pile of Trumps, Trump I, the Magician. Let us concentrate on these two cards because they hold the key to all the rest.

Look at the image of the **Fool**. He is the figure who represents the Spirit of the Tarot. It is well worth while to use your imagination to build up a kind of personal acquaintance with the Fool. To get to know him almost like a real person.

We can begin this process with the help of a little meditation sequence. Imagine you are standing on a cliff top. Be aware of the sea breaking on the rocks below, with the regular beat of the tide. Feel the breeze in your face. Hear the cry of wheeling sea birds. Now, as you stand there in imagination, listen carefully with the inner ear, and imagine that you hear the very faint jingle of bells, as those in a jester's cap. You may also hear faintly the far off barking of a dog. Then, making the scene as real as possible, see the Fool coming down the cliff path to meet you. He approaches you and stops, and smiles. Try to see his face as clearly as you can. See if he does anything. Whether he stands up or sits down, or walks or jumps around. See what his dog does. Try to hear if he says anything to you. This will not come in words you can actually hear with your physical ears. It may not even come in verbal form in your imagination. It could come to you directly as ideas. You may indeed think that the ideas are your own. But think it possible that they could be ideas that are put there telepathically by the Fool. This is the most efficient method of communication there is. Remain with the picture as long as you wish, before returning to everyday awareness.

Let us think about the Fool. We have likened him to the Spirit of the Tarot. And as you get to know him, and to pick up ideas from working with him in this way, you will find you can learn a very great deal about the Tarot – and indeed many other things – without outside assistance. If we left off all tuition now, you could do very well on your own, as in time the Fool would introduce you, of his own volition, to the other cards. But this can take rather longer time than if we give you some guidance to help you on your way from what we ourselves have learned from the Fool. The other Trumps have in fact a special four-fold structure that is also a very balanced and self-harmonising system that will help you to find your way around all the images without fear of getting lost or muddled.

You already have Trump I, the **Magician**, facing you in the upturned pile of cards before you. Take him, and place him on the table just below the Fool. Now go through the rest of the Trumps and pick out Trumps VIII, XI, XIV and XXI. You should find they are Justice, Strength, Temperance and the World. (Note: in numerating the Trumps we have followed the most commonly used order in modern packs. If there is a difference with the pack you happen to be using, follow the images not the numbers.)

These four cards are very important ones. We might call them Key Cards. In one of the very early sets of the Tarot, sometimes called the Charles VI pack, after the King of France who was thought to have commissioned it, these cards were distinguished in design from the other Trumps in that each had a halo – a very distinct angular kind of halo. They are thus set apart, in a sense, from the other Trumps, and this is because they represent the Cardinal Virtues: Strength or Fortitude, Justice, Temperance, and Prudence.

Strength is usually shown as a maiden controlling a fierce lion, although sometimes as a maiden seated by a stone pillar. An alternative old version shows the hero Hercules standing with up-raised club by a crouching lion. The meaning of this card should therefore be obvious. It signifies control; either self control or the control of outward things by one's own inner authority or skill.

I suggest you now spend a little time imagining that you are standing before the maiden and the lion as they appear on the card. You can also try to identify with her. Feel as if you are backing into the picture – and then that you are effortlessly holding the lion in check. It should give you a feeling of strength and self control. And this may well be useful to help you in daily life – as well as teaching you a great deal about the meaning of the card.

The next cardinal virtue is **Justice**, seen holding a balance and sword. This card stands for getting things evenly balanced, or an even handed assessment of decisions to be made. Stand before this figure as you did the figure of Strength and then also try to identify yourself with her. It can bring you cool detachment and a balanced view of the right thing to be done in any difficult situation or where a decision needs to be made for or against some course of action. This too can be very useful in daily life.

Now we come to the cardinal virtue called **Temperance** – an angel pouring water from one cup to another. In olden times before dinner forks were invented, a servant used to come round the table like this to enable the diners to wash their hands, so Temperance also means cleansing, as well as getting things in right proportion, which includes our opinions, our feelings and our actions. Failure to do this at the level of the emotions is what we call having a bad temper. A temperate person is one who is neither too personally involved, nor, on the other hand, coldly distant. But as Goldilocks said about the baby bear's porridge, not too hot, not too cold, but just right. Seek to experience what this card stands for by standing before the angel or identifying with it, in just the same way as you have with the other cards. You should find this helps to make you a nicer person!

The last cardinal virtue is traditionally called Prudence, and is represented in the Tarot by the Trump we call the **World**. In matters of material well being, prudence or good commonsense must rule our actions. So this card means well balanced action, leading to attainment of an aim, or completion of a process in a successful manner. Speak to the figure in the centre of this card, or alternatively identify yourself with it. Surrounded by the four images around the oval wreath of victory you should experience integration and harmonious success.

We have now made the personal acquaintance of the Fool and also of the four Cardinal Virtues. The Fool, as we have seen, is the introductor to the Tarot, and as such he represents going on to meet and discover new things. He is an inexperienced innocent, a child like figure, but also one who, like a miraculous child in legend or mythology, has a higher wisdom to impart. Thus the meaning of this card in any spread is the embarking on new ventures, that some might consider foolhardy, but which on the other hand might be very wise moves indeed, if perhaps a little unorthodox or unexpected. You never know, with the Fool, until you try!

The **Magician**, on the other hand, Trump I, is someone who is wholly in control. Take this card and place it in the middle of the table. Place about him the four cards of the Cardinal Virtues. Strength just above him. Temperance a little below him. Justice to the right, and the World to the left. He is the controller of these virtues.

Imagine you are entering a room in which he stands, behind his table, in the centre. It is a large circular hall, dimly lit, and from above his head great power can be felt to flow, descending from a high point in the roof, and which he directs by movements of his wand and his arms and hands. About the room at the same positions that you have placed the other cards about him, you can see life-sized figures of the four Trumps who represent the Cardinal Virtues. The maiden and the lion can be seen behind him at the far wall. The figure of Justice is seated on a throne to your right. Behind you, as you stand before the Magician's table, is the angel of Temperance. And to your left is the dancing figure of the World.

Within this Hall of the Magician and the Four Cardinal Virtues try to make personal contact and communion with the Magician, and feel also something of his controlled and balanced power, bringing it down from above and distributing it in controlled four-fold expression. For this is also the meaning of the card. He is a very effective human being, as you too can be if you learn all that he has to teach you.

Just as the Magician is the controller of the four cards of the Cardinal Virtues that we have laid about him – so each of these cards, in turn, controls and balances four others. This is simply demonstrated if you lay out the rest of the Trumps in the numerical order in which they appear from the pile of remaining Trumps that lies face up before you. Start with the Magician in the centre of the table, take the four Trumps we have already met and lay them out face upwards at a convenient distance about him, as before.

Now take Trumps II, III, IV and V and lay them immediately around the figure of Strength. You should have the II (the High Priestess) above it; the III (the Empress) to its right; the IV (the Emperor) below it; and the V (the Pope or Hierophant) to its left.

Now take Trumps VI, VII, IX and X and lay them about the figure of Temperance in similar fashion. You should therefore have the Trump of Love above Temperance; the Chariot to its right; the Hermit below it; and the Wheel of Fortune to its left. *(We have of course already used Trump VIII as it is one of the Cardinal Virtue cards.)*

Now take Trumps XII, XIII, XV and XVI and lay them about the figure of Justice. *(Trump XIV has of course already been used.)* You should have the Hanged Man above it; the Devil to its right; Death below it; and the Lightning Struck Tower to its left.

Finally lay the remaining Trumps, XVII, XVIII, XIX and XX around the figure of the World. This should give you the Star above the World; the Moon to its right; the Sun below it; and the Last Judgement to its left.

You now have before you the ground plan for further study, not only of all the Tarot Trumps, but of the numbered Suit cards as well.* This is because the Trump of Strength is related to Wands, Justice to Swords, Temperance to Cups, and the World to Coins or Pentacles.

The four Trumps grouped about **Strength** are all different modes of strength or power, and Strength in some of the old hand-painted cards was represented by a man with an uplifted club. **Justice**, as can be seen, holds a sword, and so as well as ruling over the somewhat malefic images around her, she also rules over the suit of Swords. **Temperance** holds two cups, and so, with the Trumps that represent various qualities of life about her, she rules over the suit of Cups. And the **World**, with the figure standing in a round frame, represents the suit of Coins. Again, in the older designs the picture was very much more coin or medallion like in appearance.

However, we will leave consideration of the numbered suits until we have worked through the rest of the Trumps. We can do this in much the same way that we introduced ourselves to the Trumps we already

---

* Do not worry if you have limited space in laying out all the cards in the way we describe. Do the best you can and remember that the important work is done in the imagination. If you like experimentation with large layouts and have space problems, try purchasing a mini version of the pack.

know. And then it is only a matter of practice to become familiar with them, as with old friends.

The Hall of Strength

Let us start with the Trumps associated with Strength. These are the Emperor and the Empress, the Hierophant and the High Priestess. Each of these represents strength, power or authority, but expressed in a different way. Either in a masculine or feminine mode, and in either an inner, spiritual or hidden way, or in an outward material and openly expressive way. We can meet each of these four figures in an imaginary journey to them, so prepare yourself for a short meditation in order to visualise doing this.

The Magician picks up the wand from his altar top, and indicates with it the figure of Strength who stands at the doorway behind him. We make our way toward this figure, who stands with her lion at her doorway.

The maiden bids us welcome, and turning to go through the doorway, invites us to follow her. We find ourselves in another circular hall, and led by the maiden and the lion we proceed to its centre. There we stand and gradually become aware of four figures, seated on thrones at the four quarters.

The maiden indicates that we go toward the seated figure of the **High Priestess**. We approach her, conscious of a smell of incense, and she gravely acknowledges our presence. There is an aura about her of great quietness and inner wisdom. Be aware of her in the form depicted in the pack of cards with which you are most familiar, but let your imagination run free enough to enable her to take on a form that is most congenial and appropriate to your relationship towards her. This may change slightly at various meetings. Spend some time communing with this powerful, peaceful figure. And also take time to feel what it is like to take on her image. It does not matter if you are male or female, we each have elements of both sexes within us, and taking on the figure of the High Priestess will bring you to a great inner peacefulness and wisdom, and this exercise will serve to increase your powers of intuition and to tap the fount of inner wisdom within you.

When you are ready, you can proceed to the next figure in the Hall of Strength. This is the **Empress**. We make our acquaintance with her and will also take time to identify with her. This will bring you the contact of outwardly expressed feminine power, in caring and protecting, not only in motherhood but in all areas of life, be it persons or projects. And once again, this feminine power is not an exclusive province of women, nor need they themselves be limited by it. These masculine and feminine powers can be expressed by men and women alike, which is the hallmark of a balanced and mature human being. If you are lacking in any of these respects then meeting with the Tarot figures, and by identifying with them from time to time, will be a healing, balancing process, bringing out your full potential. So take time to feel the power and strength of the Empress and make yourself at one with it. And, as with all the figures of the Tarot Trumps, you may also find it helpful to converse with her, be it by actual words or the simple exchange of ideas that come into your mind.

We can now go to the third throne. Here we meet the **Emperor**, who mediates the expression of strong, outwardly expressed, masculine power. If you should feel this to be somewhat overpowering, particularly if you are a woman, then summon the figure of Strength to your side and ask for her aid – perhaps by taking on her image yourself. She controls all the powers within this hall, and you will find that you can soon come to terms with the way power is expressed through the Emperor. Coming to familiar terms with the Emperor is a way to overcome any hang-ups about figures of authority. He can be a figure of great strength and support – a true father figure, or perhaps elder brother or favourite uncle. And by identifying with him you can develop your own self confidence and ability to assert yourself and what you stand for in the outside world.

The final figure that we meet in the Hall of Strength is that of the **Hierophant** or Pope. There is no specific religious meaning to this figure but he does represent spiritual power and inner wisdom in a similar fashion to the High Priestess. With him, however, it is more outwardly expressed. He is therefore more of a teacher or giver of sage advice or moral counsel. In one sense he could be regarded as something of a psychotherapist. You can go to him as guide, philosopher and friend, or father confessor. If you take on this figure yourself you will find your powers of sorting out personal problems, for yourself or others, is greatly enhanced.

This completes our work in the Hall of Strength, where we have now made the acquaintance of four more of the Tarot Trumps. Our familiarisation with the remaining Trumps is done in a similar way. So let us go, in imagination, to the Hall of Temperance.

The Hall of Temperance

We start as before in the Hall of the Magician, but this time he raises the emblem of the Cup from his altar and indicates that we go to the doorway that is immediately behind us, where stands the angel figure who represents Temperance. As we approach, the winged figure invites us in through the doorway into another circular hall, where we stand in the centre, before going to meet the first of the four figures who are to be found there.

The first we go to is in fact a group which together form the picture on the Trump known as the **Lovers**. Here are the pair of lovers, faced by a priestess of Venus, the goddess of Love, and above them hovers a winged figure of Cupid, the son of the goddess Venus, holding a bow and arrow, and with a quiver full of the arrows or darts of love. We go up to this group and feel the aura of love that emanates from them. By standing here, and feeling ourselves as part of this group, we can contact the healing power of human love that they mediate. You can also, at your leisure, take time to identify yourself with any of the four figures here. Each can give you a particular insight into the forces of love.

We pass now to the next Trump, where we come upon a young man, or a young woman, in a chariot. It is a festive rather than a warlike chariot, with a decorative canopy, just as might be seen in a carnival procession or to celebrate some triumph or great occasion. The figure in the chariot represents **Victory**, and by contact with this image, you can come to terms with the feelings of success and progress in whatever you do, or gain encouragement in times of difficulty of seeming failure.

We now proceed to the third position within this Hall where we find the **Hermit**. He stands with staff of wisdom and upraised lantern to guide people on their way. He is a protector of travellers, in all senses of the word, which includes mental and spiritual travellers too. His lantern can also take the form of an hour glass, because time is one of his significations. Thus he can help us to be patient in times of boredom or stress. Also, if we are called upon to guide others in any way, we could do well to take time to commune with this figure and try to take on some of his vast experience and knowledge of the patterns and paths of human life, which can help us to take the longer view, and to guide their immediate steps in the right direction.

Finally, in the Hall of Temperance, we come to the **Wheel of Fortune**, a slowly turning wheel, moving in a clockwise direction, with human figures upon it that rise to good fortune and success and then descend to make room for others, in the ups and downs of the cycle of life. Be aware also of the female figure who turns the wheel. This is the goddess of fortune, Fortuna. She is a figure to come and commune with when confronted with the ups and downs of life, for she can teach the wisdom that is to be gained by the acceptance of life experience, whether we be on the ups or the downs. You may also at times care to identify with or talk to any of the figures about the wheel. Originally there were four of them, and they were all human beings, not strange animals. You can thus be at one with another who is on rising fortunes, at the pinnacle of success, or gone over the top, or who seems completely lacking in good fortune. Each one has a lesson to teach and a lesson to learn, and this is where you can learn it, from being gracious and humble in victory to being philosophic and undespairing in defeat.

The Hall of Justice

The next Hall that we shall visit from the Hall of the Magician is the Hall of Justice. As we stand before the Magician he holds up his sword, and indicates that we pass toward our right to meet the figure of Justice who stands at a doorway there. She scrutinises us closely, and then allows us to enter with her into the centre of her hall. Here about the walls we see the four figures that are under her control. Although they seem to have an awesome or even unpleasant aspect in some ways, there is no reason for us to fear them. They are all simply expressions of forces that lie within ourselves, and they are held in balance and check by the figure of Justice, in whose hall they reside.

At the far wall we see a wooden framework, or gallows. From it is suspended a young man, hanging upside down by one foot. As we approach the **Hanged Man** we find that he is smiling, and seems perfectly at ease. A golden radiance like a halo surrounds his head. In his company we feel a strength of will and dedication, a self assurance and sense of service. Here is one who follows out the right thing, and inspires with his charisma, no matter what the consequences may seem. We too can gain the courage and conviction to follow his example. Bathing in the radiance of his halo we can gain an intuitive insight into what is right for us to do, and the inner conviction to carry it out.

We pass now to the next figure, which is in the form of a skeleton holding a scythe, or **Death**. He is not a figure to dread. Rather he is one who brings things to their rightful close, ending that which is outworn, making space for new growth and for new beginnings. He is therefore a figure of hope for the future, and coming to terms with him can help us to face change and welcome the challenge of the new and the unknown. He is the sweeper away of that which is no longer required and whose presence is a drag upon new burgeoning life. Every seed that enters the ground has to die to bring forth more fruit, which in turn continues the cycle, by coming into flower, fruition, and then again to seed. Dying to new birth. This is the place to come to think upon these things, especially when faced with imminent and seeming irreversible change.

The third figure in this chamber is the **Devil**, and he represents our own illusions. It is usually very easy to see the falsity of the illusions that other people have, but not so easy to identify our own. That is why the two figures seem chained to the base of the Devil's pedestal. They could quite easily escape if they wanted to, for the rings about their necks could be lifted off, did they but realise it. Here, on a pedestal, is the image of our own follies and delusions. No doubt he seems a beautiful figure to those who are standing in voluntary chains at his feet. This figure is sometimes called the Dweller on the Threshold, because he represents our own faults that we must face up to and eradicate before we can make any spiritual progress. So in a sense, when we look at the figure of the Devil we look at ourselves in a ruthlessly accurate reflecting glass. This is the place to come and meditate upon our follies and how to recognise and overcome them.

The fourth image to which we now pass is known as the **Lightning-Struck Tower**. Standing before this image is rather like standing before a moving picture show, or a film loop. We see the tower standing before us. It is struck by lightning and falls to the ground in a shower of falling masonry and human figures. It then rapidly builds itself up again, before being struck by lightning once more. If we watch carefully though, we see that the top of the tower is like a crown, and that it lifts to receive the lightning flash. It is only a scene of devastation therefore for those who resist change, or who are unprepared for new insights. The lightning is in fact a shaft of inspiration, or self-revelation, that can transform our lives, even though the immediate consequences may not always be too comfortable. It may be this lightning bolt, or shaft of enlightenment, that allows us to see the next image in a true light.

The Hall of the World

We now proceed to the last of the doorways in the Hall of the Magician. He holds up a great golden disc from his altar and indicates that we go towards our left to the figure of the World who awaits us there. The four emblems that are about the wreath in which she stands were originally four bright stars called the Watchers or Guardians of the Heavens, in the zodiacal constellations of Leo, Scorpio, Aquarius and Taurus. Hence they are in the form of a lion, an eagle, a man and a bull. The stars are nowadays known as Regulus, Antares, Fomalhaut, and Aldebaran. I mention this because in the Hall we about to enter we shall encounter what is sometimes called the starry wisdom. That is, intuitive and spiritual perceptions that lie beyond our physical senses and everyday understanding.

We pass into the Hall and proceed to its centre, and then address ourselves to the first of the images found here. We find we have approached a naked star maiden, commonly called the **Star**, who is pouring the dew of the stars upon the earth and the sea. Behind her are birds and trees and flowers springing forth from a desert landscape, and a pattern of brilliant stars shines overhead. By communing with this figure we acquaint ourselves with hope, and the opening of our lives to the gentle influences of the higher wisdom and the plan for our lives as they should and could be. This is a place to come for the gentle prompting of our own higher intuition, and realisation of our spiritual selves and own true destiny.

We go on to the next station within this Hall and find ourselves gazing at a landscape which lies beyond a stream in which we can see submarine life. Two dogs, or a wolf and a dog, bay at the **Moon** that hangs low in the sky between two towers. This is a scene for opening up our psychic faculties. The moon is the ruler of tides and of growth, and the great matrix of powers behind the natural world, that is sometimes called the astral plane. This is the realm of dreams and visions, and those who spend time contemplating this scene may become aware of the hidden springs of motivation that lie behind all events in outer life.

Now we turn to the third place in this Hall and see before us two children in a garden, dancing under a blazing **Sun**. This is an image of light and health and warmth, and also of the everyday world lived in conditions of openness and harmony. It is thus a fitting scene to contemplate when we are depressed or tired, or otherwise in need of some inner radiance and sunshine. It can also bring to us an awareness and knowledge of our own higher self, or what has been called by some our Holy Guardian Angel. The archangel Michael is one who is said to stand in the Sun and so this is a scene to contemplate when beset by any major or minor evil, for here is the place of the angelic warrior and champion of God against all error and misrule.

Lastly we turn to the final quarter where the angel of the **Last Judgement** leans from a cloud, bearing a great trumpet. This is the archangel Gabriel, the angel of annunciation, come to awaken the dead from their long sleep. This is a scene of spiritual awakening, of transformation, or transfiguration, of rousing ourselves from lethargy and getting up and going – not only in physical but in spiritual ways. The angel represents a whole new world and comes with a message of new life. This is an image to contemplate when we seek new horizons and new opportunities, and we can also identify ourselves with those who are awakening from their graves to respond to the angel's clarion call. Similarly, by identifying with the angel, we may be able to take on something of his powers to arouse and inspire others in need of awakening or inspiration or simply hope of better things to come.

A Narrative Approach to the Lesser Arcana

W E ARE NOW going to make the acquaintance of the cards of the numbered suits. So take up the rest of the pack that contains all these cards and go through it, separating it into four piles, one for each suit. That is to say: Wands, Cups, Swords and Coins.

You should now have four stacks, each of 14 cards. Take from each the Court Cards. That is the King, the Queen, the Knight and the Page.

To learn the meanings of all these cards in a simple way we are going to put the cards of each suit into a special order. We will deal with one suit at a time. Let us take the suit of Wands first. We are going to make a pile of the Wands cards face upwards in this order.

Lay down the Ace first – face upwards.
Now upon the Ace put the King – also face up.
Now the 2 and then the 3.
Now the Queen.
Next lay on the 4, then the 5, and then the 6.
Follow this with the Knight.
Now the 7, the 8, the 9 and the 10.
And lastly, on the top, still face upward, the Page.

Now do the same for each of the other three suits.

You should now have four stacks of cards before you, each one comprising a separate suit – and with the Page on top of each, and all face upwards.

We are now going to take each suit in turn and make up a story about it. The story will be very simple, but will illustrate the meaning of each card in the suit. It is easy to recall a story to mind, and so in this way you will easily remember the significance of each card. As we go through the story, try to build each picture, person or event, vividly in your mind.

And it is worthwhile going over each story a few times, visualising the scenes vividly, until you can recall and recount it to yourself. You may be surprised to find how easy this proves to be, even if you neglect the practice for some time, because the mind always remembers a story sequence easily.*

Wands: The Organisation of the Camp or the Founding of Camelot

The story we have chosen for the suit of Wands is about building and organising the defence of an ancient hill camp or fort. So settle yourself comfortably and visualise the scenes described.

We are standing before a large green hill that could form the basis for a hill fort. A fair youth comes up to us, dressed as a **Page** of the court. He carries a **Wand,** which is the symbol of his office and also a device for carrying messages, which can be clipped on to the end. He takes a message from his rod and gives it to you. It is an invitation and safe conduct to go with him to witness the building of Camelot in its first foundation as a hilltop stockade.

We follow the Page up a steep path overgrown with bushes that leads up the side of the hill. As we do so we overtake a man who is heavily laden. He is struggling to carry a load which is almost too heavy for him, consisting of no less than ten heavy staves, almost like young tree trunks. He is struggling to carry them up to the top of the hill where the stockade is to be built. This image signifies the **10 of Wands,** that signifies *Oppression*, or being over-burdened.

We pass on before him to the top of the path, and here we come upon an overseer or guardian of some kind, who is standing before a gateway that has been constructed in a newly made stockade. The man carries a quarter-staff and is immensely strong, and the gateway in which he stands consists of two rows, each of four staves, planted in the ground, so that one has to pass between them, having got past the guardian. Thus with the staff that he himself carries, there are nine staves in all. This is the image of the **9 of Wands,** one that signifies *Great Strength* and sure defence.

* The stories we have chosen roughly follow the pictures to be found on the A E Waite pack. But any other choice of story or pictures would be just as valid. And even better, to make up one of your own!

As we stand looking at the scene before us, which is simply a huge clearing on the flat top of the hill, with a strong stockade being constructed all round, eight men come running past, shouting for all to hurry. They each snatch up a stave from the ground and rush quickly towards the other side of the hilltop. We follow hastily behind them. The sight of the eight men running brandishing their staves is an image of the **8 of Wands**, that signifies *Swiftness.*

As we reach the other side of the fortification we see below us a little way down the hillside a young man defending himself against six rough looking men who have apparently been trying to get into the camp by stealth. He even pursues the six as they take to their heels upon our coming. This image is that of the **7 of Wands** and signifies courage or *Valour.*

The young man ceases to bother to pursue the gang as a Knight comes riding up on his horse. He carries a long lance upon which is a pennant. He congratulates the young man and then starts to give orders to all the men standing about, organising them into quickly finishing the work of the stockade. The work is soon completed under his *skilful direction*, which is a function of the **Knight of Wands.**

The work of building now complete, the assembled company of workmen run beside the knight as he trots round on a tour of inspection of the palisade. There are five particularly stalwart men around him who attach bits of bunting to their staves which they wave in the air, and these impromptu banners along with the pennant on the lance of the knight comprise the image of the **6 of Wands**, which signifies *Victory* after struggle or labours.

The circuit of inspection complete, the five who have accompanied the knight decide to organise themselves into games of skill, practising the martial arts that they may be called upon to exercise in defending the camp. Therefore they set to in an impressive display of mock fighting, that nevertheless can give some hard knocks to the unskilful. One young man is particularly good, and successfully takes on no less than four others at once to prove his skill. This is an image of the **5 of Wands,** which signifies trial or testing, or a proving of skills, either in examination or practice or even in actual *Strife.*

Having worked off their exuberance in their trials of skill the men gather round to make a symbolic structure in the centre of the clearing. It consists of four staves stuck four square into the ground, and covered with garlands. Some women and children join them, and they dance around it in celebration. This is the image of the **4 of Wands** and represents *Completed Work.*

Before this structure they now place a throne, and then line up respectfully at the gateway to the stockade, to welcome the **Queen**, who comes to join in the celebration of completion. She walks graciously between them, carrying a sceptre that is topped by a golden lion that holds within its paws a sunflower. She stops to speak to several of the men, women and children who are there assembled, and then sits on the central throne with the people gathered about her.

There now follows a high ranking official of the court, who seems to be some kind of inspector of the works that have been carried out. He goes round the entire circuit of fortification testing that all is secure. To do this he carries a short stave or baton, and he goes up to each pair of stakes in turn and tries to push them apart, to test their strength. The image of the baton testing the strength of the upright staves is an image of the **3 of Wands**, and signifies *Established Strength*.

There now follows a chamberlain of the court, gorgeously arrayed, and carrying two ornate sceptres, one of silver and one of gold. He strikes them ceremoniously into the ground and calls upon all to stand in silence for the coming of the King. All obey his command. With his two sceptres he presents an image of the **2 of Wands**, which signifies *Dominion* or command or head-ship.

The **King** now enters, carrying a sceptre upon which is emblazoned a dragon. He regally inspects all the assembled company and then proceeds to a space in the centre. He is obviously the monarch of all he surveys and yet he has a keen knowledge and interest in all the feats of skill and organisation that have gone to prepare the foundation of his eventual palace.

Standing alone in the centre, the king raises his dragon headed sceptre on high above his head, and then strikes it into the ground. To the wonder of all it bursts forth into leaf and blossom, shooting forth before our eyes to grow into a young and thriving wondrous tree. This is the emblem of the **Ace of Wands**, which represents the springing forth of new things into energetic thriving life.

This concludes the story of the Wands.

I recommend that you now try going over this story yourself. You can do so by taking up the Wand cards in turn, which are in their correct order in the pile before you. As you do so, reflect especially on the meaning that goes with each picture image. We will then proceed to the story of the Cup cards.

Cups: the Romance of the Runaway Apprentice

We find ourselves standing on a sea shore, where we are approached by a young Page who offers a cup to us. We look inside the cup and see there is a fish swimming within it. As we watch the fish a feeling of peace and reverie comes over us, in which certain wisdom or realisations may come to us, just as if we were looking into the calming waters of a slow moving river or a deep lake. This is how one tends to receive any message that may be brought by the **Page of Cups.**

We get the feeling that we should accompany the Page in walking along a little watercourse that flows nearby across the beach and into the sea. We follow its course inland along its curving bank, and as we do so we see a beautiful rainbow high in the sky before us, and as we turn a bend in the stream, a happy crowd of people pointing up to it joyfully, with little children dancing merrily. It is a scene of ideal happiness and of people living in harmony together. We see a group of people, who are five happy couples. One pair is standing in the centre, and it would seem are newly married. The four other couples stand in congratulation about them. All raise their cups in convivial greeting. This is the image of the **10 of Cups**, and signifies *Harmony* and *Success.*

Now a portly merchant calls over to us, and invites us to go into his house. Here, in a rich drawing room, he proudly shows us, upon a shelf, three sets of three golden vases. They are beautifully wrought and obviously worth a fortune. He sits before them with great satisfaction as if wanting his picture to be taken, which would indeed be a fitting image of the **9 of Cups**, signifying *Material Happiness* or *Contentment.*

We pass from the merchant's house into a quiet lane that runs behind it. The sun is beginning to descend in the sky and we see a young man coming down the lane. He looks disconsolate. We ask him what it is that ails him, and he replies that he is dissatisfied with life in the village. He is going off to seek far adventures. He is not sure which way to go but says he has a compass to guide him which he made himself as part of his apprentice work. He takes out and shows us a beautifully wrought little compass which, at the eight cardinal points upon it, has engraved a little golden cup. It seems to us a pity that a lad so gifted should give up his apprenticeship for wild adventures. And we reflect upon this as an image of the **8 of Cups**, and its meaning of *Abandoned Success.*

We ask him what it is that he seeks. He looks around cautiously to see if we are observed, and then says he has a secret of great power, which he will show to us if we wish. He leads us down to a deserted cove on the nearby shore and draws a seven pointed star on the sand. He places a little cup at each point with incense burning within it, and then announces to us that he can, by the power of magic, make the moon disappear. He stands and makes mystic signs and after a while a cloud does indeed obscure the moon, although we see that it will soon pass. The young man looks upon us however with an air of triumph, an image of the **7 of Cups,** and its meaning of *Illusory Success*.

We are interrupted by the sound of galloping hooves upon the sand, and turning, we find that a **Knight** has ridden up. He holds a golden cup in his hand and says that he is off in search of wisdom and adventures, on a quest to find another cup that is just like the one he has, and which is in the keeping of a most beauteous maiden, whose fair portrait is enamelled upon the cup he holds. He says that he is looking of a squire to accompany him, and the young apprentice eagerly offers his services. They go off together in happy comradeship.

The following day they come to a fair house. One that is almost grand enough to be called a castle, although it does not have fortifications. Two children are playing in the garden before it, running back and forth and around six large urns which are filled with blossoming flowers. These urns give us the image of the **6 of Cups** and the playing children signify that it stands for childlike *Happiness* and *Joy*.

The knight and his squire go up toward the house full of anticipation, for they feel that this is perhaps the place where the fair maiden will be whom they seek. However, as they pass through the rooms, all is deserted. They come back out of the house to speak to the children but find that they have gone. Indeed all but one of the urns of flowers has been overturned to spill its flowering contents onto the ground. The five overturned urns remind us of the **5 of Cups**, and the faces of the knight and squire signify its meaning, of *Disillusion* or *Disappointment*.

They remain around the house however for several days, as they find within it plenty to amuse them, and much to eat and drink. But after a while, as they are sitting at a laden table, each with two cups in front of him, undecided as to which one to drink from first, they realise that they are not content with what they have, and they are just wasting their time in idleness and lack of purpose in the midst of luxury. The four cups signify the image of the **4 of Cups** and its meaning of *Loss in Pleasure*, satiated luxury, over-indulgence, or boredom in the midst of plenty.

They ride off determined to renew their quest which they so easily forsook. They come one day to a beautiful lake in the centre of which is a wondrous island. There, seated on a throne across the waters from them, they see a beautiful Queen, who is holding a cup. It is curiously ornate, covered with emblems of fruit and flowers, with the images of angels about it. She smiles across at them and indicates that she would welcome them to cross the water to her on her island, where she has much that will please and delight them.

They see there is a little boat nearby, and they enter in to it to cross to the island. When they reach the island the Queen welcomes them and takes them up towards a fair greensward where there are many tents erected and tables laid out for feasting and celebration. In the centre, their attention is drawn to three fair maidens dancing in a ring in the midst of the tables laden with all the fruits of the harvest. The three maidens each hold an overflowing cornucopia, or shell-like cup, indicating the image of the **3 of Cups**, and its meaning of great ***Abundance***.

Their dance ended, laughing, the three maidens run toward the knight, and strewing flowers all around him, lead him to a fair young maiden who is the image of the picture upon the cup of his quest. She holds a cup just like his own and they raise them on high in plighting their mutual true love, thus giving the emblem of the **2 of Cups**, and its meaning, which is ***Love***.

A great cry of joy rises from the assembled company and at this point the **King** appears, holding a great cup, and he gives his blessing to the happy pair.

The King then takes his great cup and places it upon the ground before them. A great spout of sparkling water shoots up on high from it as it is revealed as a marvellous fountain, and a flock of doves flies over to the circle and wheels about the jet of flowing waters. This is the emblem of the **Ace of Cups**, which indicates the source and ***Fount of Love*** and joyous emotion.

That concludes the story of the Cups and you can now retell it to yourself with the aid of the cards in the pile of Cup cards before you, which you will find to be in correct order.

Swords: the Tragedy of the Murdered Lord

We are standing on a windswept hill and are approached by a young man dressed like a **Page**, carrying a drawn sword. He urges that we accompany him and there is an almost compelling intensity about him that brooks no refusal. We follow him swiftly down the hill.

We pass round the side of the hill and there in a hollow we see a terrible sight. A man, who seems by his dress to have been a lord of some kind, has been killed. He lies transfixed with a sword, and upon the ground about him are scattered other swords, as if a skirmish has taken place, and his defenders have fled, leaving their weapons. The young man gathers these up, there are nine all told, which together with the sword that pierces the man gives us the emblem of the **10 of Swords**, and its meaning, which is ***Ruin***, failure or disaster.

As we stand we are aware of a sound of a woman crying, and nearby we find, huddled upon a pile of blankets, a woman in the depths of despair. She seems to have been the wife of the murdered lord. On seeing the Page with us holding the nine swords of those who deserted their master she runs at him and flings them all to the ground in a paroxysm of grief. The woman standing stricken with grief amongst them gives us the image of the **9 of Swords**, and its meaning, of suffering or ***Despair and Cruelty***.

A little further off we come to another tragic sight, which is that of a young woman, tied and blindfolded. She is standing within a circle of eight swords that have been struck into the ground, as if a cage is about her. The Page who is with us releases her, and she appears to be the murdered lord's daughter, but she is too confused and dazed to give any account of what has happened. As she stands by the eight upstanding swords she presents a fitting image of the **8 of Swords** and its meaning of ***Shortened Force***, that is to say, restriction, confusion and helplessness.

Then we hear somebody shouting and we climb up a short way to gain a vantage point and see, a little distance from us, the ruined wagon that the lord and his ladies had been travelling in. It has been overturned and is being pillaged by a group of vagrants, who are taking advantage of the lord's disaster. There are seven of them, all armed with knives as they cut open bags to discover anything of value they can make away with, and upon seeing us they give cries of dismay and start to run off – and then having gone some little way hesitate, wondering whether they dare return and fight us or brazen things out. They form a fitting emblem of the **7 of Swords** and its meaning of untrustworthiness, and ***Unstable Effort***, or vacillation.

Their hesitation is quickly ended by the thudding of hoof beats as a **Knight** comes galloping across the plain, and they flee for their lives. The knight pursues them however and rounds them up, striking them with the flat of his sword, and then he sets them to clearing up and setting to rights the damage they have done. He then comes over towards where we stand. With grave countenance he places the dead lord across the back of his horse, and with the woman and the girl walking beside him, leads them off round the side of the mountain, to where there is a still lake, with a boat moored at its edge.

The knight places them all in the boat and leaving his horse tethered by the shore, he punts the boat across the lake. About the body of the slain lord he places six swords, stuck point downward into the wood of the boat, in token of respect. He laboriously steers and propels the heavy wooden boat, sunk down deeply into the water by the load that it carries, and as they cross the lake they serve as an emblem of the **6 of Swords** and its meanings of hard effort, or an earned respite after difficult trials, and a resulting change that will be for the better, or *Earned Success.*

Now that the knight is out of the way though, the vagabonds rejoice and resume their looting. Two of them make off on the horse, and the remaining five scrabble around and then sit on the pile of the lord's possessions, their pockets stuffed with stolen objects, and each armed with a sword that they have stolen. Together they give an image for the **5 of Swords** and its significance of loss, failure, *Defeat.*

At the far side of the lake the knight has come to a castle, where the woman and her daughter are taken care of, and the body of the dead lord is laid out in a chapel of rest, with four knights with drawn swords standing about his bier. As we regard this candlelit scene we are presented with an image for the **4 of Swords**, and is signification of *Rest from Strife.*

A figure now appears in the doorway of the chapel, and we are aware that it is the mother of the dead lord, and she is arrayed like a **Queen**. She carries a drawn sword and gravely sits on a throne at the end of the chapel in silent vigil. She sits there, not despairing, but full of dignity and grave purpose.

After a time she takes the sword in her hand and approaches the altar at the east end of the chapel. There she places the sword upon it at the feet of a statue of the Virgin, as Mother of Sorrows, her heart pierced with three swords. Thus we have the image of the **3 of Swords** and its meaning of *Sorrow.*

Then coming behind her we see her daughter. She holds two swords, with her arms crossed across her breast. She sits thus at the end of the chapel as an indication and supplication for maintaining calm, and refraining from hasty action. Thus is she the image for the **2 of Swords**, and its meaning of opposing forces in balance, or *Peace Restored.*

Finally the **King** enters, gravely carrying a mighty sword of state. He is obviously a man of great will and power who will see that ultimately justice is done.

He raises the great sword on high, in dedication to the rule of law, and as he does so, at the point of the upraised sword there appears a circle of light that becomes a golden crown with evergreen branches of fir and the magical mistletoe hanging from it. In all it is an emblem of *New Beginnings* in the form of the **Ace of Swords**.

So ends the story depicted by the Sword cards, and you should now take up the cards one by one from the appropriate pile and retell the story to yourself to fix it within your mind.

Coins: the Visit to the Castle of Riches

We find ourselves standing on a broad plain, and there comes to meet us a **Page** who is bearing a great golden medallion. He invites us to look upon it, and we see in its shining surface the message: "Whoever follows me shall discover something to their great advantage." Accordingly, when the Page turns and makes his way across the plain we decide to follow him.

We find we are proceeding along the broad and long drive-way of a rich mansion, and as we approach the gateway we see that there is gathered there a family group. A man and woman with their children, and also, seated beside them, their aged father. They are all richly dressed, and are also surrounded by domestic animals. Upon each pillar of the gateway are five golden disks with the heraldic arms of the family emblazoned upon them, ten in all. We realise we are in the presence of the image of the **10 of Coins**, which signifies *Wealth* and established material success and achievement.

We pass through the gate and find ourselves in an ornamental garden, laid out with the most exquisite of rare tropic flowers and fruit trees. A lady is walking there in a dress of cloth of gold and beside her there struts a peacock with all its deep blue and purple tail feathers displayed – upon which are to be seen nine bright golden disks or eyes. The lady seems very proud and perhaps unused to these surroundings of luxury, and flaunts and preens herself rather like the peacock. This is the image of the **9 of Coins** and its meaning of *Inheritance* or *Material Gain.*

Passing through the garden we come, just beyond it, to a workshop where a young man is cutting our medallions such as the Page had originally shown us. The craftsmanship is exquisite and the skills of the young man have obviously been developed over a long period of painstaking apprenticeship. He carves the precious metal with great care because of its great intrinsic value, and so he is a model of prudent application as well as skill. He has eight finished medallions in a circle round about him, like points on a compass card. This is our image for the **8 of Coins** and its significance of *Skill* and **Prudence.**

Passing the workshop we come to another young man. This one seems to be a gardener. He is, however, standing leaning on his hoe in some disappointment, before a most exotic tree. It has obviously not borne fruit as he had been hoping and there is much broken blossom about the ground beneath the tree, and upon the tree itself just seven golden nutmegs. Here we have before us the image of the **7 of Coins** and its significance of **Success Unfulfilled** or lack of reward for patient effort.

We leave him standing there and pass on to where we come to a broad green lawn. From one side of the lawn we see a **Knight** progressing, his horse laden with great moneybags in panniers by his saddle. The knight and his horse give an impression of great trustworthiness and stolidity.

The knight delivers the moneybags to a steward who waits in the centre of the greensward. He dumps them with a great thump onto the ground and lumbers off, his duty done. The steward meanwhile takes out from the bags piles of coin, which he weighs out with a balance, making out an account of it all. There are six of these bags, each one golden in colour, and serving to give us the image of the **6 of Coins**, whose significance is *Material Wealth* or *Success.*

The steward now takes up a handful of coins and walks over toward a high wall. There is a small trap door in the wall which he opens, and beyond we can see a crowd of beggars waiting for charity. The steward holds up the coins before the opening, and we see it is just five gold pieces. He throws them out to the beggars and slams the hatchway shut contemptuously. This is the image of the **5 of Coins**, and its significance is *Material Trouble* or anxiety about loss.

The steward now returns to the centre of lawn and summoning a group of servants he superintends the bags of money being carried across to a strongly fortified treasury. The money is stowed away within and then the steward firmly locks the door, with four golden locks, after which he stands proudly and possessively before the door, gloating over the four golden keys. This is our image for the **4 of Coins** and its significance of *Earthly* or *Material Power*.

After a while he goes to report that his work has been done. This he does to a lady who is arrayed like a **Queen** who is sitting on a great throne in another part of the garden beneath a bower of trees. She has upon her lap a golden disc upon which is engraved the plan of the great house and gardens sin which she lives, and upon which she gazes lovingly.

A little distance away some new work is going on. It is the building of an ornate tower, where masons are at this moment carving a keystone arch. It is a delicate tracery of stonework in the form of three interlinked circular windows. This is the image of the **3 of Coins**, and its meaning is *Material Works* or Constructive Building.

Before the tower is a man in a tall hat who appears to be the master architect of all that is being built. He has two circular plates of gold similar to the one held by the Queen, and upon them appear to be plans of what many of the old buildings were, and on the other plans of how some of them are to be altered. His eye glances keenly from one to the other. He is the image of the **2 of Coins** and its meaning of *Harmonious Change*.

Now towards him comes one who is obviously master of this place because he is arrayed like a **King** and is sumptuously dressed. He carries an enormous golden disk, and takes his seat on a great throne in the middle of another green space of perfect lawn.

We are aware that this particular space is going to be laid out as a new and perfect garden. The King steps forward and just before the throne lays down the golden disk upon the ground. It is to be the central piece and foundation stone about which all the rest of the garden will take its shape and point of orientation. The image and function of the **Ace of Coins** – the *Fount of Material Success*.

This brings to an end our story about the cards of the suit of Coins. As you have done with the other suits, take up each card in turn and tell the story through again to yourself, paying particular attention to the image associated with each one and its particular basic meaning.

Preparation for Divination

NOW YOU WILL NOT BE much of a Tarot reader if you have to keep looking up meanings in a book so we need to spend some time consolidating and revising what we have already learned about the cards.

One of the best ways to do this is to lay the whole pack face up in front of you. This of course is going to need quite a bit of space, so if you do not have a large enough table I suggest you use a clean clear space on the floor, and perhaps invest in a miniature set of cards.

We want to lay the cards out in four rows – each row 19 cards long from side to side. This means that with a normal sized pack the space you need will be just over four feet (120 cms) wide. And as we are going to lay out four rows, the space from top to bottom will be about 18 inches (50 cms).

I suggest you lay them out in this fashion. First lay out the suit of Wands, all face upwards, in the order that we already have them in the stacks before us. It does not matter whether you lay them out from right to left or left to right, as it is the order, not the direction, which is important for our purpose.

So lay out the Wands cards – Page, 10, 9, 8, 7, Knight, 6, 5, 4, Queen, 3, 2, King, Ace.

Now lay out the row of Cups beneath them, in the same order.

Now repeat the process with the suit of Swords.

Finally lay out the Coins, as a bottom row, in the same order.

You should now have before you the 56 cards of the Lesser Arcanum laid out before you with all the Aces one above the other at one end of the row, and all the Pages at the other end. And in between each numbered card and Court card will lie similarly together in vertical lines. Just check to see that you have them all correctly placed.

Now we going to add the Trump cards.

You will remember that we said the four Cardinal Virtue cards were each related to one of the suits. Strength was related to Wands. So lay Strength out at the end of the line of Wands. Whether to the right or left hand end does not matter.

To the Cups is related the Trump called Temperance. Lay that at the end of the line of Cups. It will also be just below the Strength Trump.

At the end of the line of Swords lay out Justice.

And at the end of the line of Coins put the World.

Now we can add the other Trump cards to our four lines.

Beside Strength lay out, in a line, the four other Trumps within her Hall. In a traditionally numbered pack this will be Trumps II, III, IV and V. The High Priestess, the Empress, the Emperor and the Pope or Hierophant. If you are using a pack that has different numbering, go by the name of the card in all of this.

Beside Temperance lay out the next four Trumps, which belong to her Hall. The Lovers, the Chariot, the Hermit and the Wheel of Fortune. These are usually numbered VI, VII, IX and X.

Now alongside Justice put the four Trumps of her Hall. The Hanged Man, Death, the Devil, and the Tower – which are normally numbered XII, XIII, XV and XVI.

And beside the Trump of the World on the bottom row, lay out the Star, the Moon, the Sun and the Angel or Last Judgement, which are usually numbered XVII, XVIII, XIX and XX.

We will now be left with just two cards – the Fool and the Magician. The Fool represents the Spirit of the Tarot, and the Magician the Controller of all its Forces. These you can place on their own wherever is convenient, although the most appropriate position will be at the top of the whole spread.

Below them, in the four lines of cards, are to be seen all the forces under their jurisdiction, represented by the 76 cards you have spread out before you. Take a good look at this spread. It is a language of 78 different words, or basic ideas. And it is by means of these 78 images, and the ideas that they convey, that the Tarot will have to describe various situations to you in response to questions that are asked of it – and which you will, in turn, have to interpret to the best of your ability.

We can quite easily recall the meanings of the cards when they are set out in order, by use of our story lines, and recalling our visits to the Halls of the Trumps. However, what we will need to be able to do is to recall the key idea, or basic meaning, of each card when we come upon it in isolation, or in a different order, mixed up with other cards.

By way of a little initial practice in developing this degree of familiarity with the cards, it is a good exercise to run your eye up and down the vertical lines.

For instance, look at the 3 of Wands. What does that signify? You may recall from our story it is a picture of a man testing the strength of a stockade – hence the basic meaning of Established Strength.

How about the 3 of Cups below it? That, in our story had three joyful maidens at a wedding feast, and signifies Abundance.

Below that is the 3 of Swords. We recall the scene of the grieving Queen in the chapel before the statue of the bleeding heart, signifying Sorrow.

And at the bottom is the 3 of Coins which calls to mind the scene of the workmen at the tower and the meaning of Material Works.

Try this exercise with all of the other numbered cards. Never mind the Court Cards and Trumps for the time being. We will come to them later. If you find difficulty in doing this exercise, go back to the story lines and play them over again.

When you find you can do this exercise fairly easily, start to jump about at random from card to card, seeing how quickly the basic meaning comes to mind. Keep up with this exercise until you feel really confident about any card on sight. After all, this is what you will be faced with in doing an actual reading.

Now let us turn our attention to the Court Cards. For the most part these represent actual people in any spread.

The Kings and Queens are likely to represent men or women in established positions, and these people in real life will usually be the same sex as the card that represents them.

The Knights and Pages are less sexually defined and could represent people of either sex. The Knight represents someone who is very active, someone who makes things happen. The Page is more passive, can be a dependent, such as a child, or even a childlike old person, or perhaps a customer or junior staff in a business situation. The Pages can also represent messages, whether face to face, or by phone or by mail. Thus they can represent gossip, as opposed to the activity of the Knights, or the personal qualities contributed to a situation by the Kings or Queens.

The general context of these people or their actions will take its flavour from the particular suits. Wands for business or organisational matters. Cups for social affairs. Swords where there is competition or disagreement. Coins in financial or matter of property or material things.

Let us take a fairly general example for each of the Court Cards. The King and Queen of Wands could be the owners or directors of a business. The Knight could be their manager, organising things on a day to day basis. The Page could be an assistant of perhaps a customer. Build up in your mind's eye a picture of each of them. The King, the Queen, the Knight and the Page bustling about in the context of a business you know well. This will serve to fix them in your mind, which will help you when you come across them in a spread.

Turning to the Cups, the King and Queen could be the father and mother at a fairly large social occasion. The knight could then be the master or mistress of ceremonies, or even bride or groom if it is a wedding, or perhaps best man. The Page could represent any of the guests attending, especially children, or one of the helpers with the catering. Imagine each of the four cards now, performing this function.

In Swords the King and Queen could be in the legal profession or else simply people whose attitudes are aggressive or argumentative, or who could in some other way have some kind of unpleasant effect. The Knight will be one who is actively involved in argument or disruption, and the Page could represent threatening or other unwelcome communications, or even those who pass on hurtful gossip. Again the Page, if a child, would be one perhaps the cause of dispute or some kind of difficulty. Once again, make a picture in your mind of each card performing the appropriate function. The more vivid a picture you make the better will you remember it.

And with the Coins the King and Queen may represent those who own or control the flow of money in some way, or other property or possessions. The Knight would be likely to be their agent, possibly a bank official or estate agent. The Page once more could represent messages relating to this kind of activity, or one who passes them on, or could also represent a financial dependent, or alternatively someone about to inherit or come into some financial windfall. Once again, use you imagination to make relevant pictures.

Now that I have briefly described the general principles to you, go over the Court cards yourself as they are laid out before you, thinking or brooding about each one, and visualise in your mind's eye the type of person that could be represented by each one. When you come to doing a reading for somebody else you may well need to find a card to represent them, so this is a good exercise for when you have to do that.

Let us now turn our attention to the Trumps. The Lesser Arcana, or suit cards, tend to represent activities and people in everyday life. The

Trumps tend to represent more inner, hidden, spiritual or psychological influences, which are likely to be of quite a powerful nature.

We have made the acquaintance of each of the Trumps in our earlier work. Let us now revise what we did then by casting an eye over the cards laid out as part of the complete pattern before us.

Along the top row, alongside the **Wands** cards, we have **Strength**, and the four Trumps that likewise represent power in four modes of expression, the **Emperor, Empress, Hierophant** and **High Priestess**. In this they are similar to the Kings and Queens of any of the four suits, but you will need to interpret the specific details according to how and where they appear in any spread. Basically though, they mean much the same kind of thing, but expressed in slightly different ways.

Passing down to the next line, the Trumps beside the **Cups** cards represent various conditions of life as we experience it. **Temperance** itself represents good temper or expression of controlled and civilised behaviour, inwardly and outwardly. The meaning of the **Lovers** should be obvious; and the **Chariot** represents how we handle progress, ambition or success. The **Hermit** represents good advice or guidance, and this can also be the passage of time, which also brings wisdom through experience or patience. Finally the **Wheel of Fortune** represents change of fortune for better or worse, according to how the rest of the spread indicates.

In the third row, alongside the suit of **Swords**, **Justice** represents evenly balanced attitudes, without fear or favour. The **Hanged Man** is one whose ideals may not match up too well with circumstances in worldly terms. **Death** rarely indicates physical death but rather an ending of a particular set of circumstances. The **Devil** represents illusions, or mistakes being made, perhaps blind prejudices or just plain wrong information. The **Tower** represents a sudden bolt from the blue that, like the Wheel of Fortune, may be for better or for worse.

On the bottom row, alongside **Coins**, the **World** represents completion of a process, four-square success. The **Star** is a card of high hopes and faith in the future. The **Sun** is a good card of general favourable circumstances. The **Moon** indicates that hidden forces are at work, just as the invisible forces of the actual moon affect the tides of the sea and growth of plants. The **Last Judgement** represents a breaking through to new realisations or circumstances in life.

This leaves just the two Trumps we began with, the Fool and the Magician. The **Fool** is one who knows a great deal intuitively although he may not always appear wise, particularly to the 'worldly wise'. He can usually be interpreted as the beginning of fresh enterprises and a state of innocence or inexperience, or facing up to new situations, which is always a situation of certain risk, even if one of exciting possibilities. The **Magician**, on the other hand, is one who is fully and demonstrably in control of circumstances and a master of his craft and of his won destiny, and possibly of others as well.

Take a little time now to run through the Trump cards in your mind as they lie before you, so that you can confidently state the basic meaning of each one, in whatever order you look at them.

Reversed cards

We are now almost in a position to undertake our first reading, but first we must consider the meaning of reversed cards.

Many people are a little nervous about using reversed cards. This is understandable. To the beginner it seems quite difficult enough to become acquainted with the ordinary meaning of the 78 cards, without complicating matters further.

However, things are not quite so difficult as they seem. The basic meanings of the cards do not change very much when reversed. It is more a question of the influence represented by the card being likely to come into play in a slightly unbalanced or awkward way.

Another reason why people may be reluctant to use them is because they associate them with trouble or difficulty of some kind. And whether they are reading the cards for themselves, or for somebody else, they are naturally reluctant to find themselves forecasting problems.

However, no Tarot reading is going to predict unavoidable disasters, and the presence of a card in the reversed mode can in fact be a very useful indicator of what to concentrate on to avoid specific difficulties. A useful device is to recommend the Enquirer to meditate upon that card, to try to identify its influence in their life, and to visualise it becoming right way up, and the effect this would have on resolving or easing their problem.

So while you have all the cards spread out before you, take time to do a final run through for yourself of the basic meaning of each card, right way up and also reversed. You can do this on several sheets of paper. List out all the cards down the left hand margin. Then draw two wide columns down the rest of the page, and jot down your ideas for each card in the appropriate space; right way up in one column, and reversed in the other column.

When you have done this you will have a complete run-down of the Tarot pack that is in your own words, and this will be far superior to anything you are likely to get out of a published book. You will in fact have started to construct your own workbook. And you can put these pages into a loose leaf file and add to it from time to time as you discover further things about the Tarot from your own readings and experience.

Before we proceed further, it may be as well to check out the designs of the pack you are using to see if all the cards are readily identifiable as being reversed or right way up. Some packs have a little mark to indicate which is the right way up if they have been produced with divination in mind. However, some old packs that were manufactured mainly as playing cards may look identical whichever way up they are, at any rate on certain cards. So take a look through the pack before you, and make a mark on any cards if necessary, so that you will be able to tell which way up they are when you are using them.

Divinatory Methods

WE ARE NOW in a position to perform an actual Tarot reading. But first of all let us emphasise that half the battle in successful divination is to have the right attitude of mind. This should be of sincere personal enquiry, as if you were consulting a wise and trusted friend – as indeed you are. So only approach the Tarot if you genuinely wish to learn from it, and do not treat it in a frivolous way. It is not a party game or light entertainment for the idly curious. If you do approach it in a silly way then you will simply get from it misleading answers.

There are many methods laid down for the actual reading of the cards. They will all, or most of them, work if approached in the right manner. So do not be confused by conflicting advice from various books. Decide which approach suits you best and then stick to it, and only modify it as a result of your own experience or developing realisations as you actually work with the cards. This is your only real authority. Your own experience. All that any book or course can do for you is to help you make the first steps in more or less the right direction. The rest is up to you.

So collect up all the cards that you have laid out before you and mix them up very thoroughly together, as we are now going to do a reading. And when you have the cards thoroughly shuffled, take a look through the pack to ensure that they are all the right way up. We are going to undertake a reading that personally concerns you. So prepare yourself for this by trying to ensure that you will not be disturbed for thirty minutes or so, and that you are in an alert and receptive frame of mind before proceeding further.

Now when we consult the Tarot we must always define quite precisely what our question is. If we have a muddled question we should not be surprised if we get a confusing answer. So take a clean sheet of paper, write your name at the top, as the subject of the reading is you, and also put the date and the time. Underneath this, write out the question. It is going to be: ***"What influences will be affecting my life in the next four weeks?"***

You can now put the sheet of paper to one side, but keep it handy as you will be going to write on it in the course of the reading.

Significator

Our next task is to choose a Significator. This is a card to represent the Querent, which in this case is yourself. From what we have earlier discussed and practised you should have no difficulty in selecting one of the Court cards to represent you. Alternatively you can, if you think it more appropriate, choose one of the Trump cards. Or even one of the numbered suit cards, especially if you are using a fully pictorial pack. Take your time over this. Once you have chosen your Significator, place it face up in the centre of the table before you.

1st Shuffle

Now you can undertake the first part of the shuffle. Concentrate your mind on the question, and while you do so, shuffle the rest of the 77 cards. After a while, when you have an inward feeling that it is time to do so, stop shuffling, and fan out the cards on the table before you, face downwards.

Reversals

From the fanned out pack select at random about half a dozen cards. The precise number depends on how you intuitively feel about it. Do not look to see what they are, but simply turn them top to tail and put them back in the pack. These will be the reversed cards that may turn up in your actual reading.

2nd Shuffle

Now take up the pack and shuffle it some more, still thinking about the question, and when you feel the time is ripe, stop shuffling and place the pack face down upon the table.

The Cut

Now we perform the cut. Use your left hand if you are right handed, or your right hand if you are left handed, and divide the pack into three piles one beside the other, still face downward. Then, using any order you choose, put them back together to form one stack, still face downward.

Layout

We are now ready to lay out the spread. There are many ways in which you could do this, and in time you may develop your own favoured method. But for this first time we shall use one of the most famous and most popular, the ten card Celtic spread, first publicised in 1911 by A.E. Waite (see Figure 37).

Take the top card from the pack that lies before you, and lay it face up on the table before you so that it covers the Significator. You can place it slightly off centre, so that you can still partly see the Significator underneath it. As you do so say: *"This covers me."* This card will represent the general tone of things affecting you, in broad general terms, over the next month. In other words, it is a general response to your question.

(If this card turns out to be reversed, by the way, it is worth checking that you are holding the pack the right way up before proceeding, otherwise the rest of the cards, or most of them, will turn up reversed as well! Also, as you are working by yourself I suggest that you make notes as you go. Although if you were doing a reading for someone else it might be better and more practical to leave any note taking until afterwards. To do this fully comprehensively, write the figure 1 on your sheet of paper, to represent the first card that you have laid down, and write the name of the actual card beside it. You can also jot down any ideas that come to you as to what you feel it means. It can be worthwhile to jot down any fleeting impressions that do not at first seem to make too much sense or to have much logical reason, as these may turn out to be accurate psychic impressions.)

Now take the next card from the top of the pack and lay it face up on the first card, and it will be appropriate to lay it across horizontally, so that you can still see much of the first card. As you do so, say *"This crosses me."* This card will represent various obstacles that you may come across in the next four weeks. Make a note of it, against a figure 2 on your note pad, together with your basic interpretation of it and any other comments that seem appropriate in the circumstances.

Now take a third card and place it face upwards on the table a little above the cards you have already laid. As you do so, say *"This crowns me."* This card will represent the aims and ideals that are appropriate for the period in question, but which may or may not actually come to fruition in this time. Note it down against a figure 3 on your record sheet, together with your interpretation and any other thoughts about it.

Now take the fourth card and put it before you, just below the cards that you have already laid, and say *"This is beneath me."* This card

Figure 37

will represent general factors that are available to you for use now, or which are affecting you now – the fruit of the past we might say, or the foundation upon which any future development will take place. Put down the name of this card and your thoughts upon its significance against the number 4 on your record sheet.

The fifth card that you take from the pack should be placed behind the direction in which the Significator is facing. However, if you have a Significator which is facing straight ahead out of the card, simply put this new card to the left or right of the central cards, as seems fit to you at the time. As you do so say *"This is behind me."* Make a note as before of this card and your impressions about its meaning, against the figure 5 on your pad. It will signify things in the immediate past, or perhaps that are still here in the present but which are rapidly passing away.

Take the sixth card and place it to one side of the central cards, this time in the direction towards which the Significator is facing – or in the remaining vacant space in your layout. As you do so say: *"This is before me."* Make a note against the figure 6 on your record sheet. This one will signify what is coming into play in the immediate future.

We now proceed to the next stage of this spread. The six cards already laid out on and around the Significator indicate the general forces operating that are concerned with the question. The four remaining cards to be laid represent you yourself, or the enquirer if you were reading the cards for somebody else. These four cards, which are sometimes called the Branch, will be laid in a vertical line, starting from the bottom and working upwards, to the right hand side of the cross of cards that are already laid out before you. So take the next card, and put it face upwards to the right hand side of the table, and as you do so, say *"This is Myself."* Make a note of this card against the number 7 on your sheet of paper together with any ideas that come along with it. This card will represent yourself, and so, in a way, is a direct comment upon your general standing in relation to the question. In one sense it is another form of the Significator, or the kind of attitude or action that is likely to be expected of him or her.

The next card you lay just above the one you have just put down. As you do so, say *"This is my House."* This card represents the general surroundings in which you find yourself, and so can well represent your place of work, or colleagues there, as well as your home and the effect that those who live with you are likely to have upon the matter. Make your notes on this against the figure 8 in your record.

Now take another card and lay it in line above the last two, and say *"These are my hopes and fears."* Make a note of the card and your interpretation against the figure 9 in your notes. This card will represent your inner feelings, which may possibly be somewhat repressed, or which if strongly and openly felt may have some kind of effect upon what is going to happen. In other words, you might be worrying, or alternatively getting excited about things that might well not happen. Yet these attitudes might well determine your attitude to what actually does occur, or which tries to occur.

Now take the final card for this spread, and lay it above the last card that you laid, and say as you do so *"This is what will come."* Record this card and your feelings about it against figure 10 in your record. This is a very important card and represents the general outcome to the question. In other words, as we are asking about general trends in the next month, this card will, in a nutshell, represent the keynote or highlight of the period ahead.

Now that you have the whole spread laid out before you, take some time to contemplate its meaning as a whole, instead of card by card. See if you can see any relationships between various parts of the spread. This will enable you to build up a more coherent general picture. Some of these ideas may be no more than hunches or feelings, but make a note of them just the same. Then you can come back to your notes at a later date and be able to recall the actual impressions you had at the time.

When you come back to your notes after a period of time you may well find that there were indications in the cards that were plainly indicating something that subsequently happened but which you missed at the time. However, if you develop the habit of keeping a record of what you do, and coming back to check how well you did in your interpretation, this will, more than anything else, develop your skills and facility in reading the Tarot. For divination is a skill and an art which, like any other, is developed by dedicated discipline and practice. The more you work at it, the better you will be. The more you put into it, the more you will get out of it as reward for your labours.

Examples of much that we have described and discussed here are elaborated in my book *The Magical World of the Tarot – Fourfold Mirror of the Universe* (Aquarian Press 1991 & Samuel Weiser 1996) giving example readings, answers to students' questions, and suggestions for developing more complex layouts.

As a useful exercise in which to develop real familiarity with the Tarot you can hardly do better than to place yourself in its position, so to speak, and take any simple story or situation you know, and try to express it in terms of Tarot cards. From this you will achieve real facility and be able to go on to design your own layouts to suit your style or different projects that may come your way. You will then really have mastered the Magic of the Tarot!

Index of Trump Images

(in Marseilles order)

Fool, 16, 17, 25-28, 30, 34, 75, 78, 84, 86, 87, 92, 102, 112, 116, 118, 119, 124-28, 131, 132, 139, 140, 141, 147, 163, 171, 172, 173, 174, 179, 195, 196, 198, 220, 223

Magician, 28-30, 34, 85, 86, 87, 92, 107, 113, 114, 119, 121, 167, 172, 178, 195, 196, 198, 200, 202, 203, 205, 220, 223, 224

High Priestess, 30-33, 34, 39, 85, 86, 87, 93, 95, 109, 113, 114, 159, 172, 176, 199, 200, 201, 220, 223

Empress, 33-35, 37, 39, 84, 85, 86, 87, 95, 106, 107, 113, 114, 167, 172, 178, 199, 200, 201, 220, 223

Emperor, 35-37, 39, 84, 85, 86, 87, 95, 105, 109, 113, 115, 153, 155, 157, 171, 172, 177, 199, 200, 201, 220, 223

Hierophant, 37-39, 85, 86, 87, 93, 95, 110, 113, 115, 155, 172, 199, 200, 201, 220, 223

Lovers, 39-41, 85, 86, 87, 113, 115, 151, 172, 177, 178, 202, 220, 223

Chariot, 17, 41-44, 61, 65, 85, 86, 87, 110, 113, 115, 151, 172, 177, 199, 220, 223

Justice, 15, 44-45, 50, 51, 56, 57, 84, 85, 86, 92, 110, 113, 114, 119, 162, 164, 165, 172, 173, 176, 177, 196, 197, 198, 199, 203, 220, 223

Hermit, 45-48, 50, 85, 86, 87, 91, 92, 105, 109, 113, 114, 151, 172, 173, 176, 177, 199, 202, 220, 223

Wheel of Fortune, 48-50, 61, 65, 85, 86, 92, 110, 113, 114, 142, 172, 175, 176, 199, 202, 220, 223

Strength, 10, 50-52, 57, 84, 85, 86, 87, 92, 109, 110, 113, 115, 146, 172, 173, 177, 196, 197, 198, 199, 200, 201, 220, 223

Hanged Man, 15, 52-54, 85, 86, 87, 92, 110, 113, 115, 146, 154, 172, 175, 176, 199, 203, 220, 223

Death, 54-55, 85, 86, 87, 92, 113, 115, 136, 172, 180, 199, 203, 220, 223

Temperance, 15, 50, 51, 56-57, 84, 85, 86, 87, 92, 109, 113, 116, 132, 172, 180, 196, 197, 198, 199, 201, 202, 220, 223

Devil, 57-60, 62, 85, 86, 87, 95, 113, 114, 136, 172, 180, 199, 204, 220, 223

Tower, 17, 60-63, 70, 85, 86, 87, 92, 109, 113, 114, 136, 139, 172, 173, 199, 204, 220, 223

Star, 61, 63-65, 66, 67, 85, 86, 91, 92, 109, 113, 114, 132, 135, 172, 180, 199, 205, 220, 223

Moon, 61, 65-67, 70, 85, 86, 87, 92, 104, 109, 113, 115, 124, 129, 131, 132, 172, 177, 180, 199, 205, 220, 203

Sun, 17, 67-69, 70, 72, 85, 86, 87, 92, 99, 109, 113, 115, 129, 131, 132, 172, 180, 199, 205, 206, 220, 223

Last Judgement, 69-71, 73, 85, 86, 92, 109, 113, 115, 129, 172, 180, 199, 206, 220, 223

World, 14, 50, 56, 57, 71-73, 75, 85, 86, 87, 92, 104, 113, 116, 118, 124, 172, 180, 195, 196, 197, 198, 199, 205, 220, 223

other forms

Bacchus, 95

Crocodile, 17

Fortitude, 15, 52, 196

Juno, 95

Jupiter, 95

Prudence, 15, 196, 197

Spanish Captain, 95

Index of Books Cited

Alice in Wonderland, Lewis Carroll, 194

Alice Through the Looking Glass, Lewis Carroll, 194

Art of Memory, The, Frances Yates, 102

Book of Thoth, The, Aleister Crowley, 20, 193

Chymical Marriage of Christian Rosencreutz, The, Anon., 47, 63, 64,

Clef des Mystères, Le, Eliphas Lévi, 16

Dogme et Rituel de la Haute Magie, Eliphas Lévi, 16, 19

Encyclopaedia of Tarot, The, Stuart Kaplan, 7

Encyclopaedic Outline of Masonic, Hermetic, Qabbalistic and Rosicrucian Symbolical Philosophy, An, Manley P. Hall, 20

Equinox, The, Aleister Crowley, 19

Flight of the Feathered Serpent, The, Peter Balin, 92

Game of Tarot, The, Michael Dummett, 7

Greater Trumps, The, Charles Williams, 27, 75, 77, 100, 109

Golden Dawn, The, Israel Regardie, 96

Histoire de la Magie, Eliphas Lévi, 16

History of Magic, Paul Christian, 17

History of White Magic, A, Gareth Knight, 13

Idiot, The, Fyodor Dostoevsky, 27

Inferno, The, Dante Allighierri, 60

Inner Guide Meditation, The, Edwin Steinbrecher, 99, 109

Joseph and his Brothers, Thomas Mann, 62

Key to the Tarot, A. E. Waite, 19, 21, 122, 182

King Lear, William Shakespeare, 27

Les XXII lames hermètiques, R. Falconnier, 18

L'homme rouge des Tuileries, Paul Christian, 16

Magic and the Power of the Goddess, Gareth Knight, 77, 118

Magical World of the Tarot, The, Gareth Knight, 231

Magick of the Tarot, The, Osborne Phillips & Melita Denning, 100

Maison acadèmique des jeux, La, 12

Monde Primitif, Le, Court de Gebelin, 12, 13

Mystical Tower of the Tarot, The, John D. Blakely, 100

Mystic Rose from the Garden of the King, The, Sir Fairfax L. Cartwright, 100

Occult Review, The, article by J.W. Brodie Innes, 82

Practical Guide to Qabalistic Symbolism, A, Gareth Knight, 21, 97, 172, 183, 193

Practice of Ritual Magic, The, Gareth Knight, 77

Rose Cross and the Goddess, The, Gareth Knight, 77

Sacred Tarot, Elbert Benjamine, 20

Sanctum Regnum, Eliphas Lévi, 19

Science des Esprits, Le, Eliphas Lévi, 16

Screwtape Letters, The, C. S. Lewis, 59

Secret Tradition in Arthurian Legend, The, Gareth Knight, 109

Sorcerer and his Apprentice, The, R. A. Gilbert, 82

Tarot des Bohemiens, Le, Papus, 18, 19

Tarot Hieroglyphique Egyptien, Dulora de la Haye; 18

To the Heart of the Rainbow, Gareth Knight, 174

Transcendental Magic, Eliphas Lévi 19

Theatre of the World, Frances Yates 102

Treatise on the Seven Rays, Alice Bailey, 183

Underworld Initiation, The, R. J. Stewart, 108, 118

Index of Packs Cited

A. E. Waite, 22, 23, 24, 25, 27, 28, 29, 30, 32, 33, 35, 36. 37, 38, 41, 43, 45, 47, 49, 50, 51, 53, 55, 56, 57, 59, 60, 62, 64, 66, 69, 70, 72, 187-93, 194

Aleister Crowley, 20, 22, 193

Beaux Arts, 24, 46, 48, 52, 68, 69, 71

Belgian, 15

Brera-Brambilla, 24, 35, 48

Cary-Yale, 24, 35, 39, 54, 69, 71

Castello Ursino, 24

Catania, 24, 42, 71

Catelin Geofroy, 11, 24, 28, 33, 46, 52, 54, 56, 61, 69

Colonna, 24, 40, 42

Court de Gebelin, 22

de Laurence, 20, 22

D'Este, 24, 25, 28, 38, 56, 63, 65, 68, 71

Dion Fortune (SIL), 187-93

Elbert Benjamine, 20, 22

Falconnier, 18, 20, 22, 23

Fournier, 24, 31, 35

Golden Dawn, 20, 22, 23, 24, 25, 28, 29, 30, 32, 34, 35, 36, 37, 39, 41, 43, 45, 47, 49, 50, 51, 53, 55, 57, 59, 62, 64, 66, 69, 70, 72

Grand Etteilla, 14-15, 22

Gringonneur, 9, 24, 25, 35, 38, 39, 42, 44, 46, 50, 52, 54, 56, 57, 60, 61, 65, 68, 71,

Guildhall, 24, 71

Italian, 10, 24, 42, 48, 54, 57, 60

Lenormand, 16

Manley Palmer Hall, 20, 22

Mantegna, 173

Metropolitan Museum of Modern Art, 24, 48

Oswald Wirth, 18, 20, 22, 23, 25, 29, 31, 33, 36, 38, 40, 41, 42, 43, 45, 47, 49, 50, 51, 53, 55, 56, 58, 62, 64, 66, 68, 70, 72

Parisian printed, 24, 25, 28, 31, 33, 36, 38, 40, 42, 44, 46, 48, 51, 54, 58, 61, 63, 66, 68, 72

Paul Christian, 22, 23, 26

Piero Tozzi, 24

Rosenthal, 24, 35, 44, 63, 67

Rosenwald, 24, 28, 31, 33, 35, 38, 39, 42, 44, 46, 50, 52, 54, 56, 58, 61, 63, 65, 68, 69, 71

Rothschild, 24, 35, 42, 54, 57, 61, 63, 65

Sicilian, 84

Swiss, 10, 24, 61, 63, 66, 68

Victoria & Albert, 24, 54, 63

Visconti-Sforza, 10, 24, 25, 28, 30, 31, 33, 35, 37, 39, 41, 43, 44, 45, 48, 50, 51, 52, 54, 56, 63, 64, 65, 66, 67, 69, 71, 72, 73, 91

Von Bartsch, 24, 38, 41, 48, 56, 69

Printed in the USA
CPSIA information can be obtained
at www.ICGtesting.com
CBHW022047080924
14268CB00008BA/96